Politics, Planning and the City

Michael Goldsmith was educated at Trinity School, Croydon, and at the universities of Reading and Manchester. Since 1963 he has taught politics at the University of Salford, where he was appointed Senior Lecturer in 1973. Between 1970 and 1972 he was Visiting Professor in the Department of Political Studies at Queen's University, Kingston, Ontario, where he also undertook research into aspects of housing and planning. The author of numerous monographs, articles and papers, Michael Goldsmith is currently research co-ordinator for, and a member of, the Social Science Research Council panel on central–local government, and Convenor of the Political Studies Association's Urban Politics Group. He, his wife and three children live in Leyland, Lancashire.

The Built Environment Series

Series Editors

Michael J. Bruton, *Professor of Planning in the University of Wales Institute of Science and Technology*
John Ratcliffe, *Head of Department of Estate Management, South Bank Polytechnic, London*

In association with the Open University Press

Politics, Planning and the City

Michael Goldsmith

Senior Lecturer in Politics,
University of Salford

Hutchinson
London Melbourne Sydney Auckland Johannesburg

Hutchinson & Co. (Publishers) Ltd
An imprint of the Hutchinson Publishing Group
24 Highbury Crescent, London N5 1RX

Hutchinson Group (Australia) Pty Ltd
30–32 Cremorne Street, Richmond South, Victoria 3121
PO Box 151, Broadway, New South Wales 2007

Hutchinson Group (NZ) Ltd
32–34 View Road, PO Box 40–086, Glenfield, Auckland 10

Hutchinson Group (SA) Pty Ltd
PO Box 337, Bergvlei 2012, South Africa

First published 1980

© Michael Goldsmith 1980

Set in 10pt Times Roman

Printed in Great Britain by The Anchor Press Ltd
and bound by Wm Brendon & Son Ltd
both of Tiptree, Essex

British Library Cataloguing in Publication Data
Goldsmith, Michael
    Politics, planning and the city. – (Built environment).
    1. Municipal government
    I. Title   II. Series
    352′.008   JS78

ISBN 0 09 141370 2 cased
        0 09 141371 0 paper

to Anne, Christopher, Samantha and Helen

Contents

Figures and tables

Figures

Tables

Preface

Like the world of cities that they seek to describe and analyse, both urban studies generally and urban politics specifically have been changing and developing rapidly over recent years. For example, the first post-graduate courses in urban studies were not introduced until the late 1960s, while as late as 1975 one author, R. A. W. Rhodes, could write complainingly about the 'lost world of local politics'. At the same time town planners were struggling to grapple with the 'new-fangled public participation', largely unaware of the political nature of much of their activity or of the cold winds of economic and population decline which have recently made their tasks difficult if not impossible. In the housing arena, developers and others were just recovering from the slump of 1973, when the 'property bubble' burst, sending more than one developer to the bankruptcy courts. Unemployment had begun to climb, and the first cuts in public expenditure were being made, hitting those services largely provided by city governments.

Since the mid 1970s, changes in the real world of the city have had their impact on those academic disciplines that seek to understand it. In urban sociology, for example, Pahl's 'managerialist' thesis, stressing the importance of both private and public gatekeepers in allocating resources in the city, has largely been superseded by Marxist analyses. In Western societies at least, such analyses lay the burden of explanation of urban politics on the imperatives of the capitalist system, suggesting that it is the pursuit of capital accumulation and profit that explains resource allocation in the city. At the same time, professional officers such as planners and social workers now recognize the political nature of their work, as the reading lists for their training courses testify.

If cities have recently been undergoing rapid change, then so has our state of knowledge about them. Our understanding of city politics and policies has grown enormously over recent years, yet we are constantly changing conceptual perspectives, our focus of attention and our judgements on policies and policy-making processes. This book reflects these kinds of change, as it does something of the uncertainty of our knowledge. It attempts to pull together the main themes and changes found in our cities today, examining them in the light of three important policy arenas – housing, planning and social services – and relating them to questions of distribution and redistribution in the city.

All books owe a great debt to the work of others, and this is no exception. The series editors, Mick Bruton and John Ratcliffe, have been most helpful and tolerant, as has Rab MacWilliam on behalf of Hutchinson, in encouraging me to write this book. Graduates and undergraduate students from a variety of courses have helped through their contributions in classes and seminars, at Salford University and elsewhere. My departmental colleagues have generally been tolerant of my pursuits in this direction, as they have always been. I have particularly benefited from conversations and discussions with John Garrard and Rob Flynn in my department, and with Barry Gleave and Neville Topham in Geography and Economics respectively. Over the years I have learnt much from my professional colleagues in political science, and particularly those who belong to the Political Studies Association's Urban Politics Group, of which I am privileged to be Convenor. A number deserve specific mention: Jim Sharpe, Ken Newton, Jeff Stanyer, Ken Young, Pat Dunleavy and Peter Saunders. I owe a particular debt to Bill Hampton (over debates about normative issues); Noel Boaden (for similar arguments about empirical matters); and to Peter Stringer (arguing so well about everything) for the five years we spent in collaborative research. Of course, none of the above is responsible for what follows: all errors of fact and judgements of opinion are my own.

Joan Cooper provided invaluable typing services, skilfully working her way through various drafts and numerous 'final' corrections and amendments. The map (pages 52–3) was drawn with skill, patience and good humour by Gustav Dobrzynski, of the Department of Geography at Salford. My children, Christopher, Samantha and Helen, have tolerated the usual trials and tribulations of authorship with patience and affection, as has my wife Anne. Hence the dedication.

1 Political theory, political practice and public policy in the city

Modern man is very much a creature of the city. In most of the developed countries of the world, 70 per cent of the population or more live in towns, while in developing countries the migration from rural areas continues apace.[1]* Regardless of the state of development, the city is the modern and future way of life, which also transcends political beliefs: The modern city is a feature of both Western liberal democratic and Eastern communist political systems.

Though cities were common in ancient and medieval times, their present shape and form is very much a result of the process of industrialization associated with the technological changes that have taken place since the eighteenth century. Without the revolutions in the means of production and transportation that have occurred since that time, the modern city would not exist. There would be no factories, no electricity or oil, no cars or trains. There would be no rich suburbs to which inner-city residents could escape; indeed, there would be far fewer inner-city residents, and the whole character of modern life would be very different and geared far more to the demands of an agricultural, peasant-based economy.

Though it is not our concern here to explain how the changes of the last 200 years have occurred, or to attempt to evaluate the impact of these changes, it is worth remembering that the rate at which change has occurred is high and that it appears to be increasing.[2] The change from an agriculturally based society to an industrially based one has taken place within a time span which, when compared with the evolution of life on this planet, is minute. Yet that industrialization process has brought with it a way of life that is taken for granted by most people in developed countries and is much sought after by those in developing ones.

This suggests that the city represents some long-sought Valhalla: only set out along the road to industrialization and the city and all will be well. Would that it were so, for both the original process of

* Superior figures refer to the Notes and references on pages 178–97.

industrial change and the subsequent ones have brought with them problems no individual could have reasonably been expected to foresee and which test the patience and wit of any form of government. Because of its relative shortage of land and because it emerged from the world wars with its industrial infrastructure relatively intact, Britain particularly has had to face not only the problems associated with being at the forefront of the Industrial Revolution, but also all those that have come since. More than America, Germany or Japan, for example, Britain has had and continues to face the problems of industrial regeneration and urban renewal, as well as dealing with some of the social issues associated with these problems, such as urban poverty and relative deprivation.

In other words, the processes of urbanization and industrialization have brought with them problems with which it is impossible for any individual to cope, and which indeed may be beyond the control of city and even national governments. The resultant specialization and division of labour which is part and parcel of the process of urbanization means that the modern city resident is increasingly dependent on the actions of other people and other institutions for all aspects of his daily life and wellbeing. He depends on government for housing, transportation, education, health, even refuse collection and disposal. He depends on other individuals or institutions to provide him with food and clothing together with the other goods and services that provide him with his relatively high standard of living. In exchange, at least in Western societies, he barters with whatever skills he has at his disposal, either on his own account or together with others who possess similar skills.

What this suggests is that the individual is very much in a subordinate position *vis-à-vis* the city in which he lives. Given reasonable weather, the rural resident might produce enough food and clothing for his family with perhaps even enough left for him to barter with other producers of goods for a few extra comforts. What makes city life both tolerable and attractive is that the 'range of comforts' is enormously extended as a result of the specialization associated with urbanization and industrialization. Put simply, the village drama society does not compare with the National Theatre, any more than Leeds does with London. The possibility of having access to this 'range of comforts' is what attracts people to, and keeps them in, the city: the impossibility of actually obtaining them results either in people leaving the city or their facing the kinds of problems associated with inner-city deprivation.

But as the scope and range of possibilities available has been increased by the development of modern city life, so has the balance between what might be called private and public government. In other words, the modern city demands a much broader scope of action by governments than does a rural area: industrialization has brought with it greater responsibilities for government. No longer can the city resident provide for himself (private government), or perhaps expect the modern entrepreneur to 'look after' him in the way that the early industrial entrepreneurs 'looked after' their work forces, though modern Japanese industry perhaps provides the exception. Instead, it is to the state – in the form of either city, regional or national government – that people look today for these kinds of services. In the modern city, the activities of government impinge on all aspects of people's daily lives, even perhaps down to the colour of their front door or whether or not they can keep pets, and the process of urbanization has also brought with it demands for some form of control over that process so that its worst excesses no longer proceed unchecked.

Those critics writing from a Marxist interpretation would probably advance another explanation, seeing the urbanization process as the logical outcome of the need for capital accumulation in capitalist societies, so that the shape and form of the city, what city governments do and the condition of the individual are all the result of this imperative and its associated class-based conflicts.

The individual and government: ideas about democracy

Questions about the relationship between the individual and his government, as well as about the scope and nature of the activities of the state, have concerned philosophers, political and other social scientists from time immemorial. Understanding some of these questions is central to the task here of analysing the relationship between politics, planning and the modern city, for the problems of the latter pose difficult questions for those who are concerned with the relationship between the individual and his city government, while planning in its broadest sense often seems to promise solutions to modern urban problems, but at the apparent expense of threatening the democratic nature of Western society. In essence, this suggests that the problems of the city can be solved, but must the solution be at the expense of the individual's basic freedoms and rights?

It is perhaps strange to reflect that the very origin of the word democracy was first used in the context of city government. Aristotle's *Politics*[3] is based on the comparative analysis of 158 Greek city-states, perhaps the ancient equivalent of the modern metropolis in terms of economic and political power, as well as the military centres of the times. Furthermore, one of the problems of the city, namely the apparent apathy of its residents, was of concern then as it is now.

Aristotle's solution to this problem was that every citizen should participate in the affairs of the city – the meaning of the word 'democracy', which Aristotle contrasted with the then prevailing 'aristocracy' – meeting to discuss matters of common interest and to propose solutions to their common problems. The ancient form of government has been revived in modern times with the advocacy of participatory democracy in its various forms, such as neighbourhood government, community development, and calls for maximum citizen participation in local affairs.

The difficulty with participatory democracy as a form of government is that it is essentially appropriate only on a small scale and is not necessarily efficient as a means of delivering the level of public goods and services demanded in modern cities. It is not that the services cannot be provided for 1000 people or less, or that that number of people would not share in the process of government, but rather that the level of service provision would be below that which people have come to expect in modern times. How, for example, would it be possible to provide a fast, cheap, flexible public transport system for the 3000 different units of government that would cover Greater Manchester if such a small-scale unit of local government were to be introduced? Thus participatory democracy may well have been appropriate to the Greek city-state, the seventeenth-century New England township or the Swiss commune, but it hardly seems appropriate to the present-day city.[4] Indeed, the process of industrialization brought with it a changing form of government, one that has been the basis of the system of government in Britain since the early nineteenth century, namely representative government or representative democracy.

Representative government as we know it today owes its origins to the writings of John Stuart Mill.[5] Mill recognized the difficulties associated with participatory democracy once the scale of society becomes larger. It seems inevitable that some form of representative government is necessary in a large-scale industrial society. Though

Mill was ambiguous about the importance of participation, especially in relation to his practical proposals for representative government, the key to his idea of representative democracy lies essentially in the idea of the political accountability of the elected representative rather than in the widespread participation of the masses.[6] Mill stresses the educative benefits of participation, particularly in so far as they improved accountability: a well educated electorate would be better able to judge the performance of their representatives. Such education was, in Mill's eyes, best achieved through local political institutions – that is, through local governments – though even here Mill stressed representative rather than participatory government.

Mill's ideas about representative government recognize one of the crucial features of the modern industrial city, namely the division of labour. Representative government implies a political division of labour, under which the process of political decision-making is carried on by those for whom politics is an all-consuming passion – Dahl's *homo politicus*[7] – while the rest of the population – *homo civicus* – follows those pursuits that are of greater interest to them. It is the notion of the political accountability of the representatives – through free and periodic elections – that theoretically ensures that *homo politicus* governs in the interest of *homo civicus*, rather than in some other sectional or self-interest. Being politically educated and interested in political affairs, *homo civicus* will be well equipped, in Mill's terms, to exercise the necessary judgement at election time.

Also involved in the notion of representative government, but owing more to Edmund Burke than to Mill, is the idea that the elected representative ought to look after the individual and collective interests of his constituents, while still exercising his own political judgement. Any individual should be able to approach his local councillor or MP for help and advice on any matter of concern to him and expect the elected representative to take up the matter on his behalf. This helps to bind the elected member to his constituents more closely, providing a point of access for individuals into the local political system. Thus representative government depends on a division of labour between *homo politicus* and *homo civicus*, and on the accessibility and accountability of the former to the latter.

The system of representative government associated with John Stuart Mill was perhaps seen at its peak during the latter half of the nineteenth century. The business of government, and pace of political life, was such that it could be understood and managed largely by the amateur part-time elected representative, assisted by a small number of full-time bureaucrats. The whole scope of nineteenth-century city government in Britain was much narrower than its present-day counterpart: functions such as housing and education came to local government late in the century, while the town planning function is entirely a twentieth-century phenomenon. Many services, such as libraries and parks, owed their origins to the generosity of industrial entrepreneurs, who, as part of their ideology, saw it as their duty to provide some cultural comforts for their workers as well as housing them.

But the pace of nineteenth-century change, and the even greater rate in the present century, has meant that the business of government, both national and local, has both increased in scope and become much more complex in nature. One measure of this is the vast increase in the army of people employed by city government. Currently over 2 million people work in local authorities, and local government in recent years has been the fastest growing part of the public sector.[8]

This means that the concept of representative democracy described above has been undergoing a process of gradual modification as a result of the continuing socioeconomic changes associated with the further industrialization and urban growth of the twentieth century. No longer do national and local elected representatives debate the issues of the day at their leisure: rather, they are often caught in a situation where they appear to be responding to a bewildering series of complex events. In doing so, they are dependent on the preliminary work and expertise of highly paid civil servants and local government professionals.

As part of this process of information-gathering and advice-giving, governments, both national and local, have recognized the contribution to policy-making process that organized groups can make. Particularly at the national level, and increasingly at the local, the right to consultation as part of the policy-making process has been extended to large numbers of special groups, from the TUC and the CBI right down to the local pigeon fanciers' club. In part, the right of consultation has been extended because of the pressure that such groups have brought upon city and national governments to pay attention to their demands; but in other cases governments have recognized the interest of such groups and invited them into the policy-making process without the latter having to exert substantial pressure.

Pluralist and elitist views of the city

This change is perhaps best considered as a move towards consultative government, designed to supplement the system of representative government. As such, it comes closer to the pluralist model of democracy perhaps best described by Dahl.[9] Under this model, the process of policy- and decision-making is widely shared among different groups in society, with no group possessing sufficient resources to be able to dominate the decision-making process continuously. The city whose process of decision-making perhaps best fits this open model is New York,[10] but even here it would be true to say that some groups, most notably blacks and Puerto Ricans, remain excluded from substantial areas of policy-making.

By contrast, British cities are generally characterized as having a more closed system of policy-making, though the extent to which it is so is subject to debate. What can be said at this stage is that the scope and range of public policy-making is much wider in the British city than it is in North America, where substantial service areas, particularly in relation to health, still remain predominantly the responsibility of the private sector.

It is important to realize that models of the policy-making process involve different and often competing normative assumptions about the nature of society, both as it is and as it should be. Nowhere has this been truer than in the wealth of American literature seeking to analyse the decision-making process in American cities since the mid 1950s. Essentially two models have been used to explain the political processes of the city. On the one hand there is the liberal democratic pluralist model associated with the writings of Dahl and his followers,[11] while on the other hand there is the Marxist/neo-Marxist elitist model associated with C. Wright Mills, Floyd Hunter and others.[12]

In the first of these models, as was suggested earlier, the process of policy-making is characterized as open to a large number of groups, none of which possesses sufficient resources to dominate decisions across a number of policy areas. The model of 'dispersed inequalities' recognizes that only a minority of people are prepared to participate in the decision-making process, but it also suggests that those who in effect exercise influence over decisions do so in such a way that the passive majority do not feel a need to enter the decision-making process on their own account. In other words, the active minority recognize and anticipate the latent power of the passive majority to organize themselves, as well as recognizing the accessibility of the decision-making process to these groups. The exercise of power by the active minority in this model is thus seen as authoritative, or acceptable, by the mass: the process of policy-making is seen as legitimate and acceptable. This is because those who take the policy decisions are responsive to the changing needs of the majority, the very openness of the political system ensuring that these changes are quickly perceived by the decision-makers.

The model is one that belongs to those who essentially see society as consensual, able to secure agreement among the different interests extant in the society. The stress is on stability and gradual change, and owes much of its inspiration to the structural functional school of social theory associated with Talcott Parsons in sociology and Almond and his associates in political science.

The emphasis on stability and consensus has led to the criticism that the theory inherently supports the status quo, and critics of the consensus/pluralist theory build their own models on the assumption that conflict lies at the centre of society. As a result, their theories emphasize change and dissent. Conflict is seen as endemic because of the scarcity of resources and because of the existence of incompatible interests. For Marxists and neo-Marxists, the status quo is seen as being imposed by a ruling class or elite, which governs in its own interests, namely those of the dominant capitalist means of production. Thus, for writers such as Harvey[13] and Castells,[14] the city is the spatial manifestation of the capitalist industrial process, and the policy-making process is such that decisions and policies favour the continuation of the capitalist means of production.

Without explicitly adopting the Marxist model, many writers, mainly sociologists, have characterized urban decision and policy-making processes as elitist. From Mills and Hunter onwards,[15] writers have pointed to the extent to which the policy-making process in cities is relatively closed, with power being concentrated in the hands of a few, often those who comprise a socioeconomic elite. This model stresses the concentration of resources that elite decision-makers possess, suggesting that they exercise power in a self-interested way. As such, they are concerned with perpetrating their own existence as powerful decision-makers, and are seen as using their power in an illegitimate and unacceptable fashion. In other (Marxist) words, elitist systems of policy-making seek to perpetrate the ruling class: the continued existence of the capitalist means of production is ensured, but only at the cost of the further exploitation (consciously or unconsciously) of the working class.

It is this exploitation by one property-owning class or elite of another class that leads to the assumption that conflict is inherent in the city. Decisions about the allocation of resources – for example in relation to the allocation of council housing or permission to develop particular sites, the structure of the education system, the allocation of welfare benefits, even the organization of refuse collection and disposal – are all seen as involving conflict among competing interests, with the resolution of such conflicts seen as being generally in the interests of the capitalist class.

Indeed, much recent Marxist writing has been particularly concerned with the role of the state in maintaining the capitalist economic system, with writers stressing the extent of the state's involvement in production processes (aid to declining manufacturing industry, such as British Leyland, or parts of the inner-city programme) as well as the provision of public goods and services under the umbrella title of 'collective consumption'. Of particular concern has been the question of the 'relative autonomy' of the state, that is to say the extent to which the state is able to act independently of or against dominant capitalist interests.[16]

The idea of the state in Marxist writings often suggests a unity and homogeneity among the various and numerous institutions that comprise the modern state which belies experience. Even those who recognize the existence of different levels of the state[17] often fail to carry this distinction much further, having the impression that city governments are far more monolithic than they are in practice.

Notwithstanding many of the difficulties critics pose for Marxist writings, there is little doubt that the recent upsurge in the literature has raised a number of interesting questions and laid down a considerable challenge to those who wish to interpret urban politics in traditional liberal democratic terms.

Part of the purpose of this book will be to examine the extent to which city politics in Britain approximates in practice to these competing models, though it must be recognized at the outset that the two models are largely irreconcilable, and neither is capable of absolute proof. What is important, however, is to have an emphasis on policy and policy-making, for only through an understanding of these two can we begin to understand what is happening in the modern city. We shall be concerned here with analysing public policy in three arenas: planning, housing and welfare – all major responsibilities of central and local government.

Policy, policy-making and implementation

At the outset, however, it is necessary to have some idea of what we mean by public policy. Political scientists have long shown a concern for public policy, albeit in largely a descriptive or prescriptive fashion. More recently, the focus has shifted away from description to analysis; to a concern with understanding or explaining public policy – what causes governments to do or not to do particular things – and with examining the consequences of such policies on society at large.[18]

At a simple level, as Dye suggests,[19] 'public policy is whatever governments choose to do or not to do'. It is important to realize that what governments choose not to do may be as important for the health and vigour of a society as those things that they choose to act upon. In this sense, the concept of public policy must include all *actions* of governments, not just the stated intentions of governments or public officials, as well as an understanding of why governments sometimes choose to do nothing about a particular question. Why is it, for example, that one government (the United States) decides to arm the police, while another (Great Britain) in general decides not to do so? Why does one city decide to establish a direct works department to undertake its capital building programme while another depends on the private construction industry? Why does one local authority enforce pollution laws while another does nothing? The question of non-decisions – of those policy areas that somehow never become part of the public agenda – is as important to understand as those decisions, or policy areas, in which governments are active.

Of course, governments, both national and local, are involved in many areas: defence, education, welfare, economic planning, police and fire services, land use planning, housing and transportation, for example. Simply finding out *what* governments are doing often presents a challenge – to the policy analyst no less than to the ordinary citizen – and *explaining* what they do an even more serious one. If we are to understand policy and the policy-making process further, we need to have a more rigorous conceptualization of what policy is.

Ranney[20] has usefully suggested that public policy has the following components:

(a)   an aspect of society or physical world which is intended to be affected;

(b) a particular sequence of behaviour desired in relation to that aspect;

(c) a selected line of action – that is, a particular set of actions designed to bring about the desired course of events;

(d) a declaration of intent – that is, some statement by policy-makers of what they intend to do, how and why;

(e) an implementation of intent – that is, actions actually undertaken *vis-à-vis* the aspect of society to be affected in pursuance of the choices and the declaration.

In other words, public policy involves something to be affected in a particular way to secure a particular result, together with a statement as to how that result is to be achieved, and the necessary actions taken to implement the statement and achieve the desired results. Thus, for example, if a city council is concerned with congestion in the city owing to the presence of large numbers of cars, and decides that it wants to reduce this to more acceptable levels, then not only must it produce policies which it feels will achieve this desired course of events (the statement of intent), but it must also implement these policies. In other words, not only might the city council be expected to say it is going to charge a high price for central city parking, but it must also implement such a policy.

Having seen what public policy involves, it is helpful if we also add two further considerations at this stage. First, a distinction should be made between policy and the consequences or outcomes of policy. It is not sufficient to analyse policy alone and pay no attention to the effects of that policy on the society around it. This is because policies can have both intended and unintended consequences. They may achieve what they set out to do, or they may have other consequences, not all of which may be considered desirable. For example, many British housing policies have been designed to give private tenants both security of tenure and relatively low rents. One consequence of these policies has been that the private rental sector has virtually dried up, as landlords have found investment in private rental housing increasingly uneconomical, while another consequence has been to hasten the decline in the physical standards of much privately rented housing, as landlords have been unable or unwilling to undertake the necessary upkeep of their property. As a consequence, the need for urban renewal and rehabilitation has probably been higher than might otherwise have been the case, and it is doubtful whether these consequences of central government policy towards the privately rented sector were either foreseen or intended. Thus a concern for the intended and unintended consequences of public policy is also central to an understanding of what is happening in the city.

Second, it is helpful to make an analytic distinction between policy-making and policy implementation. Despite some interest in implementation in government circles[21] such a distinction is difficult to make in the real world of policy: policy emerges, re-emerges and is shaped and reshaped as the process of implementation is carried on, so that officials would rarely wish to maintain the distinction. Yet analytically it is valuable, for it allows us to isolate the first four components of Ranney's definition of public policy from the last stage, namely the implementation of intentions. This is particularly useful because it may well allow us to describe and account for any variations between policy intent and policy action that occur as a result of the way in which policy intentions are converted into action, that is to say as a result of the implementation stage in the policy process. Undoubtedly there are many examples of the way in which it is administratively possible to frustrate (intentionally or unintentionally) the policy-maker's intention: consider, for example, accusations, normally from the Labour Party's ranks, of civil service antipathy to socialism, or of alternative claims, sometimes voiced by top civil servants, that somehow they represent a wider political consensus or public interest which should not be threatened, least of all by governments. At the city level, the official's sense of professional duty and standards may well lead him to stress policies that support this sense of professionalism against those that his elected members sense are right for the locality. 'Good professional practice' or 'highest professional standards' have often been the claims of redevelopment schemes that have subsequently proved not far short of unmitigated disasters. Thus, for both central and local levels of policy analysis a distinction between policy-making and policy implementation is useful.

Last, in order to understand public policy and its consequences more easily, it is helpful if we can classify policies in some way, both to distinguish different types of policy and to highlight which sorts of policies are likely to have which sorts of consequences. A number of classification schemes can be found in the literature. Thus, for example, Boaden, in his book *Urban Policy Making*[22] draws a distinction between physical and personal services in terms of the activities of English local authorities. Froman,[23] in a well-known article, has drawn a distinction between what he calls 'areal policies', such as fluoridation, which affect the whole community at the same time, and segmental ones, such as welfare, which affect less than the total population or affect different people at different times.

One of the most useful categorizations is that suggested by T. J. Lowi, first outlined in a 1964 article in *World Politics*, and developed further in *Public Administration Review*.[24] Lowi distinguishes four types of policy: distributive policies, which generally benefit everybody; constituent policies, which in effect are about the rules of the game, such as election laws; regulative policies, which are designed to regulate behaviour, such as public health laws; and lastly redistributive policies, which generally take from one group and give to another, such as graduated income tax and welfare benefits.

Lowi's categorization of public policies is helpful for it draws attention to the kinds of intended consequences that public policies may be expected to have, thus providing a starting point for the analysis of the actual consequences of policy. We drew attention earlier to the idea that policies could have both intended and unintended consequences. Lowi's categorization enables us to carry distinction further, in that it permits us to ask what were the intended consequences of a redistributive policy (such as welfare); what were its unintended ones; how far the intended consequences were achieved, and to what extent unintended consequences hindered policies from fulfilling their intentions. If, for example, central government decides that the best way to aid declining and deprived inner-city areas is by improving the physical infrastructure of these areas, we may well find that such policies may well lead to a cleaner, more attractive physical environment, but that the areas are still relatively deprived because these policies have done little to arrest the process of social and economic deprivation in the areas. Or we might find that the policies trigger off decline in other unaided areas – a kind of unintended consequence.

Thus a policy focus along the lines outlined here will allow us to see what is happening in the modern city and to consider how the actions of city governments affect the lives and quality of life of city residents. It will particularly allow us to consider how far such governments are able to meet the needs and aspirations of their residents; to consider how democratic is the process of city politics. By following Lasswell[25] and asking who gets what, when and how, we shall have begun to understand how the politics of the city takes place. In making this analysis, we shall find that city politics is a complex process, involving social, physical and economic changes, as well as the exercise of power, together with the influence of differing political cultures and ideologies. Furthermore, we shall find that much of city politics takes place within an institutional framework that itself helps determine much of what happens in the city. For example, the simple fact that metropolitan government in Britain is organized on a two-tier basis has consequences for the kinds of policies and policy outcomes in those areas. Last but not least, the way in which the urban decision-making processes, both public and private, operate will affect the kinds of policies and outcomes that occur in the city. All of these are topics we explore further in the next chapter.

2 Analysing city politics

Understanding what goes on in the real world presents us with numerous problems, and this is particularly true when we consider the complexity of life in the world's cities. Indeed, a complete understanding of the social, economic and political processes of city life is beyond the capacity of any man. To help grapple with these problems, and to build up some understanding of urban phenomena, social scientists have developed a number of models, or theories, which, though analytic abstractions, hopefully help us to identify some of the key aspects, or variables, in city life, and to indicate the possible relationships between these variables. These models, or theories, range from relatively simple checklists of factors to be identified or questions to be asked, through explanations of a limited phenomenon, to broad general models which seek to identify all the important or key variables and to suggest how they are related to each other in a complex fashion. All seek to simplify the real world and reduce it to essentially manageable proportions, and all vary in their scope and level of explanation.

In their attempts to understand the political processes of the city, political scientists and others have developed a number of models, of which five may be considered here to illuminate the general political and policy-making procedures of the city. Each is suggestive of important questions to which the political scientist would seek answers when looking at city politics, though each is undoubtedly limited in its ability to explain what happens politically in the city. In part, each model provides a competing explanation of city policies, though it seems more likely that linking the models together would provide a better, complementary explanation, reflecting some of the wider issues discussed in the previous chapter.

The five models discussed here can be briefly summarized as follows. First, there is the institutional model, long dominant in the literature, which sees political processes as largely determined by the kind of institutional, constitutional and legal framework within which local public policies are made.[1] Second, there is what might succinctly be called the community power model, which dominated the literature in the late 1950s and early 1960s, and which largely provided the impetus for the revival of interest among political scientists in the affairs of city governments.[2] Third, there is the systems model of political life, which sees much of what happens in the city as the response of the political system to changes in its environment.[3] This model was essentially dominant in the late 1960s and early 1970s and still provides an important organizing analytic framework.[4] Fourth, there are those models that emphasize the role of individuals and the local political culture, ideology or values in their explanation of city political processes, models that have emerged as counters to what was seen as the very deterministic and mechanistic nature of systemic explanations of urban political life.[5] Last, there are recent Marxist analyses of the city, particularly those associated with the work of Castells.[6]

Institutions and the city

Turning to the first of these, the institutional model, it is important to realize that city governments, like all sub-national governments, are all creatures of some higher level of government, be it the central government in a unitary political system like Britain's, or federal and state or provincial governments in federal political systems such as the United States, Canada, or West Germany. Thus, city governments will be more or less dependent upon higher levels of government for their powers and functions, and their degree of autonomy will vary accordingly. In Britain, for example, it might be argued that, while local authorities have considerable discretion in the way in which they exercise their powers, they lack any real autonomy, both because of the doctrine of *ultra vires*, which requires Parliament to have passed an Act giving local authorities the power to do whatever it is they wish to do, and because of the financial dependence of local authorities generally upon central government finance.[7] By contrast, in the highly decentralized, federal United States, many local governments have a high degree of legal and/or practical autonomy of both federal and state governments, who often experience great difficulty in persuading local governments to accept particular policies.[8]

The whole question of central–local relations is itself complex and is currently subject to a number of detailed investigations,[9] so that it is beyond our scope here. Suffice it to say that the pattern of formal and informal interactions between different levels of government and between governments of the same level are important determinants of what happens in the city. Thus, for example, the present inner-city programme in Britain, designed to do something about the crucial economic and social problems of these deprived areas in the major cities of the country, is very much organized as a partnership between central government on the one hand and the particular local authorities with large-scale inner-city problems on the other. By contrast, the continual and increasing conflict between central cities and suburbs in America means that urban problems there are more severe than in Britain and are less amenable to solutions because of the general unwillingness of suburban local authorities to co-operate with city governments over what are essentially area-wide problems.[10]

Equally important in terms of city politics and policy-making are the kind and number of political institutions to be found in the city and the way in which functions are allocated to them, a point that has long been noted by the many would-be reformers of local government. In Britain, local authorities, and hence city governments, are essentially what are called most-purpose authorities, in that they are responsible for providing most of the local services in their area. Though the number of *ad hoc* single-purpose authorities and what are euphemistically known as quasi non-governmental organizations, or *quangos*, has increased in this country, our cities contain far fewer governmental institutions than do their North American counterparts.[11] Though the 1974 local government reforms in England complicated city government by introducing the metropolitan county over the metropolitan districts, most of which had previously been county boroughs responsible for *all* local government services, the organizations of city government are still both fewer and simpler in Britain than in the United States, as is the division of services.

Indeed, the reform literature, and particularly that mainly concerned with promoting service efficiency at the local level,[12] has largely seen the problems of the cities as resolvable largely in areal, organizational and service terms. 'Get the scale right and get the services at the appropriate (efficient) level of government,' appears as the main thrust of the reformers' argument, assuming that if this is done then all the city's problems will be solved almost automatically. For metropolitan areas, such a view is almost bound to lead to a two-tier structure of government, with some services such as planning, police or fire seen as area or metropolitan county-wide functions and others, such as education, housing and welfare, as more appropriate to a second, lower or district tier. In this way, undoubtedly the kind of institutional structure and the way services and functions are allocated will be important determinants of how cities deal with their political problems and make policies. Who does what will have an impact on the power of the different tiers, affecting relationships between the different levels. Thus, in Britain for example most of the functions in metropolitan areas either lie within the district level or are shared with the metropolitan county,[13] with the result that the metropolitan districts are the more powerful level of government in the metropolitan areas. By contrast, it is the county level that is the more powerful in the non-metropolitan or shire areas, with these districts, though larger and more powerful than their predecessors, still very much the junior partners.[14]

How services and functions are allocated between different levels will obviously affect the way in which public goods and services are provided by local authorities. Housing, for example, is almost entirely a district function; and, if the experience of London is any guide,[15] then we might well expect considerable variations in the quality and type of housing provided in, as well as conflicts between inner-area and suburban district authorities, with the metropolitan counties looking on virtually helpless from the outside. Varieties in service performance between and within different types of local authority have been well demonstrated in the literature in recent years,[16] though explanations for these variations differ. The point to note here is simply that the allocation of local government functions to different tiers will have an effect on the way our cities respond to the problems they face.

There is a third way in which the institutions of local government affect the kinds of policies adopted in cities, namely through the laws and rules affecting the election and appointment of both members and officials. Such things as the frequency of elections; whether they are at large or ward-based; the age or residence requirements for members; whether or not authorities are required by law to appoint to certain posts; and whether appointments have to be approved by the appropriate central government department will all affect the kind of people who run local authorities, who become the governors of our cities. But no less important, as we shall see later, is the kind of administration structure created within a particular authority, for this may well determine the balance of power between elected members and paid officials. The point here is that most recent attempts through official reports have been to try and persuade local authorities to adopt a more co-ordinated/centralized or corporate approach to policy-making. From the Maud Report to the more direct Bains and Paterson Reports,[17] British local governments have been under pressure to adopt a corporate approach, one consequence of which has been to weaken the role of the unpaid part-time amateur councillor in the policy-making process, while strengthening that of the paid full-time professional official. Corporate planning has become one of the institutions of English local government over the last ten years, with all kinds of consequences for the way in which policies are made and the kinds of things our local authorities do.

Thus, we would be wrong to ignore completely the institutional framework within which the process of local politics is conducted, though we would be equally misleading if we were to stress too strongly an institutional explanation for what our city governments do or not do. Institutions by themselves do not make policies; people do. At best, the institutions of local government provide an organizing framework within which those who seek to make, or to influence, public policies at the local level have to operate.

Community power and the city

It is the second of our models, the community power model, that focuses attention on *who* makes the decisions in terms of city policies, and on the extent to which decisions are controlled by the few (the elite) or can be influenced by many (a pluralist alternative). These alternatives were the centre of what is known as the community power debate in the urban politics literature. Much of this literature is concerned with the distribution of power in American cities, and for a variety of reasons is not strictly relevant here. For example, there have been few attempts in Britain to replicate the kind of studies made by the two leading proponents of the debate, Robert Dahl and Floyd Hunter.[18] But the debate did focus attention on a number of issues that are relevant to our purposes. The first of these was the important distinction between decisions and non-decisions, first made by Bachrach and Baratz.[19] For them a decision is simply 'a choice among alternative courses of action', whereas they define a non-decision as 'a decision that results in suppression or thwarting of a . . . challenge to the values or interests of the decision-maker'.[20] In other words, non-decisions are the means by which demands for change can be suffocated or killed before they reach the political arena, or they can be subverted in the process of implementing a policy decision.

As a number of critics have noted, [21] the concept of non-decisions presents a number of empirical problems for research. For example, how does one identify a non-decision, if by definition the purpose of a non-decision is to keep something out of the political arena? Some apparent non-decisions may well be simply non-events, in that there never was any challenge to the decision-makers' values or interests. Others may be so well hidden as to defy empirical analysis. But some researchers are beginning to tackle these problems with interesting results, [22] suggesting that there is indeed a 'mobilization of bias' [23] which favours particular interests in a community. Crenson, for example, concentrates on the way a number of American cities adopt or enforce pollution controls, or in reality fail to do so in the light of the influence or power wielded by major industry (the polluters) in the community. Again, there are no directly comparable studies in Britain, though there is some suggestive evidence from the nineteenth century concerning the willingness of local authorities to adopt and implement building and sanitary regulations which indicates that the concept of non-decision is a useful one.

The second important contribution made by the community power studies lies in the way they improved and refined the definition and analysis of such key concepts as power, influence, authority and control, even if in the end one is left with a sense of the enormous difficulties of employing these concepts empirically. Thus, the elitists, for example, tended to employ the concept of power, with all its connotations of control over decisions and the political agenda, far more readily than did the pluralists, who talked more of influencing decisions and diffused resources. In part these differences reflected different ideological and methodological positions, which led to an increasingly sterile and bitter debate between the two sides which others chose to ignore, focusing their attention on what they felt were even more important issues. [24]

But the students of community power made a third important contribution to the study of local politics through the way in which they drew attention to the extent to which local decision-making was more or less dominated by different actors, or groups of actors, within the community. Thus they distinguish between those who hold formal positions of power, such as councillors, from those who might be in a position to exercise power or control over local decision-making by virtue of, for example, their social or economic position in the community. The community power studies focused attention on issues such as the nature of the local decision-making elite, the process of elite recruitment and the extent to which the elite, if it existed, was able to maintain control over local decision-making. For those favouring the 'elitist' conception of community power (mainly sociologists) the local decision-making process was closed, dominated by a few, largely major business men, while the 'pluralists' (mainly political scientists) characterized decision-making as relatively open. Even if only a few were involved in each decision, they were unable to expand their influence or control over a series of different decision-making arenas; nor were decision-makers to be found primarily among the ranks of the business community. In other words, the elitist–pluralist debate forced us to ask questions about how local decisions were made, who made them, and the extent to which decision-making was concentrated in the hands of the few or fragmented among the many.

However, having first recognized the importance of asking the question of who made the decisions and how they were made and, second, having acknowledged the sterility of elitist–pluralist debate, political scientists then proceeded to ask whether or not who made the decisions or how they were made had any effect on the level of service provision. As James Q. Wilson so aptly put it, 'We began to learn a great deal about who governs but surprisingly little about what *difference* it makes who governs.'[25]

The city and its environment

It was in seeking an answer to this latter question that the third model, which sees local politics largely as a political system responding to environmental change, gained currency.

Systemic approaches to the study of politics have been prevalent in the literature since David Easton published his book *The Political System* in 1953 and developed more formal theoretical approaches using systems analysis in his subsequent work up to the mid 1960s.[26] Two modes of systems thinking have dominated this body of literature. [27] First, there was the functionalist approach, owing its inspiration to the sociologist Talcott Parsons and expounded most fully in the political science literature by Gabriel Almond and his associates.[28] Few attempts have been made to use the functionalist model in the study of urban politics, so it need not detain us here.[29] Suffice it to note that its stress of function rather than structure, that is on what the system does rather than on the parts of the system, represented an important step in the development of the study of politics and, by implication, for the study of city government and politics.

More important, however, it has been the development and application of Easton's ideas that have had the most impact on the study of urban politics. By the early 1970s most writers in the field explicitly or implicitly used a systems framework, based on Easton, as the conceptual or organizing framework for their work.[30] It is necessary, therefore, to present a brief explanation of this model for our purposes here.

At the outset, one must remember that systems thinking is analytic thinking, an attempt to simplify or model the real world in order to identify the most important or key variables and to indicate possible important relationships between them. Given this analytic character, systems analysis gives its proponents considerable freedom in the way they define concepts, provided logical consistency is maintained. Essentially, systems thinking is concerned with the relationship between a system, usually defined as anything whose parts interact to make a whole, and its environment, perhaps most simply defined as anything not included within the system. The central notion is that the system responds to changes in the environment in such ways as to affect that environment in turn. Figure 1 presents this idea diagrammatically. The classic example is that of a guided missile chasing a moving target: as the latter changes direction (an

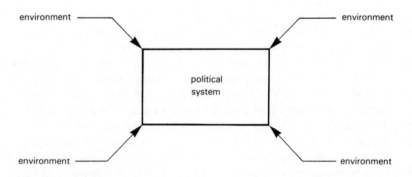

Figure 1   *The political system and its environment*

environmental change), the missile (system) also changes direction in its attempt to destroy the target. Another example is the way the human body reacts to temperature changes: as the temperature rises (environmental change), so the body (system) perspires. The two examples also contain three further central ideas contained in much of systems thinking. First, there is the idea of the system operating in such a way as to exert a greater or lesser degree of control, influence over, or ability to adapt the environment. Second, there is the notion that systems have some self-correcting or adaptive capacity in the light of environmental change. In formal terms, both the missile and the human body are self-correcting or *homoeostatic* systems.

The third notion contained in the examples is that both the missile and the body would be considered as 'open' rather than 'closed' systems, in that they are subject to influence by environmental change (i.e. open to such change) rather than detached or closed off from it. The concept of open systems suggests the idea of a boundary between the system and its environment, and it is this idea that presents one of the major problems for students and critics of systems analytic models alike in that both wish to know where this boundary should be drawn. Essentially the boundary problem is an empirical one rather than analytic, since in analytic terms one can draw the boundary between the system and its environment where one likes. But empirically, it is a very different and difficult matter: the complexity of the real world does not bend easily to fit even the most complex of systemic models.

How do these ideas apply in the field of urban politics? First, we can characterize a local administrative area as a political system, with its own members (the political community, in Easton's terms), or residents acting in their political capacity, its formal and informal decision-makers (political authorities), and its own rules of the game (or regime). Included also within the boundaries of the local political systems are such organizations as local political parties, interest or pressure groups, as well as the local media. These organizations act in a number of ways: as channels of communication between the political community or local residents and the authorities or decision-makers; as aggregators and articulators of local interest and demands; or as mechanisms concerned with the process of elite selection or recruitment, in that, for example, most elected members are now drawn from the ranks of the main political parties in their area.

We can further conceive of this political system as responding to changes in its environment – that is, the local political system is an open one – and as having some homoeostatic properties, in that it will seek to control, influence, manage or adapt its environment. But we need a better conceptualization of environment if it is to be useful for analytic purposes. Here Easton provides further guidance, by distinguishing between intra- and extra-system environments, that is between those that pertain directly to the local political system and those whose influence operates more indirectly upon it. In the former category we might distinguish analytically between the system's local social environment, in which we would include such features as the local social structure (the class structure, for example) and its socio-demographic characteristics; its local physical environment (namely its physical location, its climatic and topographical features) and its local economic environment, in which we would include such features as the local employment base, the kind of industrial and commercial undertakings, the local resource or tax base and so on.

The rest of a local political system's environment are extra-system environments: the national/international economic environment, the national social and physical environment, as well as the wider political environment. This latter is an important, but often neglected, factor influencing the way in which a local political system operates, for it comprises the whole range of intergovernmental relations in which a local government engages, be they with central government, other local authorities or statutory undertakings and quasi-governmental organizations (quangos).[31]

The relationship between a political system and its environments is illustrated in Figure 2. We can think of these environments as setting the context within which the local system operates, providing a number of opportunities or constraints as to how the local system may respond to environmental changes. These changes can be distinguished into two types: those generating support for the political system and its components (community, authorities or regime), and those generating demands to which the system must respond in terms of producing outputs. The concept of political support remains relatively under-analysed in the local context, being generally considered as any action favourable to the system, but that of demand may be thought of as having two dimensions: first, that of need, which may be succinctly defined as 'the need individuals, groups or the community has for a particular service or facility in an area',[32] and second, that of want or desires, which is more subjective in nature, being what people would like to have or achieve. In theory,

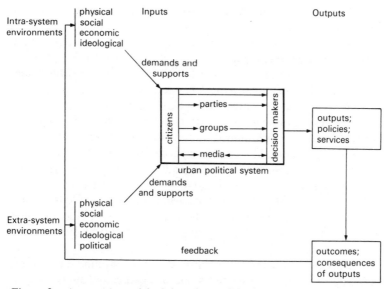

Figure 2 *A systemic model of the urban political system*

at least, need is objectively quantifiable: wants far less so. Nevertheless, the distinction is quite clear, as a simple example shows. In terms of housing, a married couple with one child will *need* accommodation that includes two, possibly three, bedrooms. The same couple may *want* a large, four-bedroomed detached house sitting in an acre of land. A clear difference between need and want exists in the example, and indeed it will be argued later that one of the reasons why public sector housing policies have been less successful than they might have otherwise been is because they have concentrated on meeting need without taking into account any element of people's wants.

As these environmental changes take place, they are picked up by the political system. Demands, however, may particularly be made from *within* the political system (what Easton calls 'withinputs'), and it is perhaps easiest to think of demands having to be articulated either by individuals in their political role (citizens in Figure 2) or by other groups and organizations within the system. In other words, environmental changes have to be perceived and articulated before the system can react to them. For example, people have to perceive traffic congestion as a problem before they will demand that something be done about it. The idea that environmental changes have to be perceived before demands can be articulated and aggregated is useful, because it allows us to use several other concepts in systems thinking which help explain why political systems do not always react as one might expect. First, there is the concept of lag, which implies both the idea of delay between environmental change and system action and also that of system under response to change. Using housing again, as an example, there was considerable delay between the consequences of and dissatisfactions with high-rise tower blocks and local housing authorities switching to other forms of building. Second, there is the concept of gain, whereby systems anticipate change or over-respond to change or demands. Governments, both national and local, rarely suffer from gain, but an example might well be the extensive use of police to marshal a National Front meeting or march, when often the number of police involved has far exceeded the number of marchers and/or counter-marchers.

Demands, as Figure 2 illustrates, thus flow through the political system, some being aggregated, some losing force and diminishing, if not disappearing, until they reach the authority's decision-makers (the elite, the authorities), those who in Easton's terms make the binding decisions for the community.

These decisions are the *outputs* (see Figure 2) of the political system. In terms of city governments, they comprise the decisions and non-decisions, the policies, the service provision levels existing in the city. Two distinctions have to be made here. First, there is that between decisions and non-decisions, to which attention has already been drawn. Second, there is the distinction between policies and service levels. This is essentially a distinction between policy-making, which culminates in a statement of intention to do (or not to do) something about a particular problem or issue, and policy implementation, which is the actual implementation of the statement of intention, and which may well differ from the intentions. This distinction is well demonstrated by Crenson's study of pollution controls in a number of American cities, which shows the extent to which they have either adopted anti-pollution policies or have successfully implemented them.[33]

There remain two more links in the system's chain, namely the concepts of outcomes and feedback. Put simply, outcomes are the consequences of outputs, both intended and unintended. It may well be that the process of policy implementation produces consequences that mean that the intentions of the policy-makers have been fulfilled; for example, a policy to cut local taxes or rates may be brought about by a reduction in service levels, thus requiring less locally financed expenditure. But there can be unintended consequences as well. For example, if we reduce expenditure on highway maintenance there may well be an increase in road accidents – surely not a consequence intended by those seeking to cut local taxes.

Last, there is the concept of feedback, shown by the arrowed line in Figure 2 linking outcomes with the environment. Again, feedback is relatively under-analysed as a concept, usually shown as in Figure 2, and explained as the process by which outputs and outcomes are 'fed back' into the different environments, setting off a new series of changes to which the system responds. It is this circularity that systems theorists claim gives systems analysis its dynamic quality, but in reality the nature of feedback loops is a great deal more complicated than Figure 2 suggests. At the very least, the figure should contain loops that join all the parts to each other, but even this is difficult to handle analytically.

Herein lies one of the weaknesses of systems thinking as it has been used to study urban politics. I have dealt with it at length because it has been and remains the predominant model in much of the literature. Nevertheless, it has a number of serious weaknesses, of which three concern us here.

First, there is the criticism that systems analysis is not an explanatory theory which explains how or why city politics operates as it does, but simply a heuristic device for organizing and identifying variables and suggesting relationships between them. As a model it 'explains' either nothing or everything, depending on one's perspective. From our point of view, systems thinking may be defended for its organizing and suggestive qualities, if for nothing else. It provides a useful starting point and may help hypothesis formulation and theory-building.

Second, systems thinking may be criticized because it is empirically untestable. The real world is not made up of little black boxes, as Dearlove has so aptly noted;[34] and besides which it is empirically impossible to distinguish environment from system or to identify the boundary between them. All one can do is rather arbitrarily allocate real-world data to the categories one employs within the systems model.

The last weakness with which we shall deal here arises from the findings of those who have employed systems models in the study of

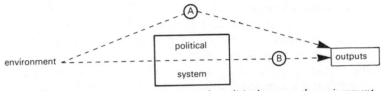

Figure 3   *Possible relationships between the political system, the environment and outputs*

urban politics, which suggest a strong measure of environmental determinism in city politics, removing political explanations of outputs and outcomes. In essence, this criticism sees systems thinking as a form of sociological reductionism, in which much of what happens in the city is seen as the result of environmental change, with the political system and political variables playing little or no part in deciding outputs and outcomes. Figure 3 illustrates this point, with the causal link marked A, rather than B, as suggested in Figure 2.

It was this weakness that has led some writers to reconsider systems thinking as an appropriate model and to introduce ideas about political ideology, disposition or assumptive world as important variables helping to explain the city political process: in so doing, these writers are putting politics back into explaining what happens in the city.

Urban managers and the city

It is this stress on the ideology and values of (particularly) decision-makers that is central to this fourth model of urban politics. Boaden, in *Urban Policy Making*, was perhaps the first British political scientist to stress the importance of what he called the 'political dispositions' of elected members and officials in the policy-making process, by which he meant the disposition of a local authority to meet needs for a particular service or to take a specific form of action. This disposition was seen as having three dimensions: the perceived gap between current and desired standards of service provision; the scope of local needs, and concern with both 'the desirability and the legitimacy of government action'.[35] The first dimension is important because it stresses the importance of perceiving the gaps or changes in the nature of environmental demands. Failure to perceive them, or to judge them as being of sufficient scope, will mean that decision-makers will not produce policy change or amend service levels, or will take inappropriate action: in systemic terms, the political system will either not respond or else will respond inadequately to environmental changes.

Boaden's third dimension, concern about the nature of governmental action, was essentially developed by John Dearlove in *The Politics of Policy in English Local Government*, using the concept of *political ideology* to do so. In his study of Kensington and Chelsea, Dearlove showed the extent to which the local council acted in relation to particular issues, such as planning and housing, in terms of what the local councillors thought appropriate according to their perception of the problem, its causes and appropriate action. Councillors' reactions to local groups were similarly conditioned by their outlook, or 'political ideology', as Dearlove called it. Dearlove also shows the way in which newly elected councillors in this largely one-party Conservative borough were socialized into an acceptance of the prevailing ideology, and though the ideological perspective of officials is neglected in the book, his work remains an important contribution to the literature.[36]

The ideas of political disposition and political ideology have been further developed and utilized by K. Young in his concept of the 'assumptive world' of the local decision-maker. Specifically, Young has been concerned with the use of the concept of values as an explanatory factor in the analysis of public policy-making, and he uses the concept of the assumptive world to describe policy-makers' 'subjective understanding of the environment in which they operate'.[37] The assumptive world provides political actors not just with their audience, backcloth, and other props, but also with their stage directions, lines and cues! As such, it is a closely interwoven mixture of perceptions, images, action precepts and so on, comprising ideology, attitudes and opinions, which, mixed together, determine the way policy-makers perceive and react to policy problems.

Significant as the idea of the 'assumptive world' is, the major problem with the concept lies in its empirical unravelling. Just how do we unpack the different layers that make up the individual's assumptive world, and, what is more, determine the relationship between these and the collective actions of a group of local decision-makers in a local authority? In his work on suburban housing with Kramer, Young has gone some way in showing how the assumptive worlds of Bromley's politicians were important in determining how that authority managed to resist providing overspill housing for inner London, despite the efforts of both the GLC and central government (of all party hues) to achieve the opposite.[38]

Quite clearly, what the work of people like Young and Dearlove shows is that the kind of perceptions that local decision-makers have of their environment and the kind of ideological framework that they have are important determinants of the policy decisions that they are likely to make. Other examples can be drawn from the planning field, where the idea that planning or planners' ideology has been an important factor in planning policy is well documented. One of the best examples is Jon Gower Davies's study[39] of Rye Hill and Newcastle, which clearly demonstrates how planners' ideas about the 'nature of the good society' were the dominant factors in determining planning policies in the area; Dennis's work on Sunderland[40] implies rather similar findings.

Davies's and Dennis's work, however, are both from a discipline other than political science, namely sociology. Yet it is in the field of urban sociology that we find what is perhaps the strongest statement of the view that councillors and officials, as well as other public and private agents and institutions, are important determinants of what happens in the city. The 'urban managerial' thesis, as it is called, is associated essentially with the work of Ray Pahl. Drawing on the work of people like Davies and Dennis, and more importantly that of John Rex, Pahl explained areal inequalities in the city and in their access to resources in terms of the values and goals held by the various urban managers of the urban system, a category including not only councillors and officials, but also estate agents, building society managers, etc.[41]

Pahl has substantially revised his thesis in the light of a number of criticisms, of which two are particularly relevant. First, Pahl was originally not clear on how the managers/gatekeepers were to be defined and their relative power assessed; and, second, the thesis seriously under-emphasized the extent to which market forces and the activities of central government seriously constrained the managers' actions. In reformulating his thesis,[42] Pahl continued to stress the managers' role in resource allocation, but recognized that they had little control over resource availability.

The city and class struggles

Urban sociology provides yet another theoretical perspective on urban politics, one that has been seen as undermining the managerialist thesis.[43] This is the neo-Marxist perspective, associated with particularly the writings of Manuel Castells,[44] and known as the structuralist perspective. Space does not permit a full discussion of this important but difficult area of writing, which has rapidly become the dominant paradigm in urban sociology, and so only its essentials are presented here.[45] In essence, recent Marxist theory has increasingly recognized the growth of urban class struggles in advanced capitalist societies: in other words, the process of class exploitation continues as much in the consumption process outside work as it does in the production process. It is this perspective that is used to explain the differences in service provision, life chances and access to resources by and within different cities.

The main theoretical work in this field has undoubtedly been that undertaken by Manuel Castells. For him, cities and city politics are a direct reflection of the logic inherent in a capitalist mode of production; and most specifically the city is at the centre of the process whereby labour power is reproduced. This is achieved through the provision of the essential means of consumption – housing, education and other amenities – a function increasingly undertaken by the state in its many forms, not least important of which is city government. However, given that there is inevitably a conflict between allocating resources to the (generally profitable) process of production and to the (unprofitable but necessary) process of consumption, and given the dominance of the production function in the capitalist system, it follows that crises are most likely to develop in the provision of the means of collective consumption. Since this process is largely a function of the state, and particularly the local state, these crises are likely to occur at the city or urban level. Thus urban conflict (or city politics) is in essence a conflict over (or crisis in) collective consumption. Thus, for example, the demands of the capitalistic production process lead to crises in such areas as housing, urban transport, health, education and so on, which require massive and increasing state action. In Castells's terms, state intervention in collective consumption is necessary either to regulate the process by which labour power is reproduced and/or to deflect working-class political pressures. In simple terms, the social wage is used either to supplement real wages in the productive sector or else to alleviate its worst excesses. And crises in the provision of collective consumption are significant because they affect working and *middle* classes alike, giving rise to new patterns of inequality, and to new forms of urban political protest.

Castells's work can (and has been) criticized by Marxists and non-Marxists alike. First, his definition of urban and the urban system raises problems: to what extent is the urban system primarily one designed for labour reproduction, and to what extent is the state primarily concerned with consumption rather than production?[46] For example, is the provision of roads primarily a question of labour reproduction, or is it primarily a question of assistance to the production process? In other words, Castells can apparently be criticized for the narrowness of his definition of the urban and for his excessive focus on the consumption function. However, Castells does not deny the existence of other processes within the urban system – particularly production functions – but considers that his focus and definition are most useful in helping to understand and analyse urban problems, a point not denied by his critics.[47]

A second criticism of Castells centres around his conception of collective consumption and his subsequent use of it. For Castells, the defining element of collective consumption is that it is provided by the state, a feature that distinguishes it from individual consumption, which is provided through the market place. In other words, it is the *provision* of the facilities that determines whether or not they are collective consumption, rather than their use (that is, whether or not they are indivisible goods). Pahl[48] has attempted to deny the utility of the concept altogether, arguing that it is difficult to make a precise distinction between the individual or collective consumption of any good, whether in terms of how it is produced or how it is used. Saunders,[49] however, maintains that Castells's definition in producer terms is consistent, and that state-provided facilities can have different political effects in the urban arena from those produced in the market place. Saunders is more critical of the *way* in which Castells *uses* his concept, as for example in terms of the provision of housing – a crucial urban resource, which can be provided either collectively or individually. As a result, rather than being the means by which non-capitalist classes are brought together to confront capitalism, a crisis in the provision of collective consumption may drive the non-capitalist classes further apart. As the Cutteslowe Walls[50] show, a crisis in the provision of housing does not mean that owner-occupiers and tenants will join together to resolve it: more likely the reverse, as the owners see their homes (and their monetary values) threatened by the building of nearby council estates.

Furthermore, as Saunders argues,[51] a crisis in collective consumption does not necessarily mean that all those subject to it will react against the state and the capitalist system, as the experience of housing again shows. Not all the homeless join squatters' movements, nor do all tenants join rent strikes or all ratepayers refuse to pay inflated rate demands.

A third, more general line of criticism relates to the question of the nature of urban conflicts as class conflicts, the relationships between the economic and the political, and the central problem of the relative autonomy of the state. Castells differs from other Marxists in *not* seeing urban conflicts as themselves constituting class conflicts, a view that follows from his emphasis on collective consumption as urban. But, given the dominance of the economic (production) sector over the political in Marxist theory generally, which implies that the primary function of the state in capitalist systems is to ensure that system's continual existence and to aid the process of capital accumulation, it follows that urban conflicts *must* be primarily class conflicts. In other words, the crises in collective consumption will be felt most heavily by the working class and less so by the middle class, who anyway will be more able to make alternative provision. Thus, for example, cuts in the education service, such as increasing the price of school meals, reducing school bus services, not providing books, etc., fall less heavily on the middle class than they do on the working class.

But also central here is the question of the relative autonomy of the state, or more particularly of the various institutions that comprise the state. This is an issue central to all recent Marxist writings, instrumentalist (e.g. Miliband[52]) and structuralist (e.g. Castells) alike.

What is of concern is the extent to which the state can act independently of the capitalist system, that is to say, how far, in both the short and long term the state can undertake policies *not* in the interests of the capitalist class. For most Marxists, such action is not generally seen as a possibility, though the real world is full of examples where the state has attempted to act against what one Conservative prime minister, Edward Heath, called 'the unacceptable face of capitalism'. Furthermore, Marxists' use of the state as a concept often implies a monolithic, homogeneous, unitary entity, and as such appears to deny the very fragmentation of institutions and agencies, and more importantly the conflicts (particularly over resources) that go on within and between their different levels and parts, which in practice comprise the state. The Marxist concept almost appears to deny the existence of possible conflict between central and local government, between city and county government, and between county and district levels, let alone any other conflicts that might involve these parts of the state with such other state institutions as health boards, water authorities, gas, electricity and other nationalized industries.[53] Furthermore, the Marxists' concept of the state seems to deny the intra-agency conflicts that seem to make up so much of 'the real world of city politics'. [54]

Inter-departmental battles over the allocation of resources for Castells's collective consumption – over such services as education, housing and leisure, for example – imply a fragmented, not united, local state, which again raises questions about the theoretical relationship between the state and the capitalist system with which Marxists have still not dealt satisfactorily.[55]

Despite these criticisms, however, enough has been said here to indicate the importance of recent Marxist writings in contributing to our understanding of urban political processes and in posing questions that raise doubts about the utility of other explanations. Most Marxists, for example, would deny the place of values and individuals in the process, hence rendering the managerialist thesis obsolete, though such a claim is clearly extravagant, as Pickvance has strongly argued.[56] Non-Marxist urban sociologists have begun to respond to these issues,[57] though urban political scientists in Britain have to date largely remained either sceptical or else largely uncritical of the new Marxist urban sociology.[58]

We have now considered five analytical models of city politics, each of which may be considered as providing an explanation of what happens in the city in terms of public policies and services. Yet each alone fails to provide a complete explanation of the city's political processes: it is *not* simply a question of understanding the institutional arrangements or the community power structure; the nature of the local environment or the components of political actors' assumptive worlds. To adopt any single perspective is to close one's eyes to the possible virtues and contribution of other theoretical perspectives: the models should not be seen as competitive so much as complementary. We need to fuse our models together, stressing how each has its part to play in explaining urban political processes.

Such a model would retain strong systemic qualities: the city is still seen as a political system that responds to environmental change, but it is an environment that, in its economic and social elements at least, is strongly determined by prevailing beliefs about the relationship between economic and political sectors as well as by the dominant mode of production. In other words, in Western societies, a large part of the urban environment is shaped by its predominantly capitalist economic sector. How the system responds to environmental changes and the nature of that response is seen as being determined by the key elements of the other theories: that is, by the institutional arrangements, the power structure, the assumptive world of those in the power structure, and the interaction between individuals and institutions. Thus, for example, the political institutions and the political structure of the city may be considered as setting the parameters for political response: they provide the channels, the access points, through which political demands can be made and political support channelled. Indeed, they may well condition the rules of the urban political game.

The power structure of the city – who occupies the position of power and how it is used – is also an important determinant of the system response to environmental change. Without an understanding of the power structure we cannot begin to understand how decision-makers formulate the policies and take the decisions (or non-decisions) that they do, or even to know who the decision-makers are. And without some idea of their assumptive world – of their environmental perceptions, attitudes, values and ideology – we cannot understand why decision-makers prefer some kinds of policies or some levels of service provision rather than others.

Thus all five models have a part to play in understanding the public policies and levels of service provided in our cities. In the ultimate analysis, city politics are about demands for action or inaction; they are about institutional arrangements and interaction; above all, they are about power and ideology. Before analysing these aspects of city politics, however, we must first examine changes in the environment of British urban areas.

3   Environmental change and the city

At the end of the last chapter, it was suggested that urban political processes were essentially either responses to a changing social and economic environment or else attempts to shape or (in Young's terms) to manage that environment,[1] even though these responses were conditioned by what we called the ideological dispositions of the actors involved in the process.

The environment that city governments seek to manage is a complex and constantly changing one. The Britain of 1980 is vastly different from that of 1950, and, since most people live in or near major urban centres, it has largely been the urban authorities that have had to cope with these changes. Given the complexity of that environment, it is helpful for our purposes if we simplify it analytically. Thus, rather than attempt to discuss the changes in any detail, this chapter seeks to outline the major changes that have taken place in Britain since 1945 along three major dimensions: areal, economic and social. By implication we shall discuss some of the changes that have taken place in the political environment.[2]

Areal change, 1945–75

By areal changes we mean those major shifts in population size and distribution that have taken place over the last thirty-five years. In 1951 Britain's population was estimated at 50 million, whereas by 1971 it had reached 55 million, an increase of 10 per cent. But this increase contains changes within Britain that are also of considerable importance, particularly for the major urban areas. Thus, for example, as Champion demonstrates,[3] both northern England and much of rural Wales lost population between 1961 and 1971, but so did many of the major urban centres. At the same time, however, parts of the 'megalopolis'[4] outside London experienced population increases in excess of 10 per cent, as did many coastal/holiday areas attractive to those retiring from work.[5]

What these examples suggest is that the pattern of population change and distribution over the last thirty-five years is not a simple one. It reflects a number of important changes – the rise of megalopolitan Britain around the corridor running from London and the South-East, through the Midlands up to the North-West; the suburbanization of much of the country; the continuing decline of the Celtic fringe and many rural parts of the country, and, last but not least, different population movements among different age and social economic groups. None of these changes is particularly novel. Most were seen as important elements of population change between 1951 and 1961 and had their origins back in the 1930s, though the latter part of the period is the one that sees the most marked suburbanization process.

Writing in the early 1970s, Hall *et al.* identified the rise of megalopolitan England' as the main development in post-war Britain. Over the post-war period, the UK population has increased 10 to 15 per cent, and most of this growth has taken place within the heavily industrialized urban core of the country, namely, megalopolitan England, as Table 1 shows. Having said that, however, the centres of highly urbanized areas have generally lost population, dropping from around 64 per cent in 1931 to a little over 50 per cent in 1971. What this reflected was the process of slum clearance and urban redevelopment of the older industrial cities during the 1950s and 1960s, which, when added to the general movement of population out of these areas, has meant a massive suburban growth around the major urban agglomerations and free-standing cities. In other words, as Clawson and Hall put it, 'the growth of population in megalopolitan England has been wholly in its suburban areas',[6] which more than doubled their size in the post-war period. In practical terms, this

Table 1 *Population trends in the UK, 1931–71*

	1931	1951	1961	1966	1971
UK population ('000s)	46,038.4	50,225.2	52,708.9	53,788.5	55,349.0
Population megalopolitan England ('000s)	27,595.4	30,489.2	32,241.9	32,864.5	33,839.3
Percentage of UK population	59.9%	60.7%	61.2%	61.1%	61.1%

meant that a city like Liverpool lost almost a quarter of its population between 1951 and 1971,[7] while some of the inner London boroughs, such as Islington and Tower Hamlets, lost around 20 per cent of their population between 1961 and 1971 alone. Similarly, cities such as Manchester and Newcastle lost 18 per cent of their population, though in other places, such as Leeds and Sheffield, this population loss was much lower – in the order of 3 per cent. Yet in all cases these cities' suburban hinterland showed considerable increase in population: around London for example, towns such as Weybridge, Watford and Crawley all experienced considerable growth. Near Manchester, towns such as Macclesfield, Lymm and Wilmslow, as well as the New Towns of Runcorn and Warrington, have all experienced growth. The decentralization trend is well demonstrated by Champion,[8] who shows the different types of core–ring shift experienced by some twenty metropolitan areas for two periods, 1951–61 and 1961–71. Of these twenty, only six experienced any movement of population into the core, all in the earlier period. Since 1971, this decentralization process has slowed only marginally.

So the picture of the urban environment in megalopolitan England is one of population movement out of the core urban areas into the rapidly expanding suburban fringes. In other words, even in the main area of population growth, there have been significant and important movements of population which themselves have generated pressures for political action by urban decision-makers.

But if population growth has taken place largely in megalopolitan England (and then mainly in the suburban rings), it follows that other parts of the United Kingdom must have experienced considerable population loss and decline. This kind of change has also generated demands for political action; and since some of the changes have been particularly marked in the old urban areas of North-East England, central Scotland and South Wales, they too have posed problems for urban decision-makers.

As Figure 4 clearly shows, it is the Celtic fringe of the country that has either lost population or had the smallest increases. In Wales, Scotland, northern and south-western England, many areas lost population, and the shift from core to suburban ring is also repeated in the main urban centres – Glasgow and Edinburgh in Scotland; Cardiff and Swansea in Wales, Newcastle and the Cleveland area in the North-East. Other parts of Wales; as well as the South-West and parts of East Anglia, were attractive as retirement areas, as Law and Warnes show in their work on the elderly.[9] But some places, for example Cumbria and Northumberland, faced considerable population loss and decline as the combination of declining traditional industry and rural depopulation made itself felt.

Thus, though there has been a broad movement of population from North to South – from the periphery to the centre – the impact of this movement has not been spread evenly across the regions. Furthermore, intra-regional movements, mainly the centrifugal shifts of population within the urban areas of megalopolitan England, further complicate the pattern. It is still further complicated when some of the demographic characteristics of these population movements are considered.

We have already referred to the movement of the elderly to traditional retirement areas on the South Coast and the Fylde as well as to new destinations in the South-West, Wales and East Anglia. This mobility of the elderly clearly takes place among those who are better off – those who can afford, either through savings, pension scheme or possible sale of the family home, to retire to their bungalow by the sea.[10] In the city, by contrast, the elderly comprise a large proportion of those left behind: in Liverpool, for example, almost one in five of the population in 1971 was over 60. Furthermore, the tendency for people to live longer continues: the Central Statistical Office estimated that the number of people above retirement age rose by 9 per cent between 1970 and mid 1975, and that the number of elderly over 85 rose by double that percentage. It is this latter group that places particular demands upon medical and social services, especially in urban areas.

The retiring elderly are but one of the mobile groups of Britain's population. Even though the south-east region has become a net exporter of population since the Second World War, it still remains attractive to the 15–24-year-olds, reflecting London's magnetism for the young. Suburban growth has largely accommodated the 25–44-year-olds, together with their school-age children, and this movement has been particularly marked in the New Town areas. Again, these mobile groups have generally contained the most able, skilled working- or middle-class people, leaving the central city with still more of those least able to fend for themselves.

Since 1970 there have been a number of other important changes, prime among them being that population growth has virtually stopped, owing largely to the continually falling birth rate since 1964. This change has posed tremendous problems in a number of local authority services and planning areas. Education has been

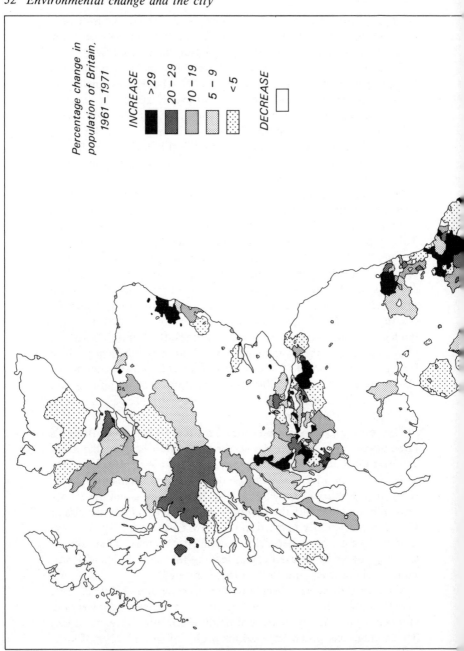

Figure 4 *Population mobility in the UK*

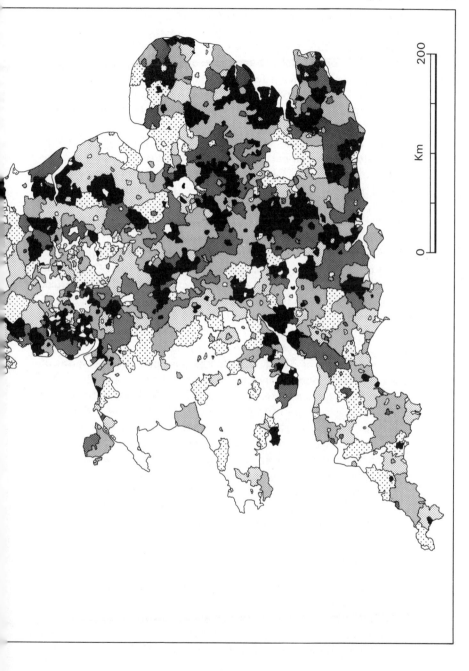

particularly affected by what is known as the 'falling rolls' problem, namely the declining number of school-age children and the consequences this poses for school and class sizes, numbers of teachers required, school building programmes, etc. Structure planning has also been affected by the rapid decline in population growth, as estimates of population size have had to be constantly revised, with all the consequences this has for jobs, house building, transport and shopping.

This latter issue has been further complicated by the continuing inter- and intra-regional population shifts. Broadly speaking, the metropolitan areas, with the exceptions of South and West Yorkshire, have lost population, a loss most heavily marked in Greater London (almost 6 per cent down between 1970 and 1975) and Merseyside (almost 5 per cent down over the same period). More detailed studies within these metropolitan counties reveal that this loss is heaviest among the inner parts of the metropolitan areas,[11] again posing particular problems for these authorities. Outside the metropolitan areas, regional population change since 1970 is varied, but generally reflects the shifts described earlier. Population growth has been most marked in East Anglia (up 7 per cent) and the South West (4.5 per cent), while the northern and north-western regions and Scotland all showed small losses of population.[12]

It is this sort of population change – a fairly quick reversal of existing trends, but not uniformly so throughout the country – that particularly places a stress on the urban political system, making it difficult to gauge appropriate responses. Some areas – Kent and Cheshire are good examples – continue to be attractive for new suburban growth, with its accompanying in-migration, whereas other areas, particularly inner-city areas, face decline and decay at a pace almost too rapid for governments, local or national, to reverse. Thus, for example, the most dismal observers of Merseyside privately offer little hope for the kind of inner-city initiatives being made there, believing the area to be beyond resuscitation.[13]

Industrial change, 1945–75

If environmental changes of the demographic kind just discussed pose difficulties for urban policy-makers, so do the kind of changes that take place in the industrial/economic environment. Currently, for example, we are being told that the development of the silicon chip/microprocessor is going to revolutionize our daily lives, causing the loss of many jobs, creating a need to develop ways and means of using increasing hours of leisure, and completely changing the industrial face of the country. Similarly, the continuing energy crisis poses all kinds of problems in areas of transportation, housing and industry, though it can be argued that governments, at both national and local levels, appear only slightly more able to deal with either of these major changes than do the rest of us.

Yet the industrial and economic structure of Britain has changed beyond all recognition since the Second World War. The country's rankings in such industries as steel, shipbuilding, aircraft construction, textiles and car manufacturing have all dropped, if not disappeared altogether. By contrast, the service sector has grown beyond all recognition, and particularly important has been the growth of public sector services and employment. Local authority employment has been one of the most marked in terms of public sector growth, rising from 1.4 million in 1949 to over 3 million by 1975.

Technological development has also played an important part in the changing picture of Britain's industrial and economic profile. The introduction of computers, the substitution of relatively cheap oil (until recently) for older fossil fuels and the development of the silicon chip have all played their part and will continue to do so.

Some idea of the nature and scope of economic and industrial change can be grasped from the following figures. Roughly speaking, Britain's gross domestic product doubled between 1948 and 1976, as did the index of industrial production. Prices, however, more than quadrupled over the same period, while the level of consumer expenditure rose from £8552 million in 1948 to £73,358 million in 1976.[14] The former figures show the slow rate of economic growth in Britain generally and in the productive sector particularly, while the latter gives some idea of both the impact of inflation on domestic prices and the tremendous increase that has taken place in consumer expenditure.

However, these changes are at the gross national level and tell us little about the kinds of changes that have taken place in particular industries. Table 2 gives us an idea about the changing employment structure in the UK and in particular selected industries. The table shows that overall employment grew by some 10 per cent, but that the manufacturing sector declined quite markedly after an initial growth in the early 1950s. Particular industries, such as agriculture, mining and textiles, are marked by very large falls in the number of people

Table 2   *Employment in selected UK industries, 1948–76 ('000s)*

Industry	1948	1958	1968	1976
Agriculture	853	643	437	395
Mining, quarrying	888	865	509	347
Textiles	1000	952	751	513
Chemicals	447	544	5C9	423
Vehicles	959	1235	821	743
Other manufacturing	248	291	360	329
Distribution				
trades	2068	2608	2890	2722
Food, drink and tobacco	756	938	853	714
Local government	*	1626	2286	2851
Total manufacturing	8241	9240	8946	7207
Total all	20,732	22,290	23,667	22,176

* Not applicable

Sources: *British Labour Statistics, Historical Abstract, 1886–1968*, London: HMSO 1971; *British Labour Statistics Yearbook, 1976*, London: HMSO 1976.

employed – of the order of around 50 per cent in all cases. Other sectors, such as chemicals and vehicles, show slower rates of decline after initial increases. The 'other manufacturing' category, which includes many industrial groupings too small to isolate into separate categories and which may thus be considered as possibly containing those sectors where rapid growth takes place following technological change, is a sector that grew only slowly.

By contrast, the non-manufacturing sector has grown throughout the period, by almost 40 per cent in the case of the distribution trades for example, though food, drink and tobacco remains constant, reflecting technological change. But by far the largest rate of growth is demonstrated by our public sector example, namely local government, which has almost doubled in terms of numbers employed over the last twenty years.

Nevertheless, changes in numbers employed may reflect technological change as much as change in the balance between production and service sectors of the economy. Agriculture, for example, which is capital-intensive and has experienced considerable technological change since the last world war, has increased output considerably while continuing to shed labour, as Newby *et al.* have clearly demonstrated.[15]

It is difficult to get fully comparative figures for output over the same period, because of the different bases of calculation, but Table 3

Table 3 *Output in selected UK industries, 1948-76* (£ million)

Industry	1948 Total	%	1958 Total	%	1968 Total	%	1976 Total	%
Chemicals	620	5.8	1584	7.2	3148	8.1	6885	10.2
Vehicles	745	7.0	2241	10.2	3821	9.9	6130	9.1
Textiles	1309	12.3	1848	8.4	2671	6.9	3423	5.1
Mining/ quarrying	509	4.8	988	4.5	1040	2.7	3093	4.6
Food, drink and tobacco	2639	24.8	4443	20.2	7567	19.6	12,569	18.6
All manufacturing	10,632		22,039		38,697		67,415	

Source: *Census of Production, 1976, Provisional Results*, London: HMSO 1978.

gives some figures for some of the industries we considered in employment terms, together with their percentage of total output. The table shows the very steady growth of such industries as vehicles, and food, drink and tobacco; the gradual expansion of chemicals, and the continued decline in textiles and, until very recently, in mining.

Summarizing both sets of tables, which reflect what is already known about the post-war British economy, there has been a decline in the manufacturing sector, most particularly in the older, heavy-goods industries based on primary raw materials, and most of the growth has taken place in the service industry sector or in terms of non-productive public employment, such as local government. Public sector employment in 1979 accounted for something like 30 per cent of the total work force,[16] of which three-quarters were outside of the nationalized industries.

Much of this change reflects state action as successive governments have become more and more involved in the problems of economic management and have concerned themselves with employment and inflation. There are various views as to the role of the state in relation to the economy,[17] and we shall consider some of them later, but here we are primarily concerned with describing some of the major consequences of state action for the economy.

Undoubtedly one of the main lines of government policy with consequences for the economy have been the successive attempts at regional policy. Regional policy had its origins in the unemployment of the 1930s and has always had as one of its major aims the reduction of levels of unemployment in the regions. Indeed, as Prest and Coppock note,[18] level of unemployment was the sole criterion used for designating areas of assistance until 1966 – the development areas, intermediate areas and so on. These areas, with generally slow rates of economic growth, if not stagnation and decay, are largely to be found in the peripheral parts of Britain – Scotland, Wales, the North, North-West and West. All have had a persistently higher-than-average rate of unemployment, as well as exhibiting most, if not all, the symptoms of economic decline as their traditional heavy industries have lost ground.

But economists suggest another argument as to why the state might adopt regional policies, namely that there may well be some divergence between the social and private costs involved in the location decisions of individual firms. For example, increased migration might result from decisions by firms to locate as close to their markets as possible. In searching for the most desirable location in terms of the balance between social and private costs, governments might well want to adopt a regional strategy. In attempting briefly to assess post-war regional policy in Britain, it is convenient to consider it in terms of two time periods: up to 1966, during which, as we have noted, unemployment levels were the sole criterion guiding the policy, and since 1966, when regional policy has been much more a part of national economic planning strategy and the criteria were much wider.

To a very large extent, regional policy has depended upon the application of the stick-and-carrot principle. The stick was generally the refusal of an Industrial Development Certificate (IDC), without which an industrial developer was unable to build new industrial floor space, while the carrots were the grants in aid given to manufacturers who set up factories in the development areas, such grants varying in amount with the relevant status of the development area.

Dividing Britain into peripheral and prosperous regions, Hall shows how well the use of the stick worked for the periods 1955–60 and 1966–70.[19] The disadvantaged peripheral regions, such as Scotland, Wales and the North, received just under 43 per cent of new industrial development between 1955 and 1960, but they fared much better (59 per cent) in the later period, 1966–70. By contrast, the prosperous regions of the South-East and the Midlands took 57 per cent of new factory space in the first period, but only just over 40 per cent in the latter. Clearly, the governmental stick operated better in

1966–70 than it did in the mid 1950s, perhaps in part at least a reflection of the different ideologies of the ruling governmental party in each period: Conservative in the late 1950s, Labour in the late 1960s.

However, the picture is not so good when the creation of total employment, rather than simply factory jobs, is concerned. In the first period, 89 per cent of all new jobs went to the prosperous regions, a figure that fell to just under 50 per cent in the second period. This result is largely due to the fact that not all newly created jobs were factory jobs: indeed, the majority were created in the tertiary or service sector of the economy.[20]

If the peripheral regions did less well in terms of both jobs and new factory space, this is also to be seen from Table 4, adapted from Hall,[21] and covering a number of indicators. In practically all cases (as Table 3 also shows), the peripheral regions fared less well during the period presented in the table, a result that would be little different either before or after the time period selected here. And these regional figures contained considerable variations within them, so that cities like Liverpool and Glasgow continued to suffer more than did the

Table 4 *Regional relations for unemployment, activity rates and household incomes, 1961–6*

	Unemploy-ment (average)	Activity rates		Weekly household income (average)
		Male	Female	
Peripheral regions				
Northern	185	96	85	84
Yorks. and Humberside	75	104	100	95
North-West	120	193	107	95
Wales	165	90	73	90
Scotland	205	100	99	94
Prosperous regions				
South-East	65 ⎱	102	106	112
East Anglia	90 ⎰			93
South-West	100	85	81	92
West Midlands	65	106	109	109
East Midlands	66	99	96	98

Source: Adapted from P. Hall, *Urban and Regional Planning,* Table 4, p.133.

regions of which they were part. Thus, while governments worked hard to provide new jobs in the peripheral regions, it is difficult to escape the conclusion that their efforts made little difference to the overall picture up to the mid 1960s: continuing prosperity and growth in the Midlands and the South-East; slightly arrested decline in much of the rest of Britain.

After the mid 1960s, however, government adopted a somewhat different strategy. The 1964 Labour Government introduced the ill-fated Department of Economic Affairs, along with the Regional Economic Planning Councils and Boards, in an attempt to introduce to Britain something akin to the indicative economic planning system of France. This story, however, is beyond our scope,[22] and we need only record that the result of the initiative 'was a mixed and not always a happy one'.[23] For our purposes, it is perhaps more important to note that the important changes that took place in regional strategy were associated with the 1966 Industrial Development Act, which significantly improved the carrots being offered to industrialists if they were to locate in the periphery. The so-called development areas were now much more widely defined, and included such black spots as Merseyside (but not North-East Lancashire), while the cash incentives and the benefits offered were much improved: 40 per cent grants against the value of plant and machinery, together with exclusion from payment of Selective Employment Tax (SET) together with receipt of the Regional Employment Premium (REP), payable for every additional worker employed and fixed at £100 per annum for an adult male worker. As Hall notes, 'SET–REP became a completely regional device to attract industry into the development areas – and a very powerful one.'[24]

The arrival of the 1970 Conservative Government led to changes, for by now it had become apparent that under-investment in the production sector generally, rather than specifically in the periphery, was a major problem facing the British economy. Thus, creation of jobs in the development areas was no longer the overriding aim: rather, it was the modernization of industrial plant everywhere, with investment grants, generous depreciation allowances and high initial allowances for buildings – even if no particular increase in jobs was expected.

Up until then, it is fair to say that regional policy had operated against the trends: certainly the disparity between regions in terms of unemployment was reduced in the mid 1960s, and things would undoubtedly have been much worse if the policy had not operated. Moore and Rhodes[25] conclude that regional policy directed over 200,000 jobs to development areas and helped the balance of payments, while stimulating national output without excessively straining national resources. But as a policy it depended (and still largely does) on private sector initiatives rather than on direct action by the state, and as a result it is largely big firms, or capital-intensive ones, and often the multinationals, who have received much of the aid from regional policy, but for whom regional differentials in the UK are largely irrelevant.[26]

Since the early 1970s, the British economy has posed more general problems which override the regional questions to which we have just referred. Reactions to the energy crises of 1973 and 1978/9 and the continuing problems of 'stagflation' pose severe problems for the state, notwithstanding the short-term cushioning effects of North Sea oil. Unemployment has almost doubled in the decade, from 792,000 to 1,506,000 by early 1978, and it is still expected to rise as we enter the 1980s. Long-term employment, especially among the older and less skilled members of the population, has particularly increased.[27] Many large companies in the private sector, such as British Leyland, Rolls Royce and Ferranti's, have found themselves in severe economic difficulties and have relied upon the state for assistance. In other words, the 1970s have produced a worsening of the economic environment in Britain, one to which central and local government has had to react.

What is significant for our purposes is that many local authorities, and perhaps particularly city governments, have not been particularly active in the economic sector, at least until recently. In part, as we shall see, the general pattern of economic growth until the early 1970s, however slow it might have been, meant that most authorities never felt the need to intervene directly in the economic sector, even if they perceived it as necessary and desirable. The colder economic climate of the 1970s has led them to become more active, precisely at the time when the private sector by and large is most unwilling to respond to their advances. Fascinatingly enough, it is city governments, with their concern over declining inner-city areas, that have become most heavily involved in the economic sector as, in partnership with the central government, they have developed strategies designed to alleviate inner-city stress and deprivation.

The previous emphasis by central government on *regional* policy, together with land use policies which implied urban containment and reduced population density, have meant that most local authorities, including urban ones, have generally not laid great stress on policies designed to promote or maintain the viability of the local economy. There have been a number of notable exceptions – Liverpool and Glasgow among them – but the continuing economic growth and the spread of the tertiary or service sector through the commercial re-development of city centres did not cause urban governors to be generally concerned about industrial and economic regeneration. It was not until the mid 1960s that the tide began to turn, and a change of policy emphasis occurred. In large part this was due to the appearance of a marked decline in the standard of life in inner-city areas, and perhaps particularly to the fact that many of these areas contained a substantial immigrant population who suffered additionally from discrimination in terms of jobs, housing, education and other respects.

At the same time, a number of explanations, both academic and bureaucratic, were provided for this situation, each of which helped shift the policy emphasis. Initially, explanations of poverty and inner-city decline were based on individualistic/cycle-of-deprivation terms: poverty arose because of *personal* problems, which could be cured essentially by positive discrimination designed to 'top up' existing services and encourage self-help. Such policies were to be found in the Urban Programme of the 1964–70 Labour Government, with its stress on educational priority areas; extra financial assistance to existing services in areas of multiple deprivation, and the Home Office's twelve Community Development Projects.[28]

This 'individualistic' style of explanation of inner-city problems has subsequently developed into a view that sees those problems as peculiar to the inner city and solvable within the existing network of administrative, political and economic relations. Indeed, this view stresses weaknesses in these relationships – the inadequate co-ordination/administration of services – together with what are regarded as poorly conceived government policies, as being as important in terms of explaining inner-city problems as is the readily recognized decline in the economic base of inner-city areas. Those associated with this view include most government departments, most political parties and pressure groups concerned with the question, as well as most of the inner-area studies and the Central Policy Review Staff (CPRS).[29]

A more critical explanation of inner-city problems is the essentially neo-Marxist one, which sees the problem as both inevitable and endemic, the result of the logic of the capitalist system. As such, the problem is not simply an inner-city one, but can be found wherever industries are in decline: it is a problem of declining capitalist industry rather than a purely inner-city phenomenon. Put simply, capitalism, in its search for profitability and accumulation, has not favoured the inner city, but, left largely unfettered, has gone where the grass is greenest.

Interestingly enough, this critique had its origins in the Home Office's Community Development Projects (CDPs), best presented in their pamphlets, *The Costs of Industrial Change* and *Gilding the Ghetto*.[30] And though they are often rather naively and simplistically presented, a number of other studies have tended to support some of their arguments, showing, for example, that job loss in inner-city areas has been caused as much by the closure of firms as by governmental dispersal policies.[31] But suffice it to say that governmental policies have rejected the CDP view that only complete state control over investment decisions and employment policies in areas of decline will lead to an amelioration of these problems. Instead, central government has preferred the first explanation: hence its concern with co-ordinated service delivery and economic regeneration through its partnerships with inner-city authorities. As a result, these authorities, and many others also concerned with the problems of economic and industrial decline in their areas, have become increasingly concerned with managing their local economics, as, for example, the attempts to rejuvenate the dockland areas of East London and Liverpool demonstrate.

We have dealt with some of these issues at some length because both regional and inner-city policy areas demonstrate the close relationship between the economic environment and the political system. Indeed, empirically it is often difficult to see cause and effect between systemic action (governmental policies) and environmental change (economic changes), though analytically the distinction remains useful. Quite clearly, what we have described in terms of the changing economic environment in post-war Britain has had important policy consequences at both central government and local authority level. Currently, with unemployment in excess of 1.5 million, interest rates at around the 20 per cent level and a continuing deterioration in the economy expected, the condition of the economic environment is likely to be an ever-increasingly important factor which urban governors will have to take into account in policy-making terms.

Social change, 1945–75

If the state of the economic environment is currently of major concern for urban governors, it is also true to say that one of the major sources of pressure on local government in Britain generally since 1945 has been the changes that have taken place in the social environment. Undoubtedly, the standard of living in Britain, although below that of many of its European partners, is much higher today than it was in 1945. Associated with these increases have been rising expectations, not only in terms of private consumption but also in terms of our consumption of public goods: yesterday's luxuries have become today's necessities. The spread of such consumer capital goods as televisions, cars, washing machines, hi-fi equipment, etc., is evidence of this point. The same kind of expansion can be seen in public service provision, for example in education, with the rapid increase in numbers undergoing further education in the post-1963 Robbins era, and with the increase in the school-leaving age to 16 in the 1970s. There has also been a tremendous increase in the number of people living in public sector housing, with currently over a third of households occupying such housing; and there have been massive increases in social services, particularly for the most disadvantaged groups such as the mentally and physically handicapped, in social security and pension benefits, as well as in health care. What has come to be known as the social wage plays a significant part in our standard of living.

Furthermore, even the changing balance between work and leisure, which means more time for leisure pursuits, has had implications for city authorities, as the major increases in the provision of leisure facilities by local authorities in the 1970s demonstrates. Since 1951, the average working week has fallen from almost forty-five hours a week to just under forty, while the number able to afford and take more than one holiday a year has also increased. According to *Social Trends*[32] the proportion of people taking a holiday away from home in the UK has risen from 25 per cent in 1951 to 36 per cent in 1977, while those going abroad rose from 2 per cent (1951) to 8 per cent (1977).

We can get some indication of how leisure patterns have changed according to changing standards of living since 1945 by looking at the growth in membership of a number of organizations involved in sport and leisure (Table 5). In all cases, activities such as caravanning, riding, yachting, golfing and visiting historic buildings all show very

Table 5 *Membership of sport and leisure organizations ('000s)*

	1951	1961	1971	1977
Caravan club	11	44	84	184
Pony club	20	30	33	50
Royal Yachting Association	1	11	31	52
English Golfing Union	n.a.*	131	279	450
National Trust	26	118	263	700

* Not available

Source: *Social Trends,* no. 9, London: HMSO 1979, Tables 12.15, 12.16, pp. 183–4.

rapid increases since 1945, and especially since 1970. All reflect increasing affluence and leisure time.

The spread of other consumer durables also reflects the social changes of the last thirty-five years. Ninety per cent of households now have television sets, over half of them colour sets. The number of telephones rented rose by two-thirds during the 1960s, while the number of cars licensed rose by ninety per cent to reach 12 million by 1970.

The effect of all these changes might most easily be summarized by saying that most people in Britain are more affluent, more mobile, and have more leisure time than was true thirty-five years ago. The consequences of these changes have posed and continue to pose problems to which city governments – indeed, the state in all its aspects – have had to respond and will continue to have to respond. The more mobile, more affluent population has, for example, broken up and spread out family networks, with all the consequences that this might create in terms of demands for more care for the elderly or the very young: the family network, no longer so closely knit, is less able to provide the support and care it might have done thirty or forty years ago. Greater mobility and affluence have also placed increased pressure on the countryside and the need to conserve places of outstanding natural beauty.

Demands such as these on the government arise from the general increase in living standards, but it must be remembered that these increases have not been shared equally, and that there have been other societal changes which have also produced demands for governmental action. Taking an example of the latter sort of change, undoubtedly the changing role of women in society, with their demands for greater independence and equality, has produced considerable changes in society and will continue to do so. In this respect, the introduction of the birth control pill and of other improved methods of contraception (notwithstanding any possible detrimental side-effects) has undoubtedly contributed considerably to the changing role of women in society, at least for those who may want such a change. Similarly, so have legislative reforms in the areas of abortion and divorce, by which both have been made easier to obtain: for example, divorces rose from just 28,000 in 1961 to 125,000 in 1976.

Not all the social changes have necessarily been for the better. Far from being abolished by the welfare reforms associated with the Labour Government of 1945–51, poverty remained to be rediscovered in the mid 1960s: currently over 3 million people are estimated to have incomes below or just above Supplementary Benefits level. The percentage of the population receiving such benefits has risen from 5 per cent in 1951 to almost 9 per cent in 1976, suggesting that more rather than fewer people are being caught in what is euphemistically described as the 'poverty trap'.

Crime – or at least reported crime – is on the increase. Serious offences rose from 547,000 in 1951 to over 2.5 million in 1978. In these figures the increase in juvenile crimes is most noticeable, rising from 25 per 1000 population in 1967 to 78 per 1000 by 1978.[33] Unemployment has remained at over 1 million for the last five years, significantly higher than earlier in the post-war period – it rarely went far above the 300,000 level until as late as 1966. Unemployment has also been most marked among school-leavers and young workers, as well as among the older, less skilled workers. Government responses include both industrial training/retraining schemes and the introduction of a number of short-term job creation schemes under the auspices of the Manpower Services Commission.

Strikes – or at least days of work lost through industrial disputes – have also been on the increase: even excluding the big miners' strikes of 1972 and 1974, there were almost twice the number of days lost through strikes between 1971 and 1976 as there were between 1966 and 1970. The miners' strike of 1974 is generally considered to have been a major contributor to the downfall of the Heath Government in the February election of that year, while 1979's 'winter of discontent' undoubtedly helped the departure of the Labour Government the following May. Not the least important protagonists in the latter period were the public sector unions, an area of considerable trade union growth in the post-war period (as is that of 'white-collar' unionism generally). Increased trade union membership and union militancy does not appear to have produced much in the way of a change in the overall distribution of wealth in Britain: 25 per cent of Britain's personal wealth remains in the hands of less than 1.5 per cent of the population, though the growth of institutional wealth-holding – by banks, insurance companies and pension funds – is one major post-war development.

All of these social changes, some of which were brought about by government action, mean that Britain in the 1980s will be a very different place from that of the 1950s. They mean that governments, both national and local, face very different and difficult problems from those faced by their earlier counterparts. These social changes, taken together with the demographic and economic ones discussed earlier, mean that questions frequently arise about the capacity of governments at all levels to cope with the many complex problems presently before them. Cries of 'governmental overload', talk of 'un-governability', fears of 'the urban crisis' have all been expressed in Britain in the 1970s. Furthermore, our discussion of environmental change since 1945 has been illustrative rather than exhaustive, and conducted largely in analytic terms. In the real world of post-war Britain, the demographic, economic and social changes, as well as much of the governmental action at all levels, have been highly interrelated and interdependent. In other words, from the point of view of local and national governments, the problems of the real world are a good deal more complex than is suggested by the rather descriptive, simplistic analysis undertaken here. It is this complexity, together with the highly interdependent and yet highly specialized nature of modern urban society in a country like Britain, that explains why there are both so many 'explanations' of and 'solutions' for the many problems facing governments today.

4 Changes in city politics 1: the reactions of the political community

The changes described in the last chapter have obviously produced policy changes on behalf of both central and local government in a whole range of different policy arenas. In this chapter, we shall attempt to see how people have reacted to the changes that have taken place around them in the city and how far they are active in city politics and in what ways. In other words, we are concerned here with analysing the ways and means of individual and group participation in city politics.

Though we are concerned here with *political* action in the city, the city is of course very much the centre of social, economic and physical activity. City residents both work and play in their town, and spend a considerable amount of time transporting themselves and their goods around it. Social and economic activity, associated with patterns of work and leisure, are very much the kinds of activity in which most people engage. By contrast, most people are not active politically, either in the partisan sense or in terms of seeking to influence political events directly. Nevertheless, it must be remembered that nearly everybody has some kind of contact with those who govern their cities. People pay their rates and rents, send their children to school, use public transport, complain about housing conditions or the lack of refuse collection. All these actions involve some degree of political contact with the authorities, albeit largely of a passive nature, often of an indirect kind.

Direct political action, in the sense of seeking to secure certain political outcomes, runs along the spectrum from voting in elections at one end to violent urban terrorism at the other end. What varies is the intensity of political action and the likely consequences for others: voting in city elections is a relatively passive, indirect way of influencing political events and many democratic theorists have experienced difficulty in demonstrating the link between the individual voter and his elected representative in terms of political outcomes. By contrast, urban terrorist activity is much more intense, involving open conflict with the authorities, violence, kidnappings and bombings, often designed to secure political outcomes that have little immediate relevance to the residents of the city in which the violence takes place. Thus, for example, the Balcombe Street seige related to problems in Northern Ireland and not to those of the City of London. Indeed, urban violence can have international consequences as well as local ones, as attempts by terrorists to free their imprisoned fellows demonstrate.

Yet urban violence can also have a local dimension: burning the ghetto is one way American blacks drew attention to their poor social and economic conditions in the late 1960s. In this country, race riots of the scale experienced in the United States are almost unknown, though violence against minority groups in the city has a long history in Britain.[1]

Voting is the majority political activity: urban violence is still very much an activity engaged in by a tiny minority of city residents. In between, there runs a whole gamut of political activities in which the individual engages and which link him to his political institutions and authorities.

Conditioning public participation

Yet in most countries the bulk of the population is politically inactive, in that the extent and nature of their political participation is very spasmodic and episodic. Political participation is conditioned by a number of factors. First, it is a reflection of the accessibility or openness of the political system: of the opportunities it allows for participation. In some cities, for example, which are little more than one-party states, the channels of political communication may be limited because of the way decisions are largely dominated by the political wishes of the party in power. In non-partisan cities, however, the channels of communication may be equally limited, because the citizen may not know who the effective decision-makers are or where to make his comments to best effect.

Second, political participation reflects the individual's motivation to become involved. People have to be interested in or by the political events of the city. They are more likely to become involved in the kinds of issues that are of immediate relevance to them. Thus, as planners have learnt from experience, it is only when the houses are about to be pulled down that local residents want to become involved, not when the possibility is first considered. Sports and recreation groups do not express much interest in structure plan proposals if the latter are concerned mainly with industry, population and housing, or touch on leisure activities only indirectly. But the threatened closure of a swimming pool or sports centre would undoubtedly rouse considerable opposition from those who either used it or thought they might do so in the near future.

Last, participation is determined by the kinds of skills that people have. Most people know what it is they want to say or do when they want to participate, but they differ markedly in the skill with which they can communicate their ideas or needs. At one extreme, there is the almost totally non-participating individual, the person who has almost no contact with the outside world in any way, or very little political contact at all. Research suggests[2] that this group is likely to contain a substantial proportion of elderly, widowed people, and single-parent families. They often have little formal education, belong to no organized groups, and do not read local newspapers or go to local libraries. Their political involvement is often secured only after costly, time-consuming work by community development workers.

At the other extreme, there are the highly articulate and skilful political activists. Members of political parties, belonging to a number of organized groups and often on their committees, such people are overwhelmingly but not exclusively to be found among the ranks of the middle class, and their participation skills reflect their wider educational and occupational opportunities. These are the people to be found often dominating public meetings on planning issues, or arguing strongly against some new industrial development on environmental grounds. But their ranks contain a substantial proportion of working-class people who are no less articulate or skilful in their political participation, skills that perhaps reflect their experience as trade union members or the extensive personal networks that they have developed.

But the majority of people undoubtedly fall between these two extremes, being much closer to Dahl's *homo civicus* rather than *homo politicus* as described above.[3] They follow social and economic pursuits because these are what interest them: politics, by contrast, is seen as a boring, fringe activity, and at best a civic duty to be performed at election time. Indeed, few could recognize their activity as political in the sense in which the political scientist uses the word: political for most people means partisan or party, and does not have the wider connotation that the political scientist uses. For them, saving houses from demolition or persuading the authorities to reroute a motorway are not political actions, but simply something important to them.

People's attitudes to politics and political participation are very much a reflection of the pattern of their political socialization and of the prevailing political values and beliefs of their society. As such, in Britain people are largely socialized into essentially non-participant political roles, but at the same time are encouraged to believe in their own political abilities. Most people can suggest ways and means by which they think they can influence political events at the city level. Getting up petitions, writing to newspapers, forming a protest group, contacting officials and councillors are all ways people suggest they would use if they wanted to influence something in their city.[4] In other words, people know how to try and influence city politics: whether they *want* to, and their expectations of success, are another matter.[5] Many certainly believe that it is often difficult to bring important issues to the attention of the authorities or to persuade the authorities to take particular decisions, a reflection of the relative lack of accessibility of British city politics as compared with their American counterpart.[6]

City elections and voting

Thus, in Britain most people's only act of political participation in city politics is by voting in local elections,[7] an act that is effectively both an indirect and a passive means of influencing events. Even voting in local elections is a minority pastime, since fewer than half the electorate bothers to turn out and vote,[8] and this figure is even lower in the main urban areas. These kinds of figures compare with an average 60 per cent turnout in by-elections and 75 per cent at general elections. Even the reform of local government, which it was claimed should lead to an increased interest in local affairs and consequently to higher levels of voting, has had little impact on voting levels. In 1973, with the first elections, turnout was 40 per cent in the county council elections, but fell to the much lower level of 34 per cent in the metropolitan district elections the following month. Figures in the next round of elections in 1976–7 were not much better: 41 per cent in the counties, 38 per cent in the districts.[9]

One reason why turnout remains low in local elections is that the electoral outcome is likely to be almost a foregone conclusion in most cases: most seats are safe seats, and indeed, until recently, many seats in the more rural parts of the country were uncontested ones. In these cases the voters are either not required to vote or else do not feel the need to do so, safe in the knowledge that their candidate or his opponent is in a virtually unassailable position. (This is not to say that electoral miracles do not occur in local elections: indeed, the swing of votes between parties at local elections is much broader than at general elections, and swings of 20–25 per cent from one party to another are not unusual.) Thus, occasionally, as in the mid 1960s and the early 1970s, even apparently safe seats can fall to the opposition, giving unexpected victory to candidates who never thought they would be required to take up the duties and burdens of office.[10]

In a small number of contests, however, the electoral outcome is likely to be much closer. In these marginal contests turnout is likely to be higher than it is in the safe seats. This leads to the question as to what it is that makes a seat marginal. One answer, suggested by Newton,[11] is that the social composition of the ward is the determining factor, and that marginal seats are much more socially heterogeneous than safe ones. A further answer, advanced by Pimlott and others,[12] is that it is party organization that makes the real difference: parties identify these socially heterogeneous seats as marginal ones and concentrate their efforts in these areas, hopeful of winning, but sure in the knowledge that they will neither lose their own safe seats nor win their opponents'. As a result of this concentration of party effort, more people are made aware of the election and its possible importance and are therefore more willing to make the journey to the polling booth, particularly if such a journey is to be made in the comfort of a car provided by one of the parties.

One feature of voting in local elections to which attention is frequently drawn is the way voters use them as a means of expressing their views on the actions of the government nationally, rather than as a means of choosing local political leaders or a local party to run the city. Given that voting in national elections has shown a higher level of volatility in the last ten years than in the previous twenty, we might expect that volatility to spill over into local elections, and such would seem to be the case. Greater uncertainty about local electoral outcomes may be expected to make the policy-making process less certain, a point to which we shall return later. At the same time, however, it might be expected to make local elections more important to the voter and less of a civic or party duty to be carried out when it is remembered, even though voting is likely to remain a relatively ineffective means by which individuals might influence local events.

Organized groups

One important way in which individuals seek to influence political events, both nationally and locally, is through their membership and activity in organized groups. Such groups have long been a phenomenon of British city politics,[13] and though perhaps less prevalent in the years immediately after the Second World War they have re-emerged in the last ten years.[14] Indeed, more and more people believe that group action is the best means by which they can influence events, as surveys in Lancashire and Cheshire show.[15] For most people, political influence means joining an organization, be it trade union, a tenants' association or an amenity society.

In the most extensive British study to date, Newton[16] identified over 4000 organized groups active in the City of Birmingham and estimated that there could be almost as many again that he had not been able to learn about. Studies elsewhere[17] have also shown that most communities have a large and varied group life; but, as Newton also shows, only about a quarter or a third of such groups are likely to be politically active in any particular time period. Most of these are likely to be sectoral groups, concerned with promoting a particular sectoral interest close to their heart, and as such are likely to become involved in a single issue or a narrow and related range of issues. Tenants' associations, ratepayers' groups, welfare rights organizations, parent–teacher associations and amenity societies all fall into this particular category. The local political system is heavily populated with this kind of single-issue group – groups that live and die around a single problem. For example, mothers may be concerned with the absence of a manned crossing outside a local primary school: they form a group to press their case, often adopting tactics designed to embarrass the local authorities and to draw attention to their problem – petitions, blocking traffic and letters to the press are all familiar tactics. But once the issue is decided one way or another, there is little to keep the group together, so it disbands, quickly to be replaced by another with some new issue it wants to bring into the political arena.

Many of such groups are not well liked by local officials and councillors,[18] largely because they have little to offer the latter, but are seen as making 'unreasonable' demands upon their local authority. Other groups, however, are much more favourably regarded: they are, in Newton's sense, 'established'[19] or in Dearlove's terms 'helpful'.[20] This is a reflection on the type and range of interaction that such groups have with local councillors and officials, and the way they are perceived by the latter. Among these groups may be found organizations concerned with welfare (such as the WRVS, old people's organizations), education (such as teachers' associations and religious organizations), housing and planning (tenants' associations, amenity societies and major entrepreneurs). All have probably shown that they have something to contribute to the decision-making process – information, expertise, for example – or else their support is regarded by the decision-makers as crucial if proposals are to be adopted and implemented successfully. In Easton's terms, such groups are very much among those 'whose views have to be taken into account'[21] in the making of decisions. In other words, such groups are likely to be co-opted into the formal decision-making process, often being formally and informally consulted on a wide range of local authority matters and having a wide range of contacts inside local authorities or a range of channels through which they are able to present their views.

Planning, particularly structure planning, provides a very good example of the kind of distinction just made between 'established' and 'unestablished' or 'helpful' and 'unhelpful' groups. Quite clearly, many structure and local planners see some groups as somehow important, or as having something to contribute to the planning process, and as such treat these groups very differently from the way in which other sections of the public are treated. Full reports of survey, rather than summaries, as well as technical reports, are sent to such groups, whereas they may be available only on request or at a price to the ordinary man in the street. Special meetings may be arranged for such groups, so that they may consult with the planners on a more personal basis; indeed, some of these groups may be incorporated into the planning process by virtue of their membership of something like a consultative panel.[22]

What places this kind of group into this privileged established position is not their own assessment of their importance,[23] but rather the authorities' (and particularly the planners') assessment. Such groups are given this privileged access not because they seek it or think they merit it, but because the planners think they are important. In other words, their support is thought necessary if a consensus on particular proposals is to be achieved, or if their opposition to them is to be blunted.

By contrast, many more groups are regarded as a hindrance rather than a help by the authorities. These are groups whose aims are most likely to be in conflict with the authority's policies and proposals. Blacks seeking recognition of their political claims and of their deprived conditions are an excellent example from recent years of one group of city residents in conflict with the city's governmental authorities; squatters seeking to occupy unoccupied property represent another. Many welfare rights groups have also been involved in many conflicts with city social workers over the kinds of welfare policies, and more particularly the implementation of such policies, adopted by local authorities. Teachers have been known to strike over such issues as the teacher–pupil ratio, or proposals for the introduction of comprehensivization, as the examples of Stockport and Tameside demonstrate. Following local government reorganization and the subsequent heavy rate increases, many ratepayers' groups threatened to withhold rate payments: in some cases, ratepayers have been imprisoned for non-payment.

What distinguishes these different groups, all of whom are essentially in a conflict situation with their civic authorities, is the kind and intensity of action that they are prepared to adopt, something that varies with the degree of motivation and participatory skills the groups possess. Some groups, such as blacks, feel so frustrated or oppressed that only direct, often violent, action appears appropriate if they are to see their claims recognized. Alternatively, direct confrontation with the authority may be the only way they know how to present their case, in the way tenants threatened with eviction or rehousing may seek to defend themselves. For still other groups, direct action occurs as a result of the failure of all other attempts to make their case: such a tactic is often adopted by groups concerned with housing the homeless, though often such groups also enjoy reasonably good relations with local officials and councillors.

Essentially, what these groups are seeking is access to the decision-makers to make the latter aware of their demands and to secure policy outcomes favourable to their aims. Many of these groups feel that the authorities are either unaware of their problems or else are unwilling to do anything about them. For their part, the authorities, however sympathetically they may view the claims of these groups, often consider themselves unable to do much about them, either because they lack the resources to do much or because they feel it is beyond the scope of the city's responsibility. Alternatively, they may regard the activities of such groups as 'unhelpful', 'damaging', and somehow illegitimate and unacceptable, if not illegal.

Yet, as we have noted, people increasingly regard action through groups as the best way of influencing political decisions in the city. In part, this reflects people's propensity to join such groups, but to a certain extent it is also a reflection of a decline in the adequacy of other political structures in the city to act as effective channels of communication between the city resident and his elected and paid officials. In functionalist terms, institutions such as local party organizations and the press no longer act as the efficient interest aggregators that people may have believed they were in the past.

Political parties

As Bulpitt[24] rightly notes, party politics has a long history in British city politics. The work of urban historians such as Fraser and Hennock,[25] as well as political scientists such as Jones and Nossiter,[26] all testify to the fact. But it has to be remembered that local political parties perform a range of functions and are not concerned solely with activity as a channel of communication between elector and elected. Historically and currently, their prime function is that of elite recruitment and elite maintenance. Political parties are concerned primarily with seeing that their candidates are returned to or maintained in power, and with the process by which party supporters are selected to join the ranks of the candidates. Increasingly people seeking election to city councils have been drawn from the ranks of the major political parties, with the Labour and Conservative Parties providing the overwhelming majority, the Liberals a poor third, and independents almost disappearing from view.

Yet local parties are social organizations, whose activities perform a whole range of functions for their members. For the majority, they provide a social outlet, be it only a snooker game in the local Conservative club or an evening's entertainment in the Labour club. For others it provides an outlet for their organizational skills, and a sense of doing something for the party, whether it be making the tea for a ward or constituency meeting or canvassing the streets around election day. For a minority, local party politics provides a career structure of its own, in which the local party becomes an all-consuming passion, where the ideological battle between 'us' (the working class) and 'them' (the rest), or between 'Left' and 'Right', can be fought out; or else it is a route by which people can achieve political influence, not only by being elected to the city council, but also by rising to office within both the party and the council.

As part of all these functions, and particularly in terms of seeking the electoral support necessary to return candidates to the ranks of the council chamber, parties also act as aggregators of public demands. At the simplest levels, these demands are collected or tapped by the network of everyday contacts of party members, be they party leaders or simply rank-and-file members. Conversations in the party club bring matters to the attention of councillors, or the ward street collector may learn of problems as he is collecting party dues or trying to encourage people to become members. This activity is probably best illustrated by the style of community-based politics associated with the Liberal Party, particularly in Liverpool, during the early 1970s. Yet all the major parties aggregate demands through their 'routine' work of keeping in touch with the electorate.

At a more complex level, these demands are aggregated and simplified through the process of *party* policy-making carried on within the party itself. In this context the party is a miniature political sub-system, subject to all kinds of pressures, and the processes of internal party politics at the local level are both difficult to research and under-researched.[27] Part of the difficulty arises because of the complexity of structural arrangements within each party, as well as the existence of different personalities and ideologies. This is seen at its most complex within local Labour Parties, which have not only independent members but also members from affiliated trade unions and socialist societies, such as the Fabians or Young Socialists. This membership is further complicated by the organizational structure of the party, which runs from the electoral ward up, taking in constituency and city party, as well as the Labour group of councillors, on the way. To put it mildly, conflict between these different interests and groups within the party is not unknown, and these conflicts are frequently complicated by ideological differences among the party members, particularly between those who define themselves and are defined by others as being on the Left and those who place themselves and are placed on the party's right wing.

It would be wrong to suggest that such conflicts are absent from either local Conservative or Liberal Parties, or that they are no less intense or that they lack any ideological dimension. Organizationally, most city Conservative Parties are much simpler, with the constituency parties and the Conservative group as the only organizational levels, and these tend to be far less formally organized than is the case with the Labour Party. For example, research suggests that most Labour candidates at local election will have met their party's requirements about membership and party activity before being selected whereas it is possible for an individual to become a Conservative Party candidate without any record of party service and indeed occasionally without prior party membership.

The Liberal Party's situation is less complicated because there are fewer of them: research in Salford in the late 1960s suggested there were fewer than thirty or forty active Liberals in the city, which compared unfavourably with the number active in the average Labour branch party at the time, while the Conservative constituency parties were much larger still. The recent emphasis on community-based politics has undoubtedly brought with it some increase in membership, but has also brought increased conflict and difficulty when it comes to turning that membership into increased electoral support and to delivering the policy goods once elected. Indeed, the Liberals' emphasis on community-based politics, with its undertones of neighbourhood government, has been made more difficult in the face of the larger units of local government in the post-reform era. Following reorganization, the town hall is simply too large and too distant for it to respond at the neighbourhood level as the Liberals' style of community politics implies, without some special kind of institutional and organizational arrangement operating outside the central offices.

Given the larger units of local government that now exist, it is difficult to see how political parties can be effective interest aggregators. For one thing, the number of councillors was reduced by local government reorganization, while the size of area and number of people represented by each councillor was substantially increased. For another thing, the membership of both major political parties has been declining over the last ten to fifteen years, and current estimates put the average local Labour Party membership at around 500–600, with the Conservative figure at about 2000.[28] In other words, not only are fewer elected representatives responsible for more people over a larger area, but also the main organizational support they have to maintain contact with their residents is in a very weak condition. In some cases local parties have come to be dominated by a handful of hard-core, dedicated activists, with the consequence that not only local councillors, but also MPs, have had their 'automatic' right to reselection called into question.

Local political parties, then, are perhaps no longer the best means by which the demands of local residents can be translated/aggregated into political action, even though in some areas, particularly the so-called one-party states, they may represent the only effective channel of communication between the leaders and the led. In these circumstances the controlling party may be so dominant that it feels it can safely ignore or is not prepared to listen to demands that are being made upon it through channels other than its own party circles. Salford in the late 1950s and early 1960s provides the Labour example of such a phenomenon, and Dearlove's study of Kensington and Chelsea provides a Conservative counterpart.[29] The question of the implications of poor demand aggregation and limited channels of communication between leaders and led is one to which we shall return later: suffice it here to suggest that one consequence of the apparent inability or unwillingness of local parties to act as a channel of communication between leaders and led is that the latter are likely to seek and use other channels, and thus the increase in local interest group activity is hardly surprising.

The local press

In considering communications between the leaders and the led, one automatically thinks of the media as the most appropriate channel. In the context of local politics, we are essentially concerned here with the local press, for in most cases local radio and television, independent and public, are essentially *regionally* oriented rather than locally so.[30] Indeed, even among what might be regarded as the local press, there are many newspapers (particularly evening ones) that are regionally oriented.

Sociologists and political scientists have recently given considerable attention to the role of the local (particularly) weekly press and local politics.[31] In so doing, they suggest some interesting contradictions about this role, which emanates from its situation as communicator down and as communicator up. In other words, not only does the local press act as an articulator and aggregator of mass demands towards the local decision-makers, but it is also a principal source of information about the activities of the local authority itself. As Stringer has shown from his study of newspaper readership in north-east Lancashire,[32] most people read a local evening or weekly newspaper, with the other half likely to read both, while as a source of local information, the local press emerged as 'of prime importance'.[33] Certainly other related research on publicizing planning proposals supports this point: most people learn about structure and local plan proposals from the local press in the first instance.

Thus, as a channel of communication from the authority to the local resident, the press emerges as being of major importance as far as the public are concerned. Without their local evening or weekly newspaper, most people would know even less about the activities of their local authority than they do at present. There is also some evidence that suggests that this is the major role that the local press sees for itself: Murphy, as well as Cox and Morgan, repeatedly shows the willingness of local editors, reporters and newspaper owners to present the views of the local authority.[34]

By contrast, however, the local press often appears unwilling to act as an aggregator of local demands. In other words, few weekly or evening newspapers are prepared to adopt an investigatory, issue-raising posture, while those that do tend to be the small circulation community or free press. Murphy suggests a number of reasons why this should be so. Partly it is because of the legal constraints such as libel laws and organizational characteristics of both the press and local government, and partly it is because the way the journalists involved themselves see the events they report. Thus, Murphy suggests there are three kinds of story that the local press are generally unwilling to report: those involving allegations of corruption; those ridiculing or challenging the present system of local government; and those that would give a wider background to council decisions or raise issues that might challenge the council decision-making procedures and policies. The first are excluded on grounds of cost, while the latter two are excluded either out of kindness or on the grounds that they lack reader interest. 'Man bites dog' sells newspapers, not 'Is the council reacting properly to people's demands for more bridge clubs?'

But the way in which the journalist operates, and his heavy dependence on others – not only for information itself, but as possible sources and contacts for yet more information – mean that the local press is unlikely to challenge the authority, on whom it may be heavily dependent both for news and advertising. Much that is printed in the local newspaper comes to the local offices without reporters having to move to collect it, and in this sense perhaps one can see that it is all too easy to produce a local newspaper that does not really communicate or aggregate demands upwards from local residents to those who make the decisions.

Thus, far from providing a forum for ideas, or acting as a critic of authority, or even providing accurate information about local events and decisions, Murphy and others suggest that the local press is a kind of silent, toothless watchdog, whose ability to bark is almost non-existent, without considering its ability to bite.

Of course, not all newspapers can be characterized in this way. Mention has already been made of the community press, often produced by enthusiastic local amateurs, particularly those with access to a reprographic machine. Such newspapers are an increasing phenomenon of our major metropolitan areas, often starting life as a local newsletter, free advertisement handout, but growing into something more serious and more widely circulated. Cheap, easy to produce, difficult and costly to prosecute in the event of possible libel, such newspapers (for example, *Private Eye*) often print the stories that the other more established newspapers do not dare print. Thus, for example, Cox and Morgan describe such newspapers as the *Liverpool Free Press* and the *Tuebrook Bugle*, both of which essentially started because of local inability to get local issues raised in the more established local press.[35] Such newspapers are concerned more with local specific issues than with the more general coverage associated with the established press, and are also concerned less with 'the good of the community', adopting an aggressive campaigning stance rather than a blander, more consensual one.

Yet to regard such newspapers as better than the existing big city newspaper is, as Cox and Morgan rightly note, misleading. What the 'alternative' press is doing is filling a gap at the neighbourhood level and helping to articulate the kinds of demands that local citizens make of their elected representatives and paid officials. In some cases, the more established press may take up these demands: if not, local community-based newspapers of the type discussed here provide another channel of communication between the leaders and led.

This chapter has been concerned with reviewing the spectrum of the public's participation in local affairs, and has particularly noted some of the changes in modes of both participation and communication by the public to those concerned with running our cities. The scale of these changes may be considered small when compared with the idealist's dream of a fully participant urban society. Yet such a dream may be unfulfillable, and the changes that have taken and are taking place in terms of individual participation and local affairs are already producing changes unforeseen even ten years ago.

One of the most important changes to have taken place in the context of city politics has been the decline of party as a means of interest aggregation and individual political participation, particularly at a time when parties are becoming increasingly important as a means of recruiting local political leaders. If parties are out of touch with local people, then how will the city fathers be able to perform their tasks in both the representative and responsive way that is traditionally expected of them?

One way, of course, might be to react favourably to one of the other major changes in city politics, namely the emergence of local pressure groups as a primary means by which people seek to influence local events. Yet the evidence to date suggests that many such groups are regarded unfavourably if not with hostility by elected members, with only a few groups being considered as having a positive role to play in the urban decision-making process.

At the end of the day, perhaps both the continued widespread apathy in electoral terms and the increasing use of direct and often violent action are the measures of the public's concern about city government, their ability and willingness to influence it, and its relevance to their needs. For squatters, the homeless, the urban guerilla and others, city government clearly fails to be relevant: for the apathetic, city government is either irrelevant or else so successful that it, and what it does, has come to be taken for granted. On balance, the evidence – in terms of local voting levels, knowledge of and interest in local affairs – would suggest that the former judgement is the more accurate one. But city government itself is changing, and these changes can be expected to affect the public's evaluation of city politics in turn. These changes form the subject matter for the next chapter.

5 Changes in city politics 2: the regime and the authorities

All of the changes in the city that we have discussed so far have had a number of consequences for the nature of decision-making within the city. The changes have contributed to the complexity of the problems with which city governments must deal, and as a consequence the process of decision-making in the city itself has become more complex.

At the outset a distinction must be made between those decisions made in the public sector and those made privately. One of the essential changes in twentieth-century Britain is that the balance between the two sections has changed, with the public sector expanding rapidly. Even in the late nineteenth century, many of the decisions that had political dimensions in the broadest sense were still taken by men outside the formal political arena: entrepreneurs, religious organizations, temperance and co-operative societies were responsible for providing many services, particularly in the housing and welfare fields, that are now undertaken by local authorities.

This is not to say that the actions of decision-makers in the private sector are unimportant in terms of what happens in the city. If anything the reverse is true: decisions and non-decisions made by private sector actors have important consequences for the shape, size and health of cities. For example, the decision of a major employer to close his works and move elsewhere is likely to have a considerable impact on city life. Decisions by builders, property companies, estate agents and landowners have had important consequences for the continuing growth of urban areas; together with the building societies, insurance companies and the major banking interests, these groups have largely shaped the centres of our cities and encouraged continuing residential growth at their edges. Multiple retailers, such as Marks and Spencers, Boots or Woolworths, and supermarket operators such as Tesco or Asda can have large-scale effects on the shopping facilities available in a particular town simply by deciding whether or not to open (or close) a branch or store there.

All of these are examples of decisions made by private sector actors which may also involve city officials and representatives or to which they will have to react. But these officials will also have to operate within a framework that is equally shaped by the actions and decisions of other public sector organizations, and not least by central government itself. Water and health authorities, other neighbouring local governments, gas and electricity boards are all examples of statutory authorities whose actions have to be taken account of by city governments, or whose co-operation may have to be sought in the implementation of policies. Approval by the relevant minister, grant aid for a particular project, or simple advice and regulation are all ways in which central government departments may become involved, and of course the fact that British local authorities must have statutory approval from Parliament for all their actions is another form of central government involvement with the locality.

The kinds of things that we have been discussing so far can be characterized into two basic types: at one level, there are changes that affect the way in which local governments operate and the areas or boundaries of such governments. Changes in the functions, types and boundaries of local government, as well as changes at the centre itself, are all likely to have an impact on the way public sector decisions are made in the city. Changes of this type are essentially *regime* changes,[1] that is to say changes in the structure of city government, or in its functions, or possibly in what might be called the rules of the game.

The second type of change is really a change in the numbers and kinds of decision-makers, both public and private, whose decisions affect the city. The emergence of new financial institutions, the rise of the property developer and the growth of a large service sector are all examples of how new kinds of private decision-makers have come on to the stage of city politics during this century. On the public side, there has been an enormous increase in both the numbers and types of paid officials – the professionals – in city governments. Planners, social workers and housing managers are but three of the new twentieth-century professions. As we shall see, the twentieth century has also seen a change in the kind of person elected on to city councils, one who depends – in Britain at least – far more on the support of a political party for his election than did his nineteenth-century counterpart, or for that matter than his present-day American opposite. Changes of this kind are perhaps best thought of as changes in the nature of the *authorities*[2] in the city, that is to say changes among those who make the binding decisions in the city about resource allocation and distribution, or changes in those with political power. This chapter is concerned with exploring these two kinds of changes and with seeing how they have affected decision-making by city governments.

Regime changes that are important to our discussion of the city are essentially of two types: formal changes, such as those that generally change the institutions, boundaries and functions of city government; and informal changes, such as those that affect the way in which such governments are financed and changes in the means by which central government relates to local authorities.

Formal regime changes: the reform of English local government

Formal regime changes involving reform of the structure and functions of local government tend to be few and far between. As any politician knows, there are few votes to be gained from local government reform, and many to be lost. In Britain, despite considerable nineteenth-century changes in the structure of local government, the system established in 1888 was to last over seventy-five years until 1973 (with the exception of London's government[3]). In other countries the process of local government reform has hardly begun, and indeed most demonstrate a strong resistance to change: America provides a particular example where there has been relatively little structural change in local government, with some commentators arguing that this is a major reason why American urban problems appear so intractable.[4]

Second, the process of local government reform is a lengthy one. It is worth remembering that reform in Britain took almost twenty years from the establishment of the Herbert Commission on London[5] in 1956 to the implementation of the Local Government Act in Scotland in 1975.

Third, most of the reforms introduced have been gradualist rather than involving extensive change. Thus, many changes involve the introduction of *ad hoc*, special-purpose authorities. Indeed, these may be all too easy to introduce: American city government is full of examples, including such well-known ones as the New York Port Authority and the Chicago Transit Authority. Area health and regional water authorities are British examples. Other, more extensive, changes involve the introduction of what might best be called weak federal systems into metropolitan areas: a weak, area-wide top-tier responsible for a few 'unimportant' functions, with a stronger lower tier holding most of the powers. Such an arrangement, while allowing for a modicum of change towards some kind of city-wide government to deal with area-wide problems, continues to respect historically powerful sub-units within the metropolitan area or allows new suburban areas some protection against possible intrusion from the city. London, and the more recently reformed other metropolitan areas such as Greater Manchester, Merseyside and West Midlands, are examples of this kind of basically weak federal system, whereas Toronto in Canada provides a well-known example of a strong federal system in which the upper tier is more powerful.[6] In nearly all cases, the reforms actually introduced have generally been less radical than those that reformers have generally wanted.

The last point worth bearing in mind before we examine the recent reforms in Britain in more detail is that the introduction of most reforms has been heavily dependent upon strong action by central or state-level governments. In other words, the initiative for the intro-duction of structural reform of local government very often lies outside the scope of local government itself: as creatures of higher levels of government, city governments must await action by those higher levels.

As we have already noted, the recent British reforms took almost twenty years to reach fruition. While London provided the model for some of the subsequent reforms, we shall concentrate here on the recent English reforms, though it is worth noting that London provides an interesting case study in terms of both the politics of metropolitan reform and of providing some yardstick for evaluating the success or failure of such reforms.[7]

As far as the recent British reforms are concerned, it is clear that by the mid 1960s there was almost universal agreement that the old structure of local government, which had been largely unaltered since 1888, was no longer capable of meeting the demands placed upon it. By 1966 the then Minister of Housing and Local Government, Richard Crossman, felt that the piecemeal *ad hoc* arrangements that existed for reviewing local government were no longer adequate and that a more thorough-going reform was necessary. To make suggestions about possible reform, a royal commission on local government in England under the chairmanship of Sir John (later Lord Redcliffe) Maud was established in 1966.[8]

The process of local government reform that followed over the next eight years has been much written about and analysed elsewhere.[9] It is sufficient for our purposes simply to detail the main points in the story. When the English Commission reported in 1969 it identified a number of essential weaknesses in the existing local government system. First, the Commission felt that the continuing division between town and country, the cornerstone of the system established in 1888, was no longer relevant, with the result that the division between major urban authorities (county boroughs) and the shire areas (county councils) was also no longer meaningful. Indeed, battles between the boroughs and the counties over land and housing space had been one of the important elements in the post-1945 local government system, particularly in areas like the North-West, and was one of the main reasons why the Commission had been established.[10]

The second weakness identified was the apparently large number of authorities and the related point that many of them were too small to carry out properly the functions expected of them. Thus, the smallest county borough (Canterbury) was expected to be capable of providing the same range and quality of service as the largest (Birmingham). County and district councils varied similarly, giving rise to yet another weakness in the old system: the division of functional responsibilities between counties and the authorities under them.

In part this was a weakness brought about by the way functions had been allocated originally: thus, for example, county councils were planning authorities and districts were housing authorities. As a result, many arguments broke out over such issues as where council housing was to go, or which districts should allow new owner-occupier housing to be built. But the division of functions was also complicated and confused by the different ways counties delegated functions to their districts, particularly in relation to such services as education and highways. Put simply, some counties delegated and some could not; others delegated to some lower-tier authorities, but not all; some lower-tier authorities wanted more delegated powers, and some did not want any. The result was almost total confusion, particularly from the point of view of the local resident, whose knowledge of who did what was limited, to say the least.[11]

The lack of knowledge about local government and the apparent lack of interest people had in local government was seen by the Commission as yet another weakness of the old system, apparently undermining the very democratic justification for having a system of elected local government at all. For many, local government was seen as the very essence of democratic government, and the Commission had been warned of the 'need to sustain a viable system of local democracy'.[12] Given that so few people apparently knew which local authority did what, knew the name of their local councillor, or were sufficiently interested to attend council or public meetings, the Commission's reaction in pointing to these findings as weaknesses in the old system is hardly surprising.

In part, this weakness was seen as a reflection of yet another, final, problem identified by the Commission as bedevilling the old system. This was the relationship between local and central government. In the Commission's view, local authorities were too weak to counteract the continuing centralization of British government, with its increasing concentration of focus on Whitehall and Westminster. In the Commission's eyes, local government was unable to stand up against the 'bullying' of the centre: it could not assert its local identity – yet another nail in the coffin of local democracy. From the central government's point of view, government departments were increasingly becoming involved in detailed local matters, without really being able to control what the local authorities were actually doing – a highly undesirable state of affairs from the point of view of the centre.[13]

With these weaknesses in mind, the Commission outlined four criteria that they felt should be met by any reform proposals. First, the structure, area and boundaries of local authorities should make sense in terms of the way people live their lives: the boundaries should take into account the growing interdependence of town and country that had taken place during the twentieth century. Second, the Commission was concerned that local government should be functionally efficient: that is to say, the functions of local government should be so allocated that local authorities are capable of providing a changing standard of service as needs and demands change, and at the same time are able to provide those services economically. As we shall see, this criterion was to cause problems later. Third, it was expected that the new local government system should be democratically viable. While this is perhaps the most ambiguous and least tangible criterion, it was undoubtedly one on which considerable stress was placed by the Commission, who intended their proposals to strengthen both the representative nature and the consultative position of local government, as well as making the system more meaningful to local people, so that it could attract and hold their interest.[14]

In meeting these criteria, the Commission was faced with a number of problems, perhaps best illustrated by a brief discussion of the issues relating size of unit to efficiency. The desirable size of reformed local authorities was a major issue confronting the Commission, in that the case for multi-purpose authorities rests upon the idea that services can best be provided by one authority, and that some areal division is possible to ensure that such provision is both technically and administratively feasible. But, as Wood correctly notes,[15] for most local services particular geographical requirements are less clear: so the Commission had a problem in determining the basis for implementing the size issue – social geography or simply population size. The former caused difficulties when it came to detailed application, while the latter is a very crude measure of effective administrative units, as the Commission's own researches on the relationship between size and efficiency demonstrated. What these largely statistical studies showed was that size could not be proved to have much effect on performance: bigger did not necessarily mean better, largely because of the difficulties the researchers faced (and still do) in terms of attempting to evaluate the quality of service provision. In the end, the Commission based its recommendations on the assumption that bigger authorities *would* provide better services, though in this respect the Commission was also limited by the requirement, stressed by most witnesses, to maintain local democracy.

When the Commission finally reported in 1969, internal pressures were such that a minority report by one member, Derek Senior,[16] was almost inevitable. The main report had as its key recommendation the idea of a 'unitary authority', an all-purpose body which covered town and country and with a population size of between 250,000 and 1 million. This recommendation meant an enormous reduction in the number of councils, since the bulk of England was to be covered by fifty-eight of these unitary bodies. As a result, the concept fitted some parts of the country better than others, with particular disadvantages of both size and remoteness from the public if the population of the new local governments should exceed 1 million. Recognizing this, the Commission suggested a two-tier system for the three largest metropolitan areas outside London – Birmingham, Liverpool and Manchester. The top-tier authority should have been responsible for such functions as planning, transportation, police, fire, etc; with the lower-tier authorities (twenty in all) responsible for personal services, including education and taxation. Some functions, such as housing, would be shared between both levels.

Finally, the Commission proposed two other types of authority. Superimposed above the structure first outlined were to be eight provincial councils, concerned primarily with providing the main strategic framework within which the new authorities would work. Coming below the new structure, the Commission proposed the creation of local councils within the unitary authorities and (where desired) in metropolitan areas corresponding with the displaced county and non-county boroughs, urban districts and parishes. The local councils were designed to perform one function, namely the expression of public opinion in matters affecting their interests by making representation to the unitary authority.

In making these proposals for provincial, metropolitan and local councils, the Commission was essentially undermining its key recommendation and principle – the unitary authority. Recognizing this, Senior made the most of it in his minority report, in which he advocated a system based on the city–region concept[17] and a two-tier system. His recommendations and those of the majority of the Commission can be compared in Figure 5.

Senior's minority report provided an extremely elegant destruction of the main lines in the majority's proposals as well as a rigorous

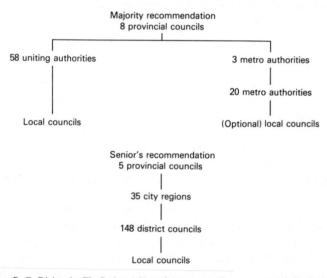

Source: P. G. Richards, *The Reformed Local Government System*, Allen & Unwin 1973.

Figure 5   *Recommendations of the Royal Commission on local government and the Minority Report compared*

justification of his proposals. Anyone seeking to oppose the Redcliffe-Maud recommendations had to go no further than Senior's memorandum of dissent to find a cogent case and alternative solution. And the Redcliffe-Maud proposals found plenty of hostile opponents. Much of the criticism of Redcliffe-Maud and of the subsequent proposals of the Labour Government in a White Paper in February 1970[18] came in fact from those authorities who were virtually to disappear under the proposals.

By and large, the Labour Government accepted the Redcliffe-Maud recommendations in making their own proposals. Public reaction was hostile, especially to the unitary authorities. Particularly critical was the Rural District Councils Association, who feared rural interests would be submerged under the new scheme, which they also felt would make local government even more remote from the public. They launched a propaganda campaign around this theme based on a character called Mr R E Mote and a slogan, 'Do not vote for R E Mote'.[19] Similarly opposed was the County Councils Association and the urban districts. Many individually elected members were also opposed, which is hardly surprising since the proposals involved a considerable reduction in their numbers. Some individual authorities that were to disappear under the proposals also launched vigorous campaigns, the most notable being that of Cheshire County Council, who produced elaborate counter-proposals and arguments as to why Cheshire should continue to exist.[20] All of the pressure was in general designed to reduce the scale of reform and to make it more 'representative' and 'democratic'. Before the Labour Government could introduce legislation to implement its proposals, however, the June 1970 election intervened, resulting in the return of the Conservative Party to power.[21]

The position of the Conservative Party *vis-à-vis* local government reform was less outspoken than that of Labour. Generally, the party favoured a two-tier system of local government, a view that had the support of most of the critics of the earlier proposals. It is hardly surprising then that the new Conservative Government should first listen to these critics and as a consequence produce a revised set of proposals in a White Paper in February 1971.[22] Wood suggests that this continued movement towards reform on the part of the Conservatives was largely due to the personal commitment to reform on the part of the Minister at the head of the Department of the Environment, Peter Walker.[23] Assuming the continued sense of willingness to change, and building on the alliance between the counties and their

districts. Walker's White Paper was very much based on their proposals for a two-tier country/district system, with a reduced scale in
the metropolitan areas and an attempt to respect existing local
authority boundaries in the county areas. While rejecting the unitary
principle advocated by Redcliffe-Maud, the White Paper accepted its
diagnosis of local government ills; its ideas on the optimum size of
authority (250,000 to 1 million); the concept of metropolitan
government (extended from three to six areas), and the idea of the
interdependence of town and country. Forty-four new counties were
proposed, including six metropolitan counties in the predominantly
urban areas.[24] These latter are smaller than the metropolitan councils
proposed by either Redcliffe-Maud or the Labour Government,
while the retention of the two-tier system throughout the country
means that the number of local governments is far larger than that
originally suggested by the Commission.

There is a considerable variation in both the population size and
tax resources among both the metropolitan and non-metropolitan
counties and their respective districts. The metro counties range from
Tyne and Wear with a population of over 1,200,000 and a (1974)
rateable value of £48,809,000, to West Midlands, with a population of
2,790,000 and a rateable value of £137,440,000. The non-metropolitan counties range from the Isle of Wight (a special case) with
109,000 inhabitants and a rateable value of £4,441,000, to Kent, with
its 1,396,000 inhabitants and a rateable value of over £60 million.
Similar differences can be found among the districts. Clearly again,
these variations will add to differences in service performance in the
future.[25]

The functional division itself is of considerable interest, revealing
as it does a difference in the importance attached to the top-tier
authorities. Thus in shire counties the top tier is the stronger and
more powerful authority, following strongly in the tradition of
county government. This is to be expected, since many of the districts
would be too small to provide a full range of services. But in the
metropolitan areas, the division of functions follows that of Greater
London, with the result that the new metropolitan counties are the
weaker level and the districts are more powerful. The districts have all
the personal services, including education, as well as local planning
and housing. The upper tier is thus left with only broad strategic
planning, transportation, police and fire, together with those
functions that are shared with the districts such as land acquisition
and recreation services.

Following discussions with the various bodies concerned, the government introduced its Local Government Bill in November 1971. Its passage to the statute books was relatively easy. Though the Labour Party opposed the Bill in Parliament, much of the force of its objections was reduced because of the unacceptability of its own proposals, and its own objections were also opposed. 1800 amendments of detail were proposed, of which the government accepted many. The government was defeated on only one item: whether or not refuse disposal should go to the county or district council. A Commons amendment was passed which gave this function to the districts; the decision was reversed by a government-sponsored amendment in the Lords.[26] Following elections in the spring and summer of 1973, the new authorities took over in April 1974, having had a 'shadow year' in which to develop new management structures and appoint staff. The old authorities dropped out of sight, but, in the end, the new system of local government came to England and the rest of Britain virtually unheralded – at least until they made their new tax demands, a topic to which we shall return.

The point behind this extensive discussion of local government reform in England, however, is to stress the idea that the way boundaries of local governments are drawn and functions are divided between authorities very much affects the political processes of the city. The Redcliffe-Maud proposals were very much urban-oriented, and if implemented would have meant a concentration of local political power in town and city hands at the expense of rural areas, which is why they found favour with the Labour Government. By contrast, the actual reforms introduced by the Conservative Government both contain the urban areas (and their political power) while largely maintaining that of the shire areas. Similarly, the fact that the metropolitan districts have most of the functions in the metropolitan areas means that the metropolitan counties are the weaker partners, facing similar kinds of problems to those faced by the GLC when seeking to secure the support and co-operation of their districts for particular county policies.[27] This situation is largely reversed in the shire areas, where the county has the bulk of the functions and where there is also a long history of two-tier government, unlike the metropolitan areas. Nevertheless, there is some evidence from the planning field that the shire counties may not get things all their own way, especially with regard to those functions that are shared between the two tiers.[28]

Informal regime changes: local finance and central–local relations

Informal regime changes, such as changes in the financial arrangements of local government or in the ways by which central government relates to the city, are perhaps as important determinants of city
politics as the more formal changes we have just examined. Both are
complicated subjects worthy of detailed study on their own,[29] so that
here we can only outline the main features of the kinds of changes that
have and do occur, and to suggest some of their consequences for city
politics.

As far as finance is concerned, local authorities in Britain raise
funds in four main ways: by 'selling' services, such as housing, leisure
facilities or transport; by levying a tax on property (the rates); by
grants from central government; and by borrowing. The important
point to grasp is that, while local government expenditure in Britain
has been growing very quickly in recent years,[30] the amount raised by
local authorities themselves has been a decreasing proportion of the
total. In other words, local authorities, and particularly the major
urban centres, have been increasingly dependent upon central
government for finance: government grants increased from 51 per
cent in 1966–7 to 66.5 per cent by 1975–6.[31]

Obviously, the availability of financial resources is an important
constraint on city governments and their ability to tackle their
problems. Given the peculiarly British way in which the property tax
is levied, in that it neither is particularly buoyant nor grows naturally,
virtually the only ways in which city governments can increase their
rate (tax) income is either by increasing the rate at which the taxes are
levied, which is generally politically unpopular, or else by increasing
the tax base, which is both slow and difficult. Many city authorities
have attempted the latter, however, through the process of city centre
redevelopment, by which older, often residential, central property
has been replaced by new office and commercial development, which
has a higher rateable value. Similarly, suburban areas have benefited
both from the continuing residential development and the process of
suburban industrial relocation that has taken place in recent years.
The result of this process has been that many inner-city areas have
been left poorer in terms of both resources and population.

The form of grants and the basis on which they are calculated also
affects the resources available to local authorities. Grants usually
take two forms – general, in that they may be spent on any service
provided, or specific, in which case the grants are earmarked for a

particular purpose. The transport supplementary grant is an example of the latter, in that it is a grant made to transport authorities to help implement their transport programmes; the largest such grant is that given to finance the police service. But throughout most of this country, and particularly since 1945, the move has been away from specific towards general grants, with the Rate Support Grant (RSG) accounting for over 85 per cent of total Exchequer grants in 1976–7.

The basis on which central government has paid grants to local authorities has altered in four main ways since 1945. First, a major objective has been that of equalizing the resources of local authorities – making good the differences between them. Second, government has increasingly sought more sophisticated measures of local needs, so as to compensate authorities for their varying needs to spend. Third, government has sought to increase the amount of local discretion that authorities have over their spending, by moving away from specific grants to general ones. Last, and most recently, government has used the grant as a means of regulating *local* tax levels, depending on its view of what proportion of the total expenditure burden local sources ought to meet.

As we have noted, the Rate Support Grant is the main one made to local authorities, and the way in which it is calculated obviously affects the resources available to a particular authority. The actual calculations are too complex to describe here, but essentially they are made around three elements. First, there is the domestic element, which is designed to cushion domestic taxpayers from the full effect of local tax increases, and which increased from under 5 per cent of average tax bills in England in 1967–8 to over 25 per cent ten years later. Second, there is the resources element, which is paid to those local governments whose rateable (taxable) value per head falls below the national average level set by the government. Last, and most complicated of all, there is the needs element, designed to compensate authorities for the amount they spend per head of population, and calculated according to a formula determined by the government and based on an analysis of past expenditure and indicators of expenditure needs that appear best to explain variations between authorities in expenditure per head. In essence, this calculation is based on the assumption that past expenditure is the best indicator of spending need. Since local government reorganization, the level of rate support grant has been subject to considerable negotiations between local authority associations and the Department of the Environment (DOE), with each side's experts attempting to convince their opposite numbers of the merit of their calculations. As a result of these negotiations and of government policy as well, there has been a considerable shift of resources away from the shire counties towards the urban and metropolitan areas, particularly London, as government has sought to shift resources to those areas where it is most needed. More recently, this trend has been reversed.

Charges for services represent another source of income for local authorities, much of it from public housing rents and transportation charges, and the total sum raised has been estimated at around 15 per cent of total current expenditure. But there has been little systematic study of authorities' charging policies, though there is little evidence of any consistent policy on either means of charging or the actual levels charged. Apart from housing and transport, local authorities charge for a wide range of services, from car parking to recreational facilities, and from school meals to licence fees. But again, clearly decisions by authorities about whether or not to charge for a particular service and how much to do so could have a significant effect on an authority's resources. For example, many urban authorities have often chosen to subsidize the level of rents out of local taxation rather than charge economic rents, thus reducing available resources.

So far we have been concerned with city government's resources for current day-by-day expenditure. But local authorities also have longer-term capital projects, the bulk of which (75 per cent) is financed by borrowing, mainly from the government through the Public Works Loans Board. Again, in recent years the volume of local government debt has risen considerably (approximately £25,000 million in 1975: under £10,000 million ten years earlier), while interest rates have also risen. Interest payments now represent the second largest item of local authority expenditure after wages and salaries. It is likely that urban authorities have the greatest indebtedness, for they have had the major capital programmes in housing, education and transport, and rises in interest rates have consequently hit city governments the hardest.

Before a local authority can borrow the money for its proposed capital expenditure, however, permission to borrow has to be given by central government. Refusal of the appropriate loan sanction, as this is known, obviously has an impact on cities' capital expenditure and is a major means by which central government is able to control the capital expenditure programmes of local authorities. By granting or refusing loan sanction, central government is both able to discourage the kind of project it does not want cities to develop and to encourage the kind of work it wants to see undertaken. Examples of the first might include the building of new town halls or civic centres, while the latter might encompass particular road or school-building programmes. Nevertheless, the centre's control over capital expenditure programmes remains weak. First, much capital expenditure has to be undertaken simply on the basis of a well established need for such expenditure, which cannot be delayed for ever. Second, once granted, loan sanction is rarely, if ever, revoked, and many local authorities seek loan sanction for projects that they do not intend to start immediately. Indeed, there may be a considerable gap between the time when loan sanction is sought and when the money is actually borrowed.[32]

Local government finance is a complex business, and we have indicated only its main features. Nevertheless, sufficient has probably been said to indicate how changes in the way city governments are financed clearly affect the resources they have available both to deal with the problems they face and to provide the many services demanded of them.

But the whole process of central–local relations is complex. Central government's primacy over local authorities derives from the doctrine of *ultra vires*, namely that the latter can only do that which has been sanctioned by Parliament. It is this doctrine that ultimately means that urban government in Britain has discretion rather than autonomy over the kinds of policies it chooses to adopt. Central government, by its powers of inspection and approval, its appellate role and its supervision of local authority accounts, and through its issuing of circulars and advice notes, has a variety of devices at its disposal *pour encourager les autres* – to persuade local authorities to adhere to its chosen policy preferences. If the financial controls act as stick and carrot, then perhaps these other devices are in some ways more subtle.

Yet, as the examples of Clay Cross over housing, Tameside over comprehensive education and various authorities over the kinds of cuts currently envisaged by Mrs Thatcher and her government colleagues all show, the centre does find it extraordinarily difficult to impose its will on the locality. In part this reflects the fact that it is the local authorities that have to implement central government policies: the latter rarely implements its own policies in the locality. It also reflects the difference between permissive and obligatory legislation: some functions all authorities are legally obliged to adopt; others they may choose whether or not to do so. It reflects differences in party-political colourings between the centre and the locality, as well as distance from London and the fact that central government cannot manage everything, even if it wanted to, which is unlikely. It also reflects the general cultural assumption that local (self-) government is a good thing *per se*, so that the large centre cannot be seen to be bullying the small local authority.

Ultimately, of course, it reflects differences between two sets of permanent, salaried officials, each with their own networks of contacts and generalized views of the world: specialists, by and large at the locality, and highly trained professional officers who are trained to oversee the day-to-day work of city government. At the centre are generalists, with no particular professional skill; professionals who might be relevant to the relationship are usually relegated to the background, so that their superior generalist administrative colleagues can dominate the centre's view of the relationship and the way it works. And while local professionals have ties that link them to their national professional associations, with their concern for service standards and codes of behaviour, and through these to their professional colleagues at the centre, the local officer also has links to his authority which encourage him to adopt a localist perspective.

Through all these channels, these points of contact and the exercise of all kinds of ploys and devices, the practice of central–local government relations is carried on, involving the exercise of power and the use of resources in what is perhaps best thought of as a kind of bargaining game with its own well understood but not infrequently changing rules.[33] Quite clearly, being involved in this game of central–local relations affects what kinds of policies city governments adopt and the way in which they implement those policies more directly under the control of the centre. Certainly the old fashioned dichotomous description of local government as either agent or partner of the centre is no longer relevant in the latter part of the twentieth century.

Authority changes: decisions and non-decisions

We can now turn to a consideration of the impact that environmental and regime changes, together with other system changes, have had on both those who take the major decisions within the city and on the nature of the public decision-making processes in the city.

At the outset we must refer back to the distinction made between decisions and non-decisions made earlier in Chapter 2, asking whether such a distinction is relevant to the modern city. Undoubtedly, for reasons to which we have already referred, this remains a difficult question to answer, but two or three points need to be borne in mind. First, the greatly increased scope of city government in twentieth-century Britain means that it is undoubtedly much more difficult for some groups of decision-makers, public or private, to exert control over the political agenda, either covertly or openly. In other words, access to decision-makers, particularly in the public sector, as well as the scope of public sector activity, has greatly increased in this century as compared with the nineteenth. It is thus much more difficult to control what issues are discussed in city politics. However, and second, this is not the same thing as saying that decision-makers treat all issues equally or that no control is exerted over how the debate on issues is undertaken. As Saunders has shown, and as Dearlove strongly implies, access to decision-makers and the nature of political debate may be severely constrained, particularly in those urban areas dominated by one political party.[34] Indeed, what is apparent from an increasing number of studies is the extent to which different individuals and groups have differential access both to decision-makers and to the services provided by city governments. What we may call major elites have a far different relationship and pattern of access to those who make the ultimate decisions: they are far more likely to be consulted; their views more likely to be acceptable to those in power, and their influence consequently is likely to be much greater than that of either the mass of individuals or minor groups who seek to become involved in the decision-making process on a far more infrequent basis.

In this way, it perhaps makes sense to talk of a mobilization of bias in English cities and in English urban politics, one that leans towards the interests of major elites and the middle classes from which the bulk of urban decision-makers are drawn.

Authority changes: elected members

Nevertheless, there have been changes in the type of person who becomes an elected representative in city governments in Britain. As a number of studies have shown, gone are the old urban squirearchy; and perhaps the old shopocracy which had its heyday in the 1920s and 1930s is not quite as numerous as it was. Even in those areas where the

Labour Party is still dominant, there are suggestions that there is a decline in working-class council membership and an increase in new middle-class professionals.[35] A number of changes in the type of person who becomes a councillor can be readily noted.

First, there is the continuing decline in the number of independent councillors, not only within the urban areas but increasingly in the shire counties, as both Grant and Bristow have documented.[36] Indeed, independent councillors, not tied to any particular party, virtually disappeared from most city governments soon after the Second World War, while their disappearance from the shire counties and rural districts has been hastened by the process of local government reform. The 1972 reforms, for example, reduced the number of elected members on councils, both as a result of reducing the total number of local authorities and limiting the number of councillors per authority. That is to say, we have larger councils with fewer elected members, a situation reinforced by the abolition of the aldermanic system, whereby the most senior councillors were freed from the chore of facing the electorate by virtue of their election to the aldermanic bench by their fellow councillors.

With fewer councils, the national parties have felt the need to extend the partisan battles of the city to the more rural parts of the country. As a result, intending councillors have been very dependent on selection as a party candidate, that is on having the appropriate party label, if they are to succeed in reaching the ranks of the council members. No longer are councillors the old social leaders so well described by Lee;[37] indeed they are not really his public persons, but rather have they become *party* persons. Now more than ever councillors owe their position to the vagaries of party selection and election.

While it is still too soon to judge accurately, there have been suggestions that local government reorganization also brought about a further change in the type of person on the city councils, driving out the old 'amateur' councillors – the old party faithfuls – and replacing them with a new, more 'professional' type of councillor. Many of the old pre-organization councillors simply dropped out at reorganization time: they either retired or else could not gain selection as a candidate by their party. Nevertheless, over 90 per cent of those people who were elected at the first elections for the new authorities had previous experience – hardly a rush of new blood. Since then, however, many of these have since dropped out, replaced by councillors of a different party label as the electorate swung against Labour in the local elections of the mid 1970s, or else retired, justifying their decision on the grounds that their work has been done now that the new authorities have been established and are working. Indeed, there is some slight evidence that the new councillors are increasingly coming from the ranks of middle-class professionals, particularly within the Conservative Party, but also in the Labour and Liberal Parties.[38]

We saw earlier how the work of people like Boaden, Dearlove and Young has been important in the study of urban politics, suggesting a change of focus towards a concern for understanding the political ideology, values and dispositions of local decision-makers. The political outlooks of councillors will very much affect the way in which they both perceive the issues and decisions in which they are involved and see their own role. A number of factors are likely to affect councillor's role perceptions, of which the most important are the councillor's length of service; the way he relates to constituents and interest groups; his focus of interest and political style, as well as his orientation to issues and other decision-makers. The type of wards represented (safe or marginal), as well as the party label, is another factor.[39]

What is necessary is some way of reducing these factors and their differential impacts on individual councillors so that their role perceptions can be classified into the most meaningful and useful types. Newton, in his study of Birmingham,[40] has perhaps succeeded best in this task, with his grouping of Birmingham councillors into five distinct types. First, there are what he calls 'parochials', whose political world consists largely of the ward and its individual constituents and problems. Parochials are 'unpaid social workers'; they are not at all ideological in their outlook, and rarely become involved in the kinds of issues that divide councils along party lines. Most tend to be found among the ranks of junior, inexperienced councillors, many of them Conservatives. Second, there are those Newton terms 'people's agents', strongly similar to parochials, but distinguishable from them in that they see themselves as protectors of citizens' interests rather than as delegates for them. Again many of them are Conservatives, with a strong ideological disposition that stresses individualism, but also allows some idea of the common interest or good.

Newton's third type is termed the 'policy advocate', showing a preference for policy matters and adopting a city-wide perspective. In classical terms, this type is perhaps closest to the Burkean representative: chosen by the electors to exercise his own judgement. Furthermore, Newton suggests that policy advocates are ideologues, operating within a 'more or less explicit set of political beliefs and values',[41] often those identified with one or other of the major political parties. Newton found a majority of Labour councillors in this category, perhaps a reflection of party control in Birmingham at the time of his work, as well as considerable length of service on the council and commitment to its work.

The fourth type is similar to the policy advocate, but is known as the 'policy broker' – moderates, compromisers, facilitators, bargainers – whose policy focus is one of striking a balance between the different competing interests associated with an issue. For them, politics consists of forging agreement, avoiding conflict and working out compromises,[42] leading to an emphasis on means rather than ends, and arriving at decisions acceptable to all. Such an outlook is likely to make them favourably disposed towards organized groups and may well lead them into conflict with the more ideologically orientated members of their party. In terms of their overall characteristics, Newton suggests that policy brokers are very similar to policy advocates, being more professional, longer-serving and more politically committed.

Newton's last type, the 'policy spokesman', comprises a small group combining a delegate perspective with an overall interest in general policy: they speak on behalf of, rather than for, their constituents, but believe in getting the policies right, even if they come into conflict with their party.

Authority changes: paid officials

Newton's classification, important though it is, represents a first step in devising a classification of the role perceptions, value preferences and policy dispositions of British elected members. More needs to be done before we have a full picture of how councillors act in the policy-making arena;[43] but Newton's work is sufficient to show that not all councillors, indeed perhaps not even the majority of them, are interested mainly in grappling with the problems of policy, even though local government reorganization and recommended changes in management structure and practice have generally been designed with the aim of encouraging councillors to become more policy-orientated.

Before discussing this point, however, we need to consider the role of the other group of major decision-makers – the paid officials. As a topic for study, the role of the local bureaucrat remains largely unresearched in British city politics: political scientists sometimes seem to think the subject unresearchable, even though they continue to argue that the old distinction between policy and administration is inapplicable. Much of the work on local bureaucrats has in fact been done by urban sociologists, largely in their exploration (and mainly rejection) of the urban managerialist thesis.[44] What this work shows is that local bureaucrats are both important gatekeepers and important actors in the policy-making process, even if the degree of their control over the environment was less than that suggested by proponents of the managerialist thesis. Nevertheless, the role of paid officials in the policy-making process remains difficult to research, if only because of the difficulties of penetrating the clichés and myths of bureaucratic power.

Given that local officials are important in the policy-making process, from where does this power come? First, it derives from the official's position as hired technical expert, as a professional. The twentieth century has seen a huge increase in both the numbers and types of professionals in local government to add to the public health and engineering professionals of the nineteenth. Town planners, educationalists, environmental health inspectors, social workers, transport specialists and most recently policy analysts and corporate planners are all twentieth-century additions to these professional ranks. In most cases, professional status implies membership of a professional association or institute, which is granted when an individual has gained qualifications recognized by the association. In recent years there has been a tendency for the standard of these entry qualifications to be raised, as the professional bodies seek to raise both the status and rewards of their members, so that even a university graduate may well be expected to work for a further qualification before being given professional status.[45]

Membership of a professional institute, however, presents a problem for the local official, namely that of dual loyalty – to the profession, and to the authority that employs him. This dual loyalty may create a problem when professional interests or standards come into conflict with those of the local authority, as expressed by the council. But it is the membership of a profession with the appropriately recognized qualifications that is the source of the local official's influence as a technical expert. Nevertheless, as much of the sociological critique of planning shows, the extent to which much of what local government does is actually technical, neutral, value-free and requires expert skills may be very much open to debate. Environmental health inspection provides a good example: judging whether a particular piece of meat is fit to eat requires certain skills for which a professional qualification is necessary. On the other hand, judging whether or not a house is fit for human habitation is less open to objective measurement.

The problem of professional expertise becomes particularly acute when the questions of establishing policy priorities, and of choosing particular strategies to achieve these priorities, are considered. As we shall see, planning is particularly a city activity in which this problem is apparent, though it is most common in those areas of governmental activity concerned with the softer, personal services. Put simply, it is difficult for a councillor to tell his city engineer how to build a new road (though not whether the road is necessary), but not for him to question whether or not a particular individual should receive social service benefits.

Having said that, councillors are often reluctant to question the advice offered by their officials or to suggest alternative strategies or priorities. In part this derives from the fact that the professional has been exclusively hired to undertake this kind of work in which he claims expertise: to question this work is to suggest either professional incompetence or else a waste of ratepayers' money. The reluctance to question advice also comes from the part-time amateur nature of the elected member: councillors often simply do not have the time or the necessary expertise to question their officials, even if they were so inclined.

Another source of the official's influence on policy-making lies in his control over the information on which policy is based, as Dennis rightly documents.[46] This control is exercised essentially in two ways. First, officials are largely responsible for the collection and presentation of materials both to committee and council. As a result of their work, many alternative courses of action are likely to be rejected as unsuitable, for whatever reason. Officials, as part of their expertise, will also be 'sources of information' in that they will know where to look or who to ask for information. They are also likely to be under considerable pressure to simplify problems and suggested solutions, and to reduce their recommendations to what their seniors would call 'manageable proportions'. Councillors are therefore likely to be presented with problem analyses and policy suggestions in a highly condensed form: their officials may well consider them either unable or unwilling to handle detailed reports.

The second way in which officials exercise control over information derives from their gatekeeper function in often controlling the access of individuals and groups to councillors and committee. Consciously or unconsciously, officials, who are often those first approached by individuals or groups wishing to make a claim on the policy-maker's time, will screen out some individuals or groups and let the claims of others through. Dearlove[47] has shown quite clearly how councillors have different perceptions of voluntary groups and their 'utility' to the policy-making process, while Dennis also demonstrates how officials controlled public access to decision-makers in relation to urban renewal schemes in Sunderland, often deflecting groups' attempts to contact councillors directly by encouraging them to deal with officials instead.

This last point reflects a third source of the official's influence in decision-making, namely the bureaucratic nature and hierarchical structure of local government work. Given the scale of modern city governments, it is inevitable that the associated division of labour will lead to the adoption of bureaucratic and hierarchical modes of decision-making. Thus lines of command and communication, along the vertical and horizontal channels associated with the usual organizational charts found in textbooks on administration, will be established which encourage delegation, specialization and isolation among the ranks of the officials. Indeed, it may well be that despite the formal responsibilities of chief officers, the actual work done under their aegis is conducted at several levels removed from them, and they may be almost as unfamiliar with the details of some of the proposals they present to committee as are the councillors who make up that committee.

Decision-making in the post-reform era

This is perhaps to exaggerate some of the changes that have followed from the 1972 reorganization of local government particularly, but there is no doubt that some of the internal structural changes in local authorities have strengthened the power of officials at the expense of that of councillors. For example, the move towards corporate planning associated with local government reorganization and the Bains report[48] has certainly had this consequence, even though the idea of a corporate approach to both policy-making and management was also designed to overcome the problems of fragmentation and lack of co-ordination associated with the old departmentalism of the pre-reform authorities. However, as Hambleton rightly notes,[49] it is still difficult to make generalizations about the extent to which authorities have fully adopted a corporate approach, both because there is a considerable variation in the number and type of corporate policy approaches adopted by local authorities, and also because the resources squeeze they have faced in recent years is very much the opposite from the situation from which corporate planning emerged. Furthermore, corporate planning implies change in attitudes by officials towards the idea of inter-departmental co-operation as much as a change in the internal structure of local authorities. Indeed, it might be said that corporate planning is all too easy to undermine: a department or chief officer unwilling to play the corporate game can find all kinds of strategies to undermine the corporate structure.

Elected members have also not been slow to undermine the corporate system. As we saw earlier, only a few councillors are likely to be policy-orientated, and many may feel their position has been undermined by the introduction of the new so-called corporate systems. In part they may also be echoing another criticism of corporate planning, namely that it tends to obscure the essentially *political* nature of local decision-making, allowing the dominance of the officers' professional values to hide behind the mask of rationality.[50]

Three further changes that have affected the internal structure of local authorities should be mentioned here. First there is the adoption by such local authorities as Liverpool and Stockport of area management schemes, whereby the corporate ideal is given an areal, neighbourhood or community focus. Under these schemes inter-departmental teams of officers work on policies related to the needs of particular geographical areas within an authority and furthermore there may be some delegation of administration and/or political responsibility for this work down to that level. Such schemes reflect American experience with its war on poverty, and model cities programmes of the 1960s, as well as British experience of the community development programme and the Inner Area Studies in the early 1970s. Probably the best known example of area management in Britain is that of Stockport, which has operated such a scheme since 1974. Stockport's area organization, which divides the city into three geographic areas, has five main aims: to prevent the authority from becoming remote and inaccessible from local residents; to promote corporate management downwards to the local level; to strengthen the elected member's role; to provide a channel of communication with local residents, and to make best use of local accommodation and officers' local knowledge. Three operational areas, defined largely in service terms and covering eight area committees, are each overseen by an area co-ordinator and designed to secure efficient service delivering to the residents in the three areas. Local residents have the opportunity of becoming involved in the process either through membership of area committees, which include the local ward councillor, or through community councils, which largely comprise organized voluntary groups in the area, and whose work is stimulated by the use of community development officers.

Passing judgement on the Stockport experiment, Hambleton notes that the area system 'is essentially advisory, and some would say toothless',[51] mainly because of lack of delegation to area co-ordinators and their teams by staff in the town hall, and by the general unwillingness of the elected members to devolve power down to the area committees. Nevertheless, the Stockport experiment, along with those in other areas, is interesting because of its attempt to deal with some of the problems of the larger local authorities brought about by reorganization.

Another experiment, this time promoted in the field of town planning, is that of planning aid, akin to what the Americans call 'advocacy planning',[52] whereby planners are employed to give (particularly disadvantaged) groups engaged in planning issues professional advice and independent support. This limited work has largely been conducted under the aegis of the Town and Country Planning Association and has involved experiments with community groups in such places as Nottingham and Manchester.

Both of these structural changes – area management and planning aid – reflect a third major pressure on the service providers at the local level, namely, a need for them to relate to their clients, the service users. As city government in particular and local government generally has grown in its scale of operation, then the need to devise institutional arrangements that make it less remote from and more in tune with the needs of local residents has increased. In some cases, as we shall see in our examination of particular services, this pressure has come from above, that is to say either from within local authorities themselves or from central government; in other cases it has come from below, a popular pressure from a public seeking to force their attentions on an unresponsive city government. Either way it reflects the kind of regime or structural change, which is also paralleled by authority change, through which local government in Britain has passed in recent years.

6 Policy arena 1: housing

In this part of the book public policy is reviewed as it affects the city in three service areas. In each case we shall be concerned with analysing the way in which government, and particularly city government, has affected a service area, and with examining the consequences, intended and unintended, of the policies for the delivery of the service under review. Of special concern in each chapter in this section will be an attempt to explore the distributional effects of the policies for the particular arena under review, in an attempt to indicate who gets what and who 'pays' what in relation to each service.

Despite innumerable attempts by successive British governments, both central and local, to define and deal with 'the housing problem', housing remains a complex subject, still difficult to understand. However, four ideas or concepts make it easier to grasp some of the essential elements of housing. First, there is the idea of different housing markets, each with their associated supply and demand. Thus, using different tenure types, we can identify the markets for owner-occupation, for public housing and for private rental, each with different levels of supply and demand. But we can also identify different housing markets as they relate to different demographic groups and to their stage in the life cycle: again this helps us identify such housing markets as those for the elderly, for married couples with or without children, and for single people.

Housing markets: access and allocation

In the case of all these different, identifiable housing markets, it also makes sense to examine the supply and demand for each, and to see how far they are affected. Thus, for example, the supply of housing for owner-occupation depends largely on the willingness of private developers to build new houses; the rate at which second-hand houses come on to the market; central government efforts at 'subsidizing' owner-occupation by either tax rebates or attempts at keeping mortgage rates low; the supply of mortgage finance, and the release of land by local authorities for new residential building, among other factors.

Already something of the complexity of housing as a subject to be analysed can be grasped: the complexity is magnified when a second idea is added, namely that of the interdependence of housing markets. Put simply, this means that changes in supply and demand conditions in one housing market have ramifications throughout the rest. Thus, for example, a rise in mortgage rates makes it more difficult for first-time buyers to get into the owner-occupier market, while also discouraging existing house-owners from possibly trading up, and releasing their own house on to the market. As a consequence, the demand for council housing is likely to increase, and indeed the way the size of council waiting lists varies according to changes in mortgage rates is well known. At the same time, assuming the supply of council housing is relatively fixed, at least in the short term, pressure for privately rented accommodation will continue to be felt.

The interdependence of housing markets has crucial implications for policy,[1] since a policy designed to assist or improve conditions in one market will have repercussions far beyond that market. Indeed, it may be argued that a failure to grasp this point explains why many governmental attempts to deal with the 'housing problem' have been less than successful. Furthermore, though successive governments have talked of housing policy, in reality there have been many housing policies, each designed to 'deal' with some aspect or other of the different housing markets, and generally lacking any real co-ordination or appreciation of the different consequences, as we shall see.

Nevertheless, this rather simple economistic way of examining and analysing housing has received considerable criticism, especially from sociologists, whose own analyses of housing depend on two further ideas: those of allocation and access, with the idea of exploring how the different agencies involved in housing control people's access to different housing tenures or how they allocate housing resources. In part these ideas owe their origins to the work of John Rex, who introduced the idea of housing classes in his work in Birmingham so as to draw attention to the way in which housing authorities might discriminate in their allocation of public housing to different racial groups.[2] Though subsequently much criticized for its essentially descriptive nature,[3] the idea of housing classes was useful as a sensitizing concept suggesting a variety of relationships to the means of residence and a tendency to conflict, which in turn led further sociologists to suggest that what was important in discussing housing was people's access to different tenure types, the way in which these were allocated and by what agencies and actors. Thus, for example, it becomes important to examine how local authorities decide who shall be given a council tenancy, in what kind of housing, where and when, and so on, and relating these findings to other actors in the housing field.

But the concepts of allocation and access are also useful in analysing what is happening in relation to private sector housing, for example, in trying to understand how building societies or estate agents also control access to certain housing tenures and also allocate housing resources. Understanding why building societies prefer to lend money on some types of property (new, or certainly post-First World War) or to lend to particular types of clients (regular savers, with steady, rising incomes) tells us a lot about the kind of people who are most likely to become owner-occupiers and what sort of houses developers are likely to build.

Despite the importance of the ideas of allocation and access, they do not replace entirely the market concepts developed previously: rather, they supplement them. In other words, having established the supply and demand conditions in different housing markets, it is then necessary to identify the allocation and access patterns there as well as the actors responsible and the interactions between them. However, even this is an oversimplification, because of the complex interrelationships between each of the markets, and because the different actors are generally involved in more than one market. This is particularly true for both central and local government. For example, city governments may be involved through the sale of council houses, allocating them for rent or building them. They may also be involved in improving older housing stock, regulating private landlords or accommodating homeless families. Furthermore, they might well be encouraging developers to build on sites within city boundaries, even perhaps trying to persuade them to build for owner-occupation on or near the city centre.

All of these are direct ways in which city governments may be involved in the various housing markets in a direct fashion. But it is also important that direct interventions in one market by city authorities will have indirect effects in the other markets. For example, by excluding some groups from access to council housing, perhaps by not allocating vacant tenancies to people on the waiting list as a result of high priority, then the authorities are likely to add to the pressure both for owner-occupation and more particularly on the declining private rental sector.

The history of city government involvement in housing dates back to the mid and late nineteenth century, when the rapid growth of the new industrial centres forced the authorities to introduce building regulations and local improvement acts in an attempt to obviate the worst excesses of overcrowded, insanitary and physically unfit housing to be found in most cities. In many cases enforcement of the new legislation and regulations proved even more difficult than introducing the new powers themselves, for many city decision-makers were reluctant to do anything that would hinder the rapid industrial growth on which not only the cities but also the decision-makers themselves depended. The overlap between city governors and the local economic elite in nineteenth-century English towns has been well documented, so the reluctance of such governors to do much to regulate housing is easily understood. The result was the gradual involvement of central government, which since the end of the First World War has increasingly been involved. After a gradual build-up in the 1920s and 1930s, the real spate of government legislation came in the 1950s and 1960s when it seemed as if there was almost an annual important piece of housing legislation. Thus Parliament passed legislation to provide housing finance, regulate private landlords, introduce fair rents/give tenants security, provide for urban redevelopment and slum clearance, encourage high-rise development, encourage low-rise development, spread home owner-ship/help the first-time buyer. This bewildering mass of legislative examples is an indication of how difficult both central and local government has found housing as a subject for state regulation. Given the complexity, we focus here largely on the way city governments have had an impact on housing since the Second World War, though it must be remembered that much local action has been in response to initiatives promoted by central government in its legislation, which has often been designed at least to encourage city authorities to move in certain directions. It is also perhaps most useful if the discussion is presented in terms of a number of different housing markets, looking at the way in which city governments have reacted to changing supply and demand conditions.

Council housing and improvement

Quite clearly, the most obvious market where local authorities exert a major influence is that for public or council housing. Local authorities, and particularly urban/metropolitan ones, are the supplier, and since public housing now comprises over a third of the total housing stock, they are a major (and perhaps the only) source of housing for many people. And since housing is a major resource, the allocation of council housing is likely to be a process full of conflict.

The supply of council housing by local authorities is dependent upon a number of factors. First, there is the extent to which there is a need for such housing, which reflects both the demand for it, as expressed in terms of numbers of people on housing waiting lists, and estimates of unfit or unsatisfactory housing in the area. Both are likely to be somewhat inaccurate, the first if only because people often leave their names on waiting lists long after they have found other housing, and the second if only because the classification of unfit or unsatisfactory housing may well vary between one environmental health inspector and another.

Most council housing in Britain's cities has been built as part of the massive urban renewal programmes of the 1950s and 1960s rather than to provide housing for waiting list candidates. The age and condition of the housing stock is a crucial factor affecting a city's housing policy, given the post-war emphasis on urban renewal. Indeed, in most cities probably more than 80 per cent of post-war council property has gone to rehouse people in slum clearance areas, leaving not more than one in five for waiting list candidates. Inevitably, this kind of situation means queueing for a home, a topic well analysed by Lambert *et al.* in their case study of Birmingham.[4] And by controlling the queueing process, the housing authorities are controlling access to public housing, a control reinforced by the allocation procedures they adopt to ensure that 'tenants and housing are matched'. The introduction of special categories for housing priority (for example, the sick or disabled); the introduction, and subsequent revision, of a points system; the need to establish one's 'homeless' condition; the grading of property, as well as distinguishing between 'serious' and 'frivolous' inquiries through various registration procedures are all examples of different ways in which access to council housing is made difficult for the ordinary man in the street. Far from simply making a visit to the housing office and registering one's name, the would-be council house tenant needs considerable patience and persistence if he is to be successful in getting the kind of housing he wants; and while accusations of 'key money'[5] may be an exaggeration, a good knowledge of the rules and regulations and an ability to 'jump the queue' may also help. Last, but not least, the would-be tenant would find it advantageous *not* to have any of those characteristics that will permit the authorities to stigmatize him as 'deviant' or 'problem', such as being a single parent, or having a history of indebtedness or a criminal record. Any of these is likely to result in an applicant falling further behind in the housing queue, or to result in poorer, older accommodation being offered.[6]

Thus city governments control access to public housing in a variety of ways and through a number of procedures. They are, however, involved in the provision of housing services in a number of other ways, perhaps most notably in recent years through their encouragement of house improvement. In practice the switch from replacement to rehabilitation of older housing since the late 1960s by urban authorities is an example of the way in which local authorities respond to central government initiatives. By the mid 1960s, central government had begun to react both to the high costs (particularly those for land) of renewal and to the burgeoning public protests against the scale of the renewal programmes in our major cities. City authorities were similarly concerned, and in some areas were further alarmed by the continuing loss of population that followed not only from voluntary migration but also from the various overspill schemes that generally accompanied the renewal programmes. Overspill – the decanting of excess population – was thought necessary if the high residential densities in the older housing areas of cities were to be reduced to more acceptable levels. Reduction in population density – dealing with overcrowding – was one of the main planks of post-war planning policy. Thus, for example, at one time it was estimated that Salford had been losing between twelve and fifteen families a week as a result of both voluntary migration and overspill, while Cox[7] has shown that between 1961 and 1971 Liverpool lost almost 25 per cent of its population, a rate that recent estimates suggest has not been reversed.

Thus, from 1968 onwards central government has encouraged a policy of improvement rather than replacement, and by an increasingly varied grant structure tied to different types of improvement scheme it has made improvement its major emphasis on the housing front. For example, schemes adopted as Housing Action Areas (HAAs), designed to improve housing in the worst areas, receive higher improvement grants than do those identified as General Improvement Areas (GIAs), which in turn are given higher grants than those to ordinary householders seeking to improve their property and who may receive 50 per cent of the cost up to a limit of £5000.

Despite the emphasis on improvement by the centre, city authorities did not all respond immediately and enthusiastically to the change. There are a number of reasons why this was so. First, the housing conditions of cities vary considerably across the country, and indeed within particular cities. Some of the areas of worst housing, such as Liverpool, Glasgow and Salford, still had much housing that was not worth saving, or else the authorities felt that improvement was not a particularly relevant policy given their housing conditions. In other cases, given the extensive clearance programmes, financial commitments and the lags involved in the normal building programme, authorities could not switch from clearance to improvement without delay: indeed, this kind of lag between policy initiative and policy implementation is common when a change of policy focus is involved.

Like getting a council house, having one's old house improved may seem a simple matter to a local resident, particularly if he is an owner-occupier and especially since half the cost will be met by government. But, as with council housing, there are a number of obstacles or barriers to improvement, some of which are erected by local or central government, others by private or quasi-public institutions involved in the provision of housing. Thus, for example, designation of an area as a GIA or HAA is far more likely to depend on decisions made by local authority procedures, such as inspection, 'lifing', etc., than it is upon the efforts of local residents. Similarly the authority may want *all* improvements to be carried out simultaneously, rather than allowing the property owner to undertake improvements at times that may be more convenient to him. Alternatively, the authority may require the work to be carried out to a standard high enough to deter the owner from incurring his part of the costs. Indeed, from an owner's point of view, improvement may simply not seem worthwhile, particularly if he is elderly or expects to move out of the area within the foreseeable future. For example, research done by the author for the Department of the Environment in one GIA in Greater Manchester revealed that the elderly particularly were unwilling to consider improving their homes, since their life expectancy was far shorter than that of the houses in which they lived. Further-

more, even the designation of the area as one suitable for improvement seemed to drive out those residents 'able to escape' from what
they felt was now stigmatized housing, and often this group
contained those most able to meet the costs of improvement. Their
exodus probably added to the continued deterioration of the area
noted by the researchers while undertaking their work.[8]

Other people may find that barriers have been erected by other
housing institutions. By definition, housing in need of improvement
is poorer-quality housing, maybe in areas not so favourably regarded
as 'good risks' by building societies, banks or insurance companies;
owners may face difficulty in raising their share of the improvement
costs from these organizations. Owners themselves may not be
regarded as good credit risks, perhaps being elderly, or poorly paid,
or immigrants. More particularly, tenants may well find that
landlords are especially unwilling to invest further capital into
something that has often given a poor return.

To counteract some of these problems, local authorities usually
involve housing associations in the task of improving the area, such
associations being willing and able, thanks to loans and grants from
government through the Housing Corporation, to buy up property
from those owners and landlords who are unable or unwilling to meet
their share of improvement costs. Having improved the property, it is
then rented back to the former owner or tenant, but, of course, at a
rent that reflects the value of the newly improved property. It is worth
noting that the interests of housing associations and local residents
may not coincide when it comes to improvement: for example,
associations have an interest in buying property at the lowest possible price, owners in selling at the highest price. The two are not
necessarily the same, as many owners of property in improvement
areas have perhaps discovered to their cost. More recently, building
societies, following encouragement both by central and local government, have been more willing to lend money for improvement and
purchase in the areas of older housing, with one society even prepared
to take on the role of landlord.[9]

Undoubtedly, many people have benefited from the emphasis on
improvement in recent years, though it has been the more
prosperous, able members of the community who have gained most.
Though the 'gentrification' process associated with Islington,[10] has
not been extensively repeated in other cities outside London, there
are pockets of middle-class improved housing in what were formerly
working-class areas in most such cities.

Another, related, phenomenon, particularly in London, has been the improvement of housing by property companies using the improvement grant system to improve their properties, hopefully being able to let them subsequently at higher rents. Nevertheless, many tenants have experienced considerable difficulty in pursuading landlords to improve property which is already showing a poor return on capital. It is partly to overcome this situation that the already mentioned housing associations have been used by local authorities; private landlords unable or unwilling to make the necessary improvements themselves may be prepared to sell the property to a housing association which is better able to undertake the improvement.

Organized groups and housing

Given the various actors involved – local authorities, owners, tenants, building societies, landlords, housing associations, etc. – it is hardly surprising that improvement schemes take time to complete, or that improvement tends to move in a rather piecemeal fashion. Nor should it be surprising that the different interests of the actors involved do not necessarily coincide all the time, so that improvement schemes are as likely to be as full of conflict as are other activities of urban governmental systems. Indeed, housing has been one of the policy arenas that has provoked more political activity among local people than perhaps any other. Tenants' associations, concerned with protecting council tenants' interests in terms of rents, maintenance and provision of amenities on council estates, have proliferated since the Second World War, many of them having long lives and developing close relationships with local councillors and officials. Owner-occupier associations, ratepayers' and residents' groups have a similar, if not longer, history of activity, though mainly such groups have been concerned with keeping rate levels down and promoting 'governmental efficiency' at the local level. Perhaps one of their more successful periods recently was during the 'ratepayers' revolt' of the mid 1970s, when many groups successfully fought local election campaigns.[11]

The organization of tenant and owner-occupier groups is very much an expression of class interests in the city, notwithstanding the fact that there are many relatively well-off council tenants and many relatively poorly-off owner-occupiers. Council tenants are still overwhelmingly working-class – though mainly semi-skilled and skilled workers. Owner-occupiers are largely middle-class – professionals, managers, etc.[12]

Homelessness

This leads to an issue so far not discussed, but one that neither the owner-occupier market nor the public sector rented market has dealt with satisfactorily in the past, namely the question of homelessness and those who, for whatever reasons, need and want cheap housing. This group, sometimes euphemistically described as the 'sub-working-class', have nearly always been and, some might argue, are increasingly dependent on the private rental sector to meet their housing requirements. Furthermore, state action, at both the central and local levels, has aggravated the problem; for example, central government has made the situation worse by the various measures it has introduced both to control the level of rents charged by private landlords and to give tenants security of tenure, both of which have made investment in property unattractive to the small-scale investor who was traditionally the type of person acting as a private landlord. Local authorities have also contributed, both through their improvement and renewal policies, which (naturally) remove the poorer (but cheaper) housing stock from the market, and by their tenancy selection procedures, which may well discriminate against the kind of person who needs and wants cheap housing. The problems of homeless families undoubtedly gave rise to one of the main public conflicts in the housing arena and to one of the many politically active movements in city politics in the 1960s and 1970s – the squatters. Seeking to occupy unoccupied private or public accommodation, the squatters helped to draw attention to the problems of homelessness that exist in Britain's major cities. Indeed, London's longest-running squat, which began in 1973 in the Tolmers Square area next to Euston Station, has only recently come to an end (summer 1979), and the development company's bulldozers moved in to clear much of old housing. Wates[13] shows that the 186 squatters there in 1975 covered a wide range of people, including students (40), professionals (10), manual workers (12), teachers (8), and unemployed (25), not to mention musicians, artists, bakers and pensioners. At its peak in the mid 1970s, when the squatting movement was well established, it has been estimated that 30,000 people had taken direct action to house themselves in London alone. At that time in Greater London there were 12,000 people living in temporary hostel accommodation and over 200,000 on the council housing lists: 100,000 houses, by contrast, were lying empty.[14]

Most of the organized squats were developed gradually, partly as a result of lessons learnt from early experience and partly because of the condition of the houses squatters sought to occupy. Squatting is a politically and socially explosive issue: the authorities, if not the property-owners, are likely to react violently, seeking eviction orders, and often using police to carry out the latter. The arrival of squatters may promote an unfavourable reaction among existing residents, breaking up the community still further. Private owners of property occupied by squatters may adopt harassing tactics to drive out the unwelcome residents: as Wates says, 'Only people who were determined, politically motivated, or absolutely desperate'[15] were able to squat for any length of time. The conditions of the housing that squatters occupy is also a problem: most likely it will be derelict and decaying, having been unoccupied for a number of years. There will be no water, gas or electricity: floorboards may have been ripped up, windows bricked in, lavatories, cisterns and hand basins smashed. Damp will be a problem, and there may be rats and other vermin. Turning this kind of property into fit habitation is a long and arduous task, notwithstanding the ever-present threat of eviction. For all these reasons, the turnover among squatters is high, most squats are relatively short-lived, and yet some have had considerable impact.

Writing about the squatting movement's early years, one of its founders notes[16] that, while it had not achieved widespread direct action, the movement had achieved better housing for some people by its actions. In London at least, a number of boroughs were prepared to let homeless families take over and occupy empty houses, and the movement also brought the problem of homelessness forcibly to the attention of central government and local authorities alike.[17]

By the mid 1970s the problems of homeless families had reached such a level that central government, as a result of pressure from groups like Shelter and the many squatting campaigns, was obliged to tighten up the housing legislation so as to ensure that local authorities would house homeless families more effectively. This was to be achieved by the Homeless Persons Act (1976), though this Act still retained a number of loopholes which some authorities have utilized to avoid housing people they consider undesirable.[18] The problem is at its worst in London and the other major cities, partly because of their honeypot nature in naturally attracting people, and partly because they still have large pockets of the cheaper older housing sought by such groups.

Normally the homeless have included people generally labelled by the authorities as 'deviant' in some way or other: 'hard-core' unemployables, single-parent families, immigrants, those with a record of criminal activities or of indebtedness, all groups unattractive to those who control access to both the owner-occupier and public sector markets. More recently, however, as a result of conditions in the housing markets and the general economic situation, as well as changing living patterns, the ranks of the homeless have been swollen by the increasing number of single young people seeking to live away from home, by young newly-marrieds unable to meet waiting list requirements or raise funds to qualify for a mortgage or pay rents for the limited private rental accommodation available, and by the elderly, who, dependent on either state pensions or limited fixed incomes, are unable to cope with the ravages of inflation. Through the provision of sheltered housing, local authorities have begun to meet the demands of this latter group for housing.[19] [19]

Who gains and who pays?

Undoubtedly, those who have gained most in terms of housing resources have been the many people who have become owner-occupiers. From constituting around 25 per cent of the total housing tenures at the end of the war, owner-occupation had become the form of tenure of over 50 per cent of the population by the mid 1970s; the 'property-owning democracy' promised by the Conservatives in the early 1950s had arrived by the time Mrs Thatcher took office in 1979. Indeed, the commitment to owner-occupation was increasingly shared by the Labour Party, with the result that governments of both complexions have sought to subsidize and protect the owner-occupier, both through the relief provided on mortgage interest payments (fully allowable against tax) and by their attempts to hold down building society interest rates. The 1974 Labour Government, for example, even went so far as to lend the building societies money for a short period in 1975 in order to stop the mortgage rate rising above 10 per cent.[20]

Owner-occupiers have also benefited in another way, however, namely from the tendency of house prices to rise faster than prices generally. This means that it is possible for an owner-occupier to realize real profits when he sells his property, notwithstanding the fact that he will have to pay more for new housing than he did originally. He may use his profits to trade up – buy a bigger house in better surroundings – or to move to an area of cheaper housing, or to trade down, as his housing needs change according to the seller's place in the life cycle. Only rarely may an owner-occupier be obliged to move unwillingly to an area where housing is more expensive – by virtue of a job move, for example – and even in these cases he may well be compensated by a higher revenue, or by substantial financial assistance from his employer designed to offset the costs of the move. Even in these cases, the owner-occupier will still probably be able to reap his profits (perhaps at a better rate) at a later date. In other words, rarely, if ever, does the owner-occupier lose money by virtue of his form of tenure: buying a house remains one of the best ways of accumulating capital, as anybody who bought and sold a house in 1972 (when house prices virtually doubled) knows full well.

From whom is the owner-occupier making his gains? Largely from the first-time buyer, who is consistently faced with a heavy premium to enter the owner-occupier market. But gains are also made from those who invest in the finance of housing, that is building society depositors, who are usually small savers, drawn disproportionately from the working class. Last, the owner-occupier gains at the expense of the taxpayer generally, by virtue of the tax relief on mortgage interest payments, and more recently through the grants for improving property made available under the various improvement schemes introduced by the government from the late 1960s onwards.[21]

The tendency for owner-occupiers to look after their interests in urban political conflict is well known. Residents' associations, along with ones for ratepayers, have long been a feature of city politics. Their desire to maintain or enhance property values, to maintain or improve residential densities, to buy up undesirables – be they individuals or activities – is well known, and their claims on local decision-makers are faithfully reported in local newspapers throughout the country. Being largely, though not exclusively, middle-class, the groups are likely to have the skills and resources necessary to mount the kinds of campaigns that will ensure the protection of their interests. By comparison, tenants' associations, which in most cases will be organized around those living in publicly rather than privately rented accommodation, frequently suffer from the absence of skills and resources, particularly leadership and money.

Though perhaps better documented in American studies,[22]

research on residents' and ratepayers' associations has been undertaken here. For example, in his recent book Saunders ably illustrates the influence of such groups in the middle-class suburbs of the London borough of Croydon, where they were well able to fight off such opponents as a major builder, a wealthy local foundation and the GLC.[23] Young and Kramer[24] have also documented the way in which the London borough of Bromley resisted all attempts to bring overspill population from London's inner suburbs into the borough's suburban pastures. In both cases, the politics of these boroughs has looked after the interests of their wealthier, middle-class owner-occupiers, who have undoubtedly benefited more than have their working-class counterparts in council or privately rented accommodation inside these boroughs or elsewhere in London. To a very large extent, this is a story that would be repeated in other British cities.

In part, problems of housing like those outlined in this chapter arise from the failure of central and local government either to dominate or to reach a mutually satisfactory arrangement with the private sector interests concerned with housing. Far too often, housing policy appears as a short-term reaction by the state to yet another housing crisis brought about by either the failure of the market or some unforeseen consequences of some other governmental policy. Often the state appears to be taking on those housing functions that the private sector finds unprofitable. At other times, the state appears as the willing partner of private interests – through its active encouragement of owner-occupation, for example. Lastly, in times of economic recession the local state has frequently been the saviour of private building firms, as public sector housing contracts provide a bedrock of work when economic conditions discourage private house building. In all these cases both central and local government appear to be following events in the housing arena rather than attempting to provide a lead.

The Green Paper of 1977

This situation was recognized by the Labour Government in 1975, which through Anthony Crosland initiated a review of housing finance, subsequently published in June 1977 as a Green Paper.[25] Its supporting technical documents have been generally recognized as providing a detailed comprehensive analysis of government policy and the housing question. The major weakness, however, of the

Green Paper lies in the fact that it proposes no radical reformulation of either policy or finance at the central level. Furthermore, it is positively euphoric about the virtues of home ownership, which is seen as a 'basic and natural desire' of all people,[26] a claim difficult to justify. Its analysis of the *private* rental sector is poor, while its suggestions for the public sector appear traditional, with one exception. This concerns the introduction of a new system of capital spending allocations for housing, whereby local authorities draw up four-year housing investment programmes (HIPs) covering all capital expenditure in the housing field for new building through acquisitions to mortgages and improvement grants. HIPs are to be produced annually, covering all housing programmes, and are supposed to give local authorities greater freedom in the way they allocate their housing funds, for they receive a block grant to spend as they see fit. In practice, the likely effect may well be to increase central government control, since Whitehall now decides not only the size of the housing cake, but also how it is divided among the local authorities. In this respect, the new HIPs are rather similar to the system devised for handling transport policy and planning. In the end, the whole Green Paper promised much and seems to have delivered little. In the words of one critic, 'the housing policy review is almost a non-event in terms of its policy recommendation, and the housing situation in future years will suffer in consequence',[27] a view with which it is difficult to disagree.

In part, as we shall see, this situation is linked to predominant views about the nature and purpose of planning, which in the 1950s and 1960s stressed redevelopment (particularly in the city centre, where commercial development replaced former housing and largely small-scale industrial users) and the decanting of population (which encouraged suburbanization and the spread of privately built owner-occupied housing, and which stressed the importance of the car as a means of transport, hence encouraging the building of motorways and land-hungry road schemes, particularly in cities). But, in all these cases, it was the private sector that made the running. This is perhaps illustrated by the example of the still largely unexplored activities of the property developer, many of whom have made vast profits from the commercial redevelopment of city centres, particularly through the provision of office space. The activities of people like Harry Hyams and his company, Oldham Estates (particularly over Centre Point);[28] of the Levy brothers and the redevelopment of the Euston Centre and the subsequent battle for

Tolmers Square,[29] as well as the less well chronicled efforts of such companies as Ravenseft,[30] Arndale, Town and Country Properties, etc., are visible for all to see in practically every major British town. And, as far as one can judge, local authorities, and even central government on occasion, have been willing partners in the property boom, though nearly always on less than advantageous terms.[31]

The point here is not so much to denigrate the success of the private sector in terms of its achievements, but to note that private sector interests, particularly the need for profit and continued capital accumulation, and those of urban and central governments do not necessarily coincide. As a result, because the latter have generally either not seized the initiative or else have not been clear as to what *their* interests exactly are, many governmental policies, at both central and local level, have failed to achieve what was intended for them – equity, justice, redistribution or whatever. As we shall see, while this has been true of other policy arenas, housing provides a particular example of the kinds of difficulties faced by central and local governments in achieving their aims. Notwithstanding the general commitment to property ownership itself, initially a main plank of the post-Second World War Conservative Party, and more recently (and almost inevitably) accepted by the Labour Party, other attempts at dealing with housing problems have largely been damaged by what are best described as 'unforeseen circumstances' or 'market circumstances'. For example, who foresaw that people would not like living in tower blocks, even though nobody asked possible tenants before they were built? Equally, who considered the possible consequences for inner-city areas of both high voluntary and overspill migration, particularly by the middle class and skilled workers, to the privately built suburbs and the publicly financed New Towns? Who considered the possible impact of redevelopment and renewal on the supply of cheap privately rented accommodation; and thus on the number of homeless?

With hindsight, it is possible to see these consequences, as well as the effects of rising interest rates and inflation on the price of owner-occupied housing and the supply of mortgage finance. All of these, of course, have consequences for people, in housing perhaps as much as in other areas of governmental activity. As in all areas of political life, some people gain and some lose.

It is, of course, difficult to assess accurately who has gained or lost most through post-war housing policy. Clearly, those with an interest in developing property – for housing or office building – have done well, as have those who were able to move up the housing market at the most advantageous times in the post-war years. Indeed, in one year, 1972, it was possible to buy and sell a new house at a handsome profit without even occupying the house at all. But inflation and rising construction costs make it increasingly difficult for first-time buyers to break into the housing market: they need both larger mortgages and deposits in order to step on to the first rung of the owner-occupier's ladder. This in spite of various attempts, both by central and local government, to persuade building societies to give first-time buyers priority for mortgages, and to introduce incentives to home ownership such as the option mortgage and saving bonuses schemes of recent years.[32]

Having said that, by and large, once on the housing ladder most owners have seen property values rise and thus have benefited from housing policies. On balance, it is probably also true to say that public sector tenants have also benefited, but perhaps not to the same extent. Despite the many criticisms of redevelopment and renewal policies, in many cases tenants have benefited from the improvement in their *physical* environment brought about by such policies, which helped to replace so much of the unfit housing in British cities after the war. Whether such policies improved the residents' social and economic environment is another matter: the creation of tower blocks of flats clearly did not replace the old 'communities' and 'neighbourhoods' based on the nineteenth-century grid system of housing layouts, with their pubs and corner shops at the end of each street. Similarly, the decline of industry in those areas, and its movement out towards the edge of the city, have left many of these areas with weak or poor economies – the so-called inner-city areas. Many of the more able residents have left these areas, or been encouraged to do so, for the suburbs or New Town sites, leaving behind an imbalanced, and particularly ageing, population. Often it is also an immigrant population. It is this group in particular that has perhaps benefited least from post-war housing policy, being least able to compete in anything like equal terms in any of the different housing markets.

It is this point that highlights the importance of control over access to housing: by looking unfavourably upon these disadvantaged groups, for whatever reason, those who control access to housing in both the private and public sectors discriminate against them. Since housing is a crucial resource in the life chances game, such discrimination lies at the centre of the political conflicts over housing that have been the subject of this chapter.

7   Policy arena 2: planning

Town planning in Britain has often been held up as an example of virtue to the world, yet in recent years the activity has been subject to extreme criticism. Planners themselves have expressed self-doubts about the nature and purpose of the activity in which they engage, while recent economic and financial conditions have severely strained the operational ability of the planning system. In a period of economic decline and financial uncertainty, planners have learned how difficult it is to persuade others to do the things necessary if a plan is to be fulfilled. In a nutshell, while planners produce plans, others implement them, and to a large extent it is this lack of control over their environment, and over the other agencies and actions whose support is necessary if plans are to be successfully implemented, that lies at the heart of what may be regarded as the current crisis in planning.

An understanding of how this transformation has occurred and why is central to an understanding of many of the political processes of the modern city. For example, if, following Williams,[1] we wish to argue that much of the political conflict in the city is about the occupancy of space, then planning, since it is primarily concerned with the use of *physical* space, is an activity central to the conflict about the allocation of, or access to, space.

Planning and planning ideology

The view that planning is, above all else, a political activity in the broadest sense has only recently and grudgingly been accepted by the planning profession itself. In part this was because the professional ideology was essentially one that claimed that planning was objective, technical, and as such non-political. For most of its history, the profession believed that there was no disagreement in society about goals, and that the means by which these goals are achieved could be decided by the technical methods available to the planner.

Given the origins of town planning, and the character of its early leading proponents such as Howard, Geddes and Unwin, such a view of planning is hardly surprising. Furthermore, of course, statutory planning on a nationwide, obligatory basis is a post-Second World War phenomenon, following the passage into the statute books of the Town and Country Planning Act of 1947. Additionally, the development of planning education, particularly on a full-time basis, came later, with many of the planning schools not being established until the late 1950s and early 1960s. Before this, most training was a mixture of part-time academic work mixed with in-service experience – most planners learned how to plan by actually doing it in post. As a result, planners had received their initial training in another discipline. In the years immediately after the war, this was usually architecture or surveying, and, after the late 1950s more usually geography, with planning skills added on subsequently.

Dependent on 'men of vision' for its inspiration, with only a recently established statutory basis and with few practitioners trained full-time as planners, planning in the early years after 1945 was as much an act of faith as anything. As a result, few members of the profession were either willing or able to question their creed, even if they were conscious of the need to do so. Similarly, with the possible exception of those who lived in either the original garden cities or their post-war descendants, the first generation of new towns around London, few people among the planned had experienced planning: they had little evidence on which to base a judgement. Thus, beyond infrequent choruses of 'new town blues', few of the planned were in a position to voice an opinion about the value of the new planning system, and it was not until the early 1960s that doubts about the system were raised – first within the profession itself[2] and subsequently from outside the profession, especially from sociologists examining particular planning proposals.[3] Both sets of criticisms led to a questioning about the purpose of planning, and inevitably this led to doubts about the non-political nature of planning.

In part, some of the critics of the planning system drew inspiration from the work of American planners,[4] where the academic development of the subject had moved much faster than had the practical application. In part, they were given an impetus by the obvious defects of the system, particularly the delays in implementation and the associated 'planning blight'. Lastly, some critics questioned the apparent autonomy of the planners, and their reluctance to take into account the views and interests of the planned. This mixture persuaded planners to modify their concern with planning solely as a question of physical land use, if not as yet to question the kinds of goals they sought to achieve. As a consequence, planners began to recognize the social and economic components to planning and also the need to secure the support of the planned for their proposals. As we shall see, this change of ethic led to reforms in the statutory basis of planning – with the introduction of the 'new planning system' in 1968. Subsequent experience and criticism has made planners much more aware of the political nature of their activities, and has focused their attention on such questions as the distributional consequences of planning proposals and the problems associated with their implementation. These changes in planning ethics and what might be called planning style have produced changes in the kinds of political processes associated with planning decisions. Through an examination of the changes that have taken place in planning since 1945, therefore, it is hoped that this chapter will also illuminate the changes that have occurred in the politics of planning, as well as evaluating the experience of planning during the post-war period.

The post-war planning system

The whole post-war package of planning legislation, from the 1945 Distribution of Industry Act to the 1952 Town Development Act, was very much part of the wider social welfare legislation associated with the 1945 Labour Government. Nevertheless, as Peter Hall has so ably demonstrated in his analysis of post-war planning in Britain,[5] the period under review was dominated by a number of limited objectives in planning terms. Underlying the objectives over which planners thought they had some control was the economic one of controlling industrial location in the interests of regional balance, reflecting the (largely false) assumption of British governments until recently that economic and physical planning are two separate activities unrelated to each other. As a result, land use planners largely regarded questions of economic planning as outside their control.

Central to the land use planning system, however, were three other, more limited but important, objectives. First was the aim of urban containment, so that the urban sprawl associated with the pattern of development of the 1930s would be stopped, an objective associated with the Barlow Report of 1940.[6] Second, and relatedly, there was the objective of protecting the countryside, a reflection of strong agricultural and rural interests as exemplified in the Scott Report in 1942.[7] These two objectives came together in a third – namely, that future population growth should largely take place in planned, self-contained, balanced communities – the New Towns concept, developed from the ideas of Howard and Geddes so strongly by people like Unwin, Sharp and Osborn, and finally given official approval in the 1946 Reith Committee Report.[8]

Associated with these three main objectives were a number of other subsidiary aims, such as the promotion of strong service centres, segregated land use, and improved accessibility, environmental quality and transportation. Most of these were essentially local matters with a strong design element, and here again a strong reflection of the major influences in the profession.

Stating the objectives as simply as has been done here is, of course, to oversimplify. Undoubtedly, as Hall notes,[9] there were other objectives and none were as clearly spelt out as they have been here. Nevertheless, underlying all these themes was a kind of (elite) consensus about the general desirability of the values implicit in them, even though these value judgements were essentially untestable.[10] The benefits were to be demonstrated by the results: the improvement in environmental quality and in the physical arrangement of land and buildings would produce benefits for all to see. And by adopting these objectives, British planning remained within its primary, land use, tradition. It continued to have a narrow physical basis, coupled with a strong belief in environmental determination: as we shall see, it was in this tradition, in the implied consensus about values, and in particular in the subsequent failure of planning to demonstrate the benefits associated with its objectives, that the seeds of later criticism lay.

In the meantime, however, the objectives and tradition were enshrined in the 1947 Town and Country Planning Act. This Act made planning a compulsory function of the major local authorities, namely the (rural-dominated) counties and the (urban) county boroughs. These were required to prepare a Development Plan for land use in the authority over the next twenty years, subject to a review every five years. The authorities were also required to control the development of land for the period covered by the Plan, once it had been approved by the Minister. All proposals to develop land or to change its post-1947 use became subject to planning permission, though the proposers had the right of appeal, via a public inquiry, against authorities' refusals to grant permission. Again, these statutory processes, which were almost inevitably lengthy, also contained the seeds of later criticism, this time largely coming from within the profession itself.

In terms of planning strategy, much of the period to the mid 1960s was dominated by the ideology of urban containment, with major population growth and dispersal of concentrated city populations going to the New Towns. As Hall notes,[11] there was strong political support for this strategy, particularly from the rural county councillors, who regarded their urban county borough counterparts as land-grabbing expansionists of the worst order. City planners found themselves in something of a dilemma – drawn professionally towards acceptance of the containment strategy, and by experience towards giving support to the more expansionist leanings of their political masters. The urban planners' 'salvation' lay in the continuing development of new and expanded towns, which would 'siphon off', 'overspill' or 'disperse' the excess population in the cities, thus improving the environmental quality of cities as places in which to live. More latterly, the contribution of this policy towards the problems of the 'inner city' today have been recognized, for it was always the most able and most skilled, in terms of both workers and employers, who were prepared to make the move out from the city.

Controlling profits from development

As with nearly all legislative proposals, the Town and Country Planning Act of 1947 had wider objectives than establishing a compulsory planning system. Not the least of these from the Labour Government's point of view was the need to control development gain, that is to limit the profits that a developer might make by virtue of a change in land use brought about by the state. An understanding of this issue is crucial, for in many ways it is central to many of the political questions that have arisen in British cities in the post-war period. Yet it is one to which social scientists generally and political scientists particularly have given little attention until recently.[12] Put simply, the question of development gains concerns who should benefit from changes in land use, particularly when such land changes imply higher values for the land in its new use: should the benefits accrue to the individual land or site owner? should they go to the state, or should they be divided between the state and individual, and if so, on what basis? Quite clearly, the answers to these questions will affect the supply of, and demand for, land in its varying uses, for landowners will sell land and developers will develop their sites only if they foresee profit at the end of the deal. This in turn implies that the interests of landowners, developers and planners (as representatives of city governments) will probably be in conflict more often than they are in agreement. In large part, as we shall see, failure to understand this conflict of interest and perhaps the development process itself is why the planners have been unable to control either the commercial redevelopment of city centres or the suburban growth of private housing estates. As Marriott, Elkin and Ambrose, as well as Wates and Cook,[13] have all clearly demonstrated, both councillors and planners have been 'beaten' in the 'development game' time and time again, and not infrequently have been the willing partners in the development process. Also, as the Poulson affair and other cases show, the vast profits to be made from the development have often provided a temptation that some elected members and planning officials have found it difficult to resist. How does this occur? In 1945 the problem was perhaps simpler to understand but essentially no different, namely, to what extent should owners of land participate in the increased value of their land when this increase has been brought about not by any action on the part of the owner, but more likely by state action through the activities of local authorities acting in their planning capacity and producing their statutory development plans? A change in approved use – from agricultural to housing, industrial or commercial – would mean greatly increased value to the owner: this is why land with planning permission for a particular type of development has a higher selling price than land without permission. The betterment issue, to give the question its technical title, was only one-half of the problem. The other half was the question of compensation – the issues of whether or not landowners should be compensated when land values depreciated because of restrictions imposed through the operation of the 1947 Act, and whether landowners should be compensated for the loss of profits that might arise from development undertaken.

The Act dealt clearly and radically with the latter: no compensation for loss incurred when planning permission was refused, because the land's development value was vested in the state. The former was to be met by a series of once-and-for-all payments for which a total sum of £300 million was allocated under the Act. The betterment issue – namely the increase in value of land resulting from the granting of planning permission – was secured for the community by the imposition of a development charge equal to the increase in value – a move extremely unpopular with developers, who saw the change as a tax on enterprise, and thus were generally unwilling to develop land, and with landowners, few of whom were willing to sell land with development value at anything near its existing use price.

Perhaps inevitably, the situation had to be changed. The 1953 Town and Country Planning Act, introduced by the Conservative Government, not unnaturally abolished the betterment charge and denationalized development rights, and a further Act in 1954 introduced complex financial arrangements for compensation,[14] which resulted in a dual market for land: private sales at current market levels, and public purchases at existing use value. This situation lasted until 1959, when another Town and Country Planning Act removed this anomaly and restored open market value as the basis of compensation for compulsory purchase. The problems of compensation and betterment were now totally unresolved, at a time when the involvement of city governments in the process of public urban redevelopment was at its peak. This costly burden, as Cherry puts it mildly, 'fell heavily on the local authorities',[15] and the following four years have been called the heyday of the private sector.[16]

Just why is perhaps most simply and starkly demonstrated from the world of such people as Harry Hyams and Joe Levy – that of speculative office building – and particularly because the spectacular boom and slump of 1973 – the bursting of the property bubble – focused attention on the question more closely than ever before. Essentially, the process is simple and common to all property developers regardless of size and complexity.[17] First, the cost of the site/land acquisition and of building construction is financed by a loan, which is repaid with interest over time. The company's profit on the building comes from two sources. The first is revenue profit, which is the surplus of income from renting space in the building over maintenance and loan repayment costs. In the 1950s and 1960s loan charges were often fixed for the whole repayment period (up to forty years), while rents would rise with inflation. Rent income, particularly after the early years, would thus exceed costs by a large margin, and obviously, the lower the loan charges (interest rates) and the higher the rate of inflation, the bigger the rate of profit.

The second source of profit is on capital. At the time of the property boom in the early 1970s, our company would have made a capital profit overnight by virtue of having built the office block, for the value of the building on the market far exceeded its construction cost. Understanding the link between the annual rental of a building and its value is crucial in understanding the development process, even though the process of valuation is a complex one. The valuation is based on what an investor would be prepared to pay for our building, given current annual rents. The following example, taken from Ambrose and Colenutt, illustrates what is involved.

Given an annual rent of say £1 million for a building, agreed for a seven-year period, and disregarding annual maintenance outgoings, what would an investor be willing to pay for the property? If he wanted an annual return of 10% on his money, he would be prepared to offer £10 million . . . he would be ready to pay 'ten-year purchase'. But that is to assume that rents will remain at current levels for the life of the building, whereas if past trends can be relied upon they should double at the next review, giving a return on capital invested of 20% (£2 million annual return on an outlay of £10 million). If this is the general expectation, there is likely to be competitive bidding for the building and the present value may be pushed up to £20 million or twenty-year purchase.[18]

While this gives an initial lower yield of only 5 per cent, the probability is that this will increase in the light of subsequent rent review increases. The purchaser is prepared to accept the initial low yield in the expectation of a much greater rate of return in later years, if the rent increases can be relied upon. And they generally can, as the examples of Centre Point and the Euston Centre indicate. The latter block, one of Joe Levy's Stock Conversion and Investment Trust properties, rose from around £15 million in 1964 to nearly £64 million in 1972 – a rise in value that came about solely from rising rent levels and falling yield rates.[19] And empty office blocks are valued at the same levels as occupied ones: hence Hyams could afford to have Centre Point empty.

Two subsequent attempts have been made to deal with the betterment/compensation problem, both introduced by Labour governments, and both something less than successful. The first was the ill-fated Land Commission, established in 1967, and abolished by the Heath Government soon after taking office in 1970. The Commission's activities had contributed to the increase in land prices, but it bought little land (mainly in areas of low demand) and sold even less, while uncertainty about the Commission's future probably also further restricted the supply of land.[20] The second was the Community Land Act of 1975, a piece of legislation so complex that few could understand it, but undermined anyway, partly because it was a permissive piece of legislation which Conservative local authorities were unlikely to adopt, but largely because economic circumstances and tightening financial resources meant that most authorities could not afford to deal in land as they might otherwise have done. The Conservative Government's new Bill proposes to abolish this legislation.

This brief examination of the development gain/compensation issue has demonstrated its centrality to the urban political processes, to planning and to the partisan political debate. It is a matter of different party-political ideology as to what should be done about the costs and benefits of development that arise largely from the ownership of land: the problem of speculation and the extent to which it should be controlled in the interests of the community at large. With this problem in mind, it is time to return to the question of how far the post-1947 planning system was able to achieve its main objectives of urban containment, protecting the countryside, and the promoting of New Towns.

The success of post-war planning in Britain

As Hall suggests,[21] two assumptions underpinned the 1947 Act: first, that much of the development would be undertaken by the public sector – by the new planning authorities themselves; second, and more important, that there would be little or no population growth. In the event, neither assumption was to hold good. It was particularly the unanticipated increase in population, together with delays in submitting and approving development plans, that undermined the development plan system. Far from having a declining population, as predicted by the planners, Britain's population rose by almost 10 million over the 1945–65 period. Pressure on land for changing use patterns was greatest where the population growth was concentrated, but it was further aggravated by the continuing suburbanization process. As living standards rose in the 1950s and 1960s people moved out of the cities to realize their goal of home ownership, and the move to the suburbs was increased by the redevelopment processes undertaken by city governments, seeking to improve housing quality and to reduce population densities by their slum clearance processes. The whole process was further aggravated by the associated changes in transportation; as more and more people were able to afford cars, and as suburban railway services were improved, more people were able to commute relatively long distances. Nowhere was (and is) this more apparent than around London, where traffic congestion and long commuting trips were (and are) common experiences.

These kinds of changes rendered totally inadequate the assumptions on which post-war planning was based. It certainly made the planning authorities' tasks much more difficult. Yet, in retrospect, this pressure for growth was also perhaps the planners' strongest weapon, since, through their control over planning permissions, they could determine where most of the growth should go. Yet, it also seems that planners were less aware of the importance of development control than they might have been, particularly once the size and spread of technological, economic and demographic changes discussed above made most development plans obsolete.[22] As a result, both city and county planners were obliged to operate a largely inadequate planning system, responding only slowly to the pressures upon it.

These pressures, taken together with the 1953 dismantling of the betterment/compensation provisions of the 1947 Act, meant increasingly that development was undertaken by the private rather than the public sector. It was in the cities – where residential re-development was too expensive for the private developer to contemplate, but where it was demonstrably most necessary – and in the new and expanded towns – which had an erratic career – that the public sector was to play its part; in the case of the former it is not obvious what the exact role of the planners has been. In many cases, once the development plan has been produced, the process of redevelopment in cities was left to a strange and often unco-ordinated mix of environmental health inspectors, architects, housing managers and social workers, with planners rarely being involved. In other cases, such as those discussed by Davies and Dennis,[23] planners were at the heart of the process, using their control over information or hiding behind their mask of technical competence to 'impose' solutions on unwitting or unwilling local residents.

Whatever the truth of the matter, perhaps it was only really in the New Towns that planners were able to plan and implement their proposals on any real scale. Despite their brief decline in the 1950s, when the Conservative Government refused to sanction further New Towns until the latter part of the decade, these towns have flourished, both the first generation of them, such as Crawley and Harlow, which were designed to help with London's containment, and the 1960s second generation, including Telford and Peterborough, and finally the major development of Milton Keynes.[24] The New Towns programme has been greatly admired, particularly by foreign observers, and even their critics would recognize the success of many individual towns. But concern about the extent to which the New Towns have become the self-contained, economically viable, socially balanced communities their original advocates intended is perhaps justified. The difficulties faced, for example, by Skelmersdale in attracting and maintaining jobs, or the dependence of Corby on steel, raise doubts about economic viability; the heavy commuting flows out of London's New Towns into London questions the idea of self-containment, while the fact that it is the most able, skilled people who have moved to the New Towns is well documented – they have not helped the old or the poor, nor have they attracted the rich.[25] Whatever else New Towns are, socially balanced they are not. Furthermore, the New Towns programme *as a whole* assisted the movement of both people and jobs out of the cities, thus contributing to the general suburbanization process and aggravating the problems of population and economic imbalance that face the major inner-city areas today. Furthermore, contrary to the intentions of the creators of the 1947 planning system, less than 5 per cent of new housing between 1945 and 1971 went to new and expanded towns. Perhaps the final comment on the 'planned communities' belongs to Peter Hall and his colleagues:

collectively, the overwhelming impression that emerges is the gap between the ideals of the generation which brought the post-war planning system into being, and the reality of the quarter century after the Second World War.[26]

Clearly, the post-war planning system has failed markedly in meeting one of its objectives – ensuring that most of the post-war development took place in the New Towns.

Having said that, the 1947 system was undoubtedly more success-ful in fulfilling its other objectives of protecting the countryside and containing urban growth. Different in practice from that intended in theory, as Hall notes,[27] the system has been, and still largely is, concerned with the control of land use rather than with promoting the development of land. And while the old development plans might represent what a planning authority wanted to achieve over a twenty-year period, in practice the implementation of that plan depended largely, if not exclusively, on the activities of private developers. The central most important fact about the planning system in Britain is that it depended, and still does, on the interaction between both the public and private sectors: between private developers and public planners. Furthermore, as some of the discussion of development gain and compensation suggested, it have been a relationship in which the planner and the planning authority has been on the weaker side. The source of its power has largely been the legislative provisions which allow it to designate land use and to give planning permission: these powers, when linked to the objectives of urban containment and protecting the countryside, have meant inevitable conflict between planners, developers and landowners.

Nevertheless, despite the conflicts, the planners appear to have succeeded in their objective of containment. In making his assessment, Hall notes that 'the amount of land converted from rural to urban use has been minimised and compacted',[28] though with the consequences of increasing suburbanization and inflationary land prices. The objective was largely achieved by a mix of Green Belts and the concentration of new developments in small towns and villages in the county areas, and by massive urban residential development in the major cities, albeit at lower densities than before. While not all the major cities favoured this policy – see, for example, the continuing search until the late 1960s for overspill sites by Manchester and Liverpool – many saw it as a way of maintaining their population, their rateable value and their grants from central government. Despite the success of containment, Hall raises the question as to how far it was the result of deliberate and conscious planning, and how far the result of the failure to react swiftly to the upwardly moving population figures and of the power of agricultural and preservationist pressure groups.[29] Certainly, if the experience of Cheshire is any guide, this judgement is valid. As Lee notes,[30] the county resisted Manchester's attempts to obtain a large-scale overspill site successfully in the post-war period, limited development to a number of villages, and listened carefully to the strong agricultural interests.

In making a final assessment of the 1947 planning system, Hall and his colleagues[31] judge that it is the developers who have gained most and lost least, followed by suburban residents and public sector tenants, though both have had to face costs in terms of higher costs and perhaps less than desirable living spaces. Again, as in housing, it was the 'poorer members of the private rental housing sector' who got the 'poorest bargain' – 'it has, simply, been left out of the urban growth process'.[32] Contrary to its intentions, the 1947 system did least for the less fortunate and most for the most fortunate.

The pressures for change

In this light, and given the continuing failure of the 1947 planning system to adapt to the twin pressures of rising population size and increasing living standards, it is hardly surprising that pressures for changing the planning system began to build up, particularly in the 1960s.

The pressures came from both within and without the profession, and understandably it was the former that had the greatest influence in the shaping of the 1968 Act. However, in the long run it may be that the external pressures for changes will prove to be more important, coming as they did from those who were more critical of planning. Over time, in practice the two sets of critics barely overlap, which is perhaps why the professional demand for change won out. The professionals were concerned on a number of grounds, some of which also concerned their critics. First, there was a shared concern over the delay between the introduction of planning proposals and their subsequent implementation: the need for public inquiries, amendments etc., often meant considerable delay which resulted in planning blight, namely the decay and deterioration of properties in areas whose future was uncertain because of the planning proposals hanging over them. Second, there was the planners' concern with the rigidity associated with the old-style development plans with their clearly designated land use maps – a factor that contributed to the inflation of land prices, and to the speculation in land in the early 1960s as planners came under increasing pressure to release more, previously unzoned land, for housing in the light of increasing population figures. Third, planners wanted to be more comprehensive in their planning – so that they would become more responsive to changes in economic and social trends, as well as to population and transportation changes.

These demands were encompassed in the work of the Planning Advisory Group, whose 1965 report,[33] with its proposal to replace the development plan system with a number of different plans, was to be largely followed in the Town and Country Planning Act of 1968.

Critics from outside the planning profession, mainly either local residents subject to planning proposals or academic sociologists concerned with urban processes, were largely concerned with three issues. First, they shared a concern over planning blight associated with uncertainty. Second, and more important, they were concerned with the power over, and apparent unresponsiveness of, the planning profession to the public and its demands. Lastly, critics have been concerned with questioning the values and consensus about planning goals that underpin the profession: in other words, critics questioned the technical expertise of the planner.[34]

Many of these criticisms were only just beginning to emerge when the 1968 Town and Country Planning Act reached the Statute Book, and as such were too late to influence that legislation. In part, the legislation, with its apparent commitment to public participation, appeared to anticipate some of these doubts, but in practice the commitment was designed more to meet planners' objections about delays and planning blight than necessarily to ensure any responsiveness to public demands. Thus planners felt that if people could be enabled to understand planning problems and their solutions, and offer their support for what the planners proposed, then objections to proposals would vanish, the process would be speeded up, and blight would be either avoided altogether or minimized. This would be planning by consensus – though apparently a consensus based on what planners felt was the 'best solution' to planning problems. The idea of public participation in planning was, however, given further blessing in 1969 with the publication of the Skeffington Committee report *People and Planning*.[35] The report made a number of useful and sensible recommendations, but in the eyes of its critics it really did not go far enough and exhibited a sense of *naïveté* about the extent to which participation would result in consensus rather than conflict, stressing the 'apparent benefits' of participation rather than its costs. Thus, one pair of critics felt that the Committee's members 'see participation as a pilgrim's progress, leading from ignorance and apathy to understanding, consensus and constructive action. The case for these assumptions is preached but never agreed. . . .'[36] Nowhere was the possibility that conflict might be inevitable considered; nor were the interests of the professionals themselves recognized; nor was there really any clear purpose outlined that participation might serve, a point that subsequent critics have also frequently made.[37]

The 1968 planning system and after

But the Town and Country Planning Act did more than simply introduce public participation into planning. It introduced a new system of planning based on essentially two sorts of plans: structure and local plans.[38] Structure plans, the first round of which is currently reaching completion – ten years after the introduction of the new system – are essentially statements of general policy concerning future development over the next fifteen to twenty years. Initially, as the 1970 Development Plans Manual suggests, structure plans were intended as broad-scale plans, covering economic and social matters as well as more traditional land use and transportation matters. In a sense, they would have been the kind of comprehensive plans that the planners seem to have wanted in the late 1960s; but in the event they have become much narrower in concept and content, being concerned with such key issues as population, housing, industry and transport. In part this narrowing down process has been brought about by the Department of the Environment, concerned both by the delay in producing these structure plans and the difficulties obviously experienced by planners in attempting such comprehensive planning.[39] The problem of broad-scale comprehensive planning was further aggravated by local government reform in 1972, with its emphasis on another form of comprehensive planning – namely 'corporate planning' – which in the early years at least appeared to undermine the planners' attempts at comprehensive planning.[40]

Local government reform further undermined the new planning system, which had been introduced on the assumption, shared and agreed by planners, that there would be a unitary system of local government and that planning would be carried on under that single roof. Not only did the 1972 Act maintain and extend the two-tier system of local government; it also split the planning functions, making structure planning the responsibility of the top-tier county authorities and local planning the responsibility of the second-tier district authorities. In some ways, as we shall see, the result has been chaos, with little effective planning being undertaken at either level.

The districts' local plans are designed to show the detailed proposals for smaller areas: a kind of backcloth against which development control decisions, as Cherry calls them,[41] can be taken. In this way they put the flesh on the skeleton of the structure plan. In practice, there have been few statutory local plans adopted; one 1978 estimate suggested that there were only fifteen plans in England at that time.[42] There are a number of reasons why progress has been slow. First, local plans can be formally adopted only when a structure plan has been approved by the Secretary of State for the Environment: in theory, local plans should be drawn up only after structure plan approval, but in practice, because of the delays in producing structure plans, local planning has proceeded alongside structure planning on an informal basis. Second, in the non-metropolitan areas, planning is a new function at the district level. The creation of new planning departments at the time of local reorganization placed a heavy strain on the supply of qualified planners in the country, and many of them were new to the areas. Thus, it was necessary to learn something about their districts and their planning problems. At the same time, districts were being asked to react to structure plan proposals, or to supply information for the structure plan, as well as having to work out a new development control system with the county. Inevitably, there have been conflicts between the two levels over what constitutes a county or district planning matter, and this in turn leads to delay in undertaking local planning.

Third, statutory local plans, like structure plans, were subject to public participation, a factor that further delayed work. Furthermore, but unlike structure plans, there was still the possibility of objection to local plans, with an attendant public inquiry, heard by a member of the Planning Inspectorate, but paid for by the district; and the district would be expected to take account of the inspector's report, or else the process would be started all over again. Lastly, of course, many of the districts already had old-style development plans not yet fully implemented: in other words, they had planning proposals which they might not wish to change, in which case the need for local plans was obviated.

The position of the metropolitan districts – the city governments – was somewhat different. Many of them, as former county boroughs, had been planning authorities in their own right. As such, they resented the imposition of the new metropolitan counties on top of them and fought long and bitterly over the question of what was a county or district matter, particularly in terms of the structure plan content. Furthermore, as ex-county boroughs, their old-style development plans were probably more relevant than those of the shire districts, while the planning departments were also likely to be involved in a number of other quasi-planning activities, such as the preparation of schemes for general improvement areas and housing action areas.

For all these reasons, district councils have engaged in little statutory local planning, preferring instead to undertake what has been called informal local planning; and indeed there has been considerable pressure on the DOE to allow plans made on this basis to be adopted, as well as pressure to review the statutory commitment to public participation.

As it stands, the removal of this commitment might produce little change, for in practice much that has been done in the name of public participation has been little more than publicity or information-giving.[43] The planners have largely been able to control both the form and content of public participation programmes, mainly because of their control over the information in the planning process and timing of it. Where changes have taken place in planning proposals, it is because planners have reacted to public pressure, rather than the public being closely involved in the planning process with the planners from the outset. Planners still tend to decide the objectives of the plan and to treat the public either as a group who have to be told about proposals so as to ensure support for them (the building of consensus again) or else as possibly having information which the planners find relevant for their proposals. And in many cases the planners themselves have been uncertain as to the role they expect the public to play in participating in the preparation of plans.[44]

By contrast, most of the public have been quite clear about their part in the proceedings: none at all, unless they are clearly affected by the proposals. Most people simply seek to find out what the proposals involve and when they discover that there is no immediate impact on them they drop out of the 'participation game'. Even so, those who become involved in this limited fashion, let alone those who become more fully involved, are unrepresentative of the population at large. Middle-class, male, owner-occupier, long-term resident – these are the characteristics of most of the individuals who can be found at planning meetings, exhibitions, and so on.

But this is to treat the public as a homogeneous group, a mistake frequently made by the planners as well. In effect, three distinct types of public have been engaged, in differing fashions, in the planning process. First, and in terms of the nature of their involvement perhaps the most important, there are the major elites: the statutory undertakers, such as gas, water and electricity boards, as well as major industrial and commercial agencies, or agricultural interests in more rural parts, and possibly environmental groups. Such groups have a history of involvement in the planning process and are frequently consulted by planners – they are among those whose views the planners have to take into account in producing proposals and whose support they consider crucial if the proposals are to be adopted and implemented.

Second, there are what might be called the minor elites – the whole plethora of organized groups whose interest might possibly be aroused by planning proposals. In many cases, it is to these groups that the planners have addressed much of their participatory effort, often producing long lists of such groups, sending them information, inviting them to meetings, even sending one of their number to speak to a group meeting. Many such groups simply ignore the invitation, but others do become closely involved.[45] Many of them frequently have the kinds of organizational and other skills that enable them to meet the planners on something like equal terms, and the subsequent interaction is often productive.

Last, there is the public as a collectivity of individuals: the few members of the public who attend meetings and exhibitions, or contact the planners, in their own right, and not as members or representatives of some organized group. If the average attendance at most planning meetings is any guide, then it is unlikely that there are many such individuals, but they do appear, and their contribution may also be useful.

What the experience of recent years has shown in terms of public participation in planning is that there are a number of people and groups sufficiently interested and willing to become involved in the planning process, if only on the somewhat narrow basis most planners currently appear to offer. Public participation has also proved costly, in terms of time, money and other resources, particularly staff, though whether it has contributed over-much to the delay in producing structure and local plans is perhaps open to doubt. Furthermore, the interplay has mainly been between the public and the planners, with elected representatives largely sitting on the sidelines. Partly this is because many planners simply interpret the requirement for public participation as little more than yet another of their technical tasks. Partly, elected representatives do not see public participation as their concern: their task in the planning process is to approve proposals in the final stages, and as such they are either unaware or unwilling to accept that public participation in planning might possibly conflict with their role or weaken their decision-making power. As planning has moved on in the late 1970s, and with less statutory planning being undertaken, the extent of public involvement has declined to the point where it is almost non-existent, and for some it is seen as an unnecessary irrelevance.

The constraints on planning

The reason why this might be so lies in the other novel experience found by planners in the 1970s, namely that of attempting to plan in a period of population, economic and social decline. Like its predecessor, the new post-1968 planning system has proved to be founded on false assumptions. This time the assumption was that the population and economic growth associated with the 1950s and 1960s would continue, an assumption very much reflected in the early structure plans of 1970–3. In reality the reverse has been true, and planners have been forced to draw up their proposals in the face of declining populations, a worsening financial climate (particularly as far as the public sector is concerned), and continuing economic decline. Though partly obscured by the benefits of North Sea oil and other possible technological change, there appears to be little doubt that the nature and style of planning in the 1980s will be very different from that of the 1960s and early 1970s. And what planners have particularly learned from the experience of the 1970s is undoubtedly how little control, how little ability, they have when it comes to implementing their proposals. Their power still resides in designating land use and giving permission to develop – and when nobody wants to develop, there is little planners can do to persuade them to do otherwise. Far from being the powerful gatekeepers or urban managerialists identified by their sociological critics, planners now appear as rather weak, perhaps irrelevant, pawns in an economic and political environment which is much more hostile than it was twenty years ago. This situation, together with those raised by the first attempts at public participation, present planners and city governments with a new challenge to their power and prestige to which they will have to respond in the 1980s.

8 Policy arena 3: social services

The rise of the welfare state, with its accompanying concept of the social wage, is undoubtedly one of the distinct features of the extension of state activity in post-war Britain. Through areas such as health, education and social services, the state has sought to develop the individual citizen and to protect him from misfortune. In Marxist terms,[1] the state has played (and still does) a major role in aiding the reproduction of labour. A detailed analysis of all the changes in the welfare field, particularly those in the health and education services, is beyond the scope of this chapter. Nevertheless, many of the changes that have taken place in the politics of the personal social services apply also in part to most, if not all, the welfare services.[2]

The provision of welfare services by the state has a long history, particularly in terms of unemployment relief. The reform of the Poor Law in the 1830s was an important landmark as far as the development of both local government and of welfare services in Britain generally.[3] Foster's Education Act in 1870 saw the introduction of a state education system, and the reforms associated with the Liberal Government of 1906–10 brought unemployment relief and old age pensions into being. Other reforms in the 1920s and 1930s extended the welfare state still further.

Nevertheless, it was really the reforms of the 1940s, and particularly those introduced by the Attlee Labour Government between 1945 and 1951, that were seen as major contributions. Through the introduction of a national health system, better provisions for child allowances, old age pensions and unemployment benefits, together with the broad state education system introduced in Butler's Education Act of 1944, it was thought at the time that nobody would ever again face the poverty and hardship that so many had suffered during the Great Depression of the inter-war years. Poverty was to be eliminated.

Within twenty years, however, poverty had been 'rediscovered' in Britain, particularly by empirically orientated sociologists such as

Peter Townsend and Brian Abel-Smith.[4] In fact, as these and subsequent studies were to show, poverty had not been eliminated by the extension of the welfare state, if only because, to use an appropriate analogy, the umbrella leaked. In other words, the welfare state either failed to provide cover for all, or else its coverage was particularly inadequate for or irrelevant to the needs of some groups in the community. Since the early and mid 1960s, there have been an increasing number of attempts to extend the coverage of the welfare state, many of them depending on different interpretations and explanations of the problem of poverty. Though we shall touch on some aspects of this debate, it is partly outside the scope of this book,[5] and our major focus here will remain principally on the provision of the personal social services and on those attempts to alleviate poverty that have had primarily an urban focus.

Normative issues and welfare: social justice, equality and equity, universality and selectivity

Before turning to this, however, it is important to remember that the provision of welfare services involves important normative issues and principles to which some attention must be paid if we are to understand some of the current debates, issues and politics involved in the social services. At least five normative ideas are involved: social justice, equality, equity, universality and selectivity. Clearly all these ideas are related, though it is helpful here if they are treated separately, however briefly.

Social justice is very much a fashionable idea of the 1970s,[6] though it is closely related to and underpins ideas about equality and equity and has its roots in the kind of ideas about the social contract developed by Locke and Rousseau.[7] The most important modern exponent of social justice theory is John Rawls, whose book *A Theory of Justice*[8] is an influential contribution to this area, not least because it has been the starting point for some fresh thinking about the problems of equality and liberty. Rawl's model is an artificial one, with no basis in reality, and purely an expository one. It is an intricate theory, with some difficult assumptions having to be maintained, but with some interesting implications for our purposes. Rawl's theory assumes rationality as the basis for decisions by a group of people coming together to decide the basic principles on which they wish to order their society, but the group's decisions are limited by certain clearly defined factors. For example, the people have a clear set of preferences – they want more social goods rather than less; they want to protect their liberties; and they are capable of ranking the possible alternatives. Furthermore, Rawls precludes the members of the group from pursuing certain activities through the concept of the 'veil of ignorance': they have no knowledge of their own position in the new society, of their own value system and so on, so that the only basis for decision-making is a rational one which coincides with what the members of the group would feel to be intuitively fair and just. Under these circumstances, Rawls argues that two principles would govern decisions made in the new society. The first principle is that 'each person is to have an equal right to the most extensive total system of equal basic liberties compatible with a similar system of liberty for all'. The second principle is a two-part one, requiring that 'social and economic inequalities are to be arranged so that they are first to the greatest benefit of the least advantaged, and second attached to offices and positions open to all under conditions of equality of opportunity'.[9]

For Rawls, the first principle – that is the advancement of equality and liberty – takes priority over the second, while equality of opportunity takes priority over ensuring that the greatest benefit goes to the disadvantaged. While space prohibits any fuller discussion of Rawls's elaborate and intricate argument, two important ideas need to be borne in mind for our subsequent discussion: first, Rawls's stress on equality, and particularly equality of opportunity, and second, his emphasis of positive discrimination towards the disadvantaged as a means of ensuring equity. Rawls's argument has important implications for the development of social policy and hence for the provision of social services: in his terms, social justice should be the goal of social policy, with the promotion of equality and equity the means by which the goal is attained.   .

A number of other writers employ the idea of social justice in their work on social policy. Writing in the early 1960s, for example, Runciman employed the term in connection with his study of relative deprivation,[10] that is the difference between expected and achieved status which different people or groups feel. Runciman uses the idea of social justice to explain how people feel about social equality, maintaining that 'the notion of social justice is implicit in every account (of equality)',[11] and goes on to suggest that a socially just society would be one in which wealth inequalities would be removed to where there would be a 'continuous transfer of wealth from the richest to the poorest'.[12] Some years later, Harvey employed the concept in his analysis of the distribution of costs and benefits associated with the development of the city and with its political processes,[13] concluding that the distribution was in effect neither socially just nor equitable. More recently, Albert Weale, in his *Equality and Social Policy*,[14] stresses the importance of analysing social policies as means of testing social justice, arguing that when the state provides a range of freely available services the most egalitarian position possible has been reached. In practice, in Britain this position has not been reached, for most social policy is effectively a mix of public and private provision.

Equality and equity are frequently seen as the possible aims of social policy, despite Rawls's claim that they are essentially the means by which a socially just society is attained, rather than the goals of a society by themselves. Equality and equity are not necessarily the same thing. In essence equality means equal shares: equity, fair shares. Unless people's needs are the same, there cannot be policies that are both equitable and equal, while if people's needs vary there are what Jones *et al.* call 'problems of degree'.[15] That is to say, there are problems in measuring both the extent of inequalities and in deciding what kind of redistribution will achieve equity.[16]

Most writers recognize that the attainment of complete equality is an impossible dream, as even the most influential critics of inequality, such as Tawney and Titmuss, allow. Thus it is the reduction of inequalities that is sought, both on moral and practical grounds, and the reduction is to be achieved largely by a mixture of social policies designed to redistribute wealth, discriminate positively in favour of the underprivileged, and promote equality of opportunity. Furthermore, ideas about equality and equity imply that such policies must apply to all rather than to only a few.

This last point links into the two remaining concepts underlying debates about social policy and particularly the personal social services, namely universality and selectivity. Universality implies that the service or benefit should be available to all, and that everybody should contribute to its cost. The National Health Service is an example of a service provided on a universal basis.

Selectivity implies that the benefit or service should be made available only to those who qualify on some definable grounds. Within this category, however, there may be greater or lesser degrees of universality, depending on how the rules of eligibility for benefit are defined. Thus, for example, child allowance is paid to all mothers of children, but rent or rate allowances, as well as supplementary benefit, vary according to some measurement of need.

As we might expect, social policy is one of the major areas of disagreement between the major political parties at both national and local levels. The Labour Party is more likely to favour policies that promote equality and equity, as well as to want them applied on a universalistic basis. In this sense, Labour's social policies are more likely to have an umbrella-like quality. By contrast, the Conservative Party is more likely to see social policy as a kind of safety net, either covering these situations with which the market cannot cope or else attempting to alleviate the worst excesses of the market system. As a consequence, Conservative social policies are more likely to be selective in nature, and less concerned with promoting equality and equity.

As recent experience indicates, the difference between the two parties is one of tendencies rather than hard and fast distinctions. Conservatives do not reject some universalistic policies, while Labour policies have elements of selectivity. Nevertheless, the gap between the two parties is now perhaps wider than at any other time since the Second World War.

A further point to note is that it is central government that tends to be responsible for those elements of the welfare state that have more universal qualities, such as unemployment benefits, child allowances and the health service, regional health authorities notwithstanding. The one notable exception is education, which remains a responsibility of local government.[17] By contrast, selective services, of which the personal social services are an example, are largely administered at the local level, the exception being supplementary benefits.

However one views them, social legislation and the social services are a central feature of the late twentieth-century state. Gough has calculated that in Britain some 24 per cent of national income was being spent on the welfare state by 1970, as compared with less than 2 per cent a hundred years previously.[18] Non-Marxists writing about the welfare state generally see its growth as the result of the more enlightened values of the twentieth century as compared with those that stressed the *laissez-faire* views which dominated the nineteenth century. Recent Marxists, however (of which Gough and Castells are excellent examples) treat the welfare state and its growth as an essential feature of modern capitalist societies. We saw earlier, for example, how Castells sees the crisis for capitalism as arising largely over the issue of collective consumption, particularly at the local, urban, level. In other words, for Castells the crisis will be one over the welfare state and the ability of the state to maintain and improve the levels at which state benefits are provided. The situation would be exacerbated if current trends in the capitalist sectors continued, such as falling rates of profit, decline in the manufacturing sector and rapid technological change leading to increased unemployment.

The personal social services

All of this is by way of a background scenario against which our discussion of the provision of the personal social services at the local level will be conducted. Within this narrower, more specific area, however, there are a number of issues that are of particular relevance. First, there are issues concerned with the reorganization of welfare services into a single social service department following the publication of the Seebohm Report in 1968.[19] Second, there are issues concerned with the emergence of the social work profession and the role of the professional social worker in the development and administration of social policy. Third, there is the question of the role of the voluntary sector, that is of organized groups, in the provision of social services, since these services are one example where the voluntary sector has a long history of such involvement. Indeed, without them many of the social services would not have grown as they have. Last, there is the question of the welfare rights groups and the issue of multiple deprivation and the social services.

Turning to the first of these, the creation of a single social services department, it is important to recognize that this is a creation of the 1970s. Before this, local social services had been provided largely in an unplanned, unco-ordinated fashion. For example, responsibility for administering poor relief had been transferred to local government from the old Poor Law Guardiancies in 1929; the Children's Act of 1948 made local government responsible for the care of children who have not the benefit of a normal life, while the National Assistance Act of the same year gave local government the task of providing accommodation and other services for the elderly, the physically handicapped and the homeless. Essentially these Acts laid the foundations for both the growth of local government's welfare and domiciliary services.

Something of the fragmentation involved in this piecemeal development of local social services can be gauged from the number of central government departments responsible for overseeing these services: the Home Office, the Ministries of Health, Pensions, and

Education, as well as the Board of Control, were all involved. Largely as a result of demographic changes, particularly the large increase in the number of elderly people,[20] expenditure on child care and the local welfare services expanded rapidly over the next twenty years. Hall estimates a 180 per cent rise (at constant prices) for both groups of services, and notes particularly the heavy increase in capital expenditure involved in providing residential facilities for both groups.[21]

Fragmentation of responsibility at both central and local levels for these services further meant that overall control and planning for these services was particularly weak, especially at the time when expenditure on the services was rising most quickly. As a consequence, this was one of the major pressures behind the demands for change, but it has also to be linked to changing ideas about the nature of social work and of the social work profession itself.

In part these changes reflect changing explanations of the nature of social problems. Until the early 1950s, most social problems, particularly that of poverty, were seen as the result of individual deficiencies, and the appropriate 'cure' was thought to lie in the institutionalization of the unfortunate. In this way the individual's deficiencies would be 'corrected', or else the rest of the community would be 'protected' from these inadequates. Care of the elderly, the mentally ill and the poor was organized along these lines until at least the early 1950s.

The growth in the children's services was perhaps most responsible for some of the subsequent changes in ideas about the causes and possible solutions to social problems. This service gave rise to an emphasis on prevention of the problems, while health and welfare services encouraged the idea of community care. Both shifts reflected a growing awareness of other possible explanations of social problems, ideas about the 'cycle of deprivation' or the 'culture of poverty', as well as more radical explanations which lay in the broader nature of society itself.[22]

The important thing is that these changing explanations of social problems led to arguments that prevention and community care were socially desirable as a means of alleviating them. Claims were also made that such an approach was also economic, an attractive agreement at a time of rapidly rising expenditure.[23]

At the same time as changes in ideas about the nature of social work were taking place, social workers were beginning to develop something of a common identity. In 1951 the Association of Social

Workers was formed, and the first general course in social work came in 1954. In the early 1960s discussions about both the nature of social work and social workers continued, so that by the time the Seebohm Committee was formed in 1965, these developments had added further weight to the general demand for changes in the organization of the social services.

As Hall correctly points out,[24] many of those who were arguing about the necessity for change were important members of the Labour Party. On its coming to power in 1974, many of them became members of the government, and a move was made towards the creation of a Family Service Department which could cover the activities of a number of government departments concerned with welfare, but which would be based on categories of clients rather than on the basis of service provided. Such a move alarmed a number of prominent academics concerned with the welfare services, most notably Richard Titmuss,[25] and counter-proposals were made by a group of academics and practitioners for a more broadly based reorganization of the social services. Out of this conflict, the Seebohm Committee was born. Three years later, in the summer of 1968, its report was published.

As far as the social services were concerned, Seebohm identified a number of shortcomings: inadequacies in the amount, range and quality of provision; poor co-ordination; difficult access and insufficient adaptability. These weaknesses were brought about by a lack of resources, inadequate knowledge and divided responsibility in the social services, for which only limited solutions were available. In Seebohm's eyes, this meant the creation of a large, personal social services department, since this was thought to be capable of both attracting extra resources and developing the necessary planning capacity for assessing needs.

In effect, however, this meant disentangling many interdepartmental conflicts at the local level and unravelling the problem of central–local relations in this area. At the local level, the new department was to take on work that had previously been the responsibility of such departments as health, education and children's. In so far as the social workers in these departments had any professional qualifications, they were likely to be in their specific area of social work, rather than of a more general kind. Training of social workers capable of dealing with all kinds of social work problems was an issue the Committee had to face, and its recommendations that such training should be the responsibility of one body, and that there should be a reduction in the specialization extent in the social work profession, were both contentious issues.

As far as central–local relations were concerned, the issue was essentially that of increasing central control versus maintaining local autonomy, an issue only partly delayed in its resolution by the existence at the same time of the Redcliffe-Maud Committee. For Seebohm, the issue was essentially one that followed from its recommendation that local authorities be given the statutory duty to create a separate social services department. Given this statutory responsibility, how far could the Committee go in terms of restricting central control, particularly over the appointment of chief officer, an issue that divided the Committee? The Committee decided that the authority should both consult the minister and note his comments.

One other matter was of particular concern to the Committee, namely the role of the voluntary sector in the newly reorganized system. Recognizing the large and important contribution that many voluntary groups had made in the provision of welfare services, the Committee stressed their continuing participation in the planning and delivery of the new services. As such, this commitment to public participation was stronger than anything suggested by Redcliffe-Maud, and predated the more detailed proposals of the Sheffington Committee report of 1969.

Two years were to elapse between the publication of Seebohm and its implementation in the form of the Local Authority Social Services Act of 1970. Since then, the scale of the work of local authority social service departments has increased immensely. Between 1969 and 1974, for example, expenditure grew by 68 per cent, while the number of professional staff grew by about 40 per cent between 1972 and 1974 alone. All categories of beneficiaries showed substantial increases: those receiving home helps rose by 30 per cent; free meals by 25 per cent; and the mentally handicapped receiving services by 30 per cent. Since 1974, however, this rate of growth has slowed as social services departments have faced successive cuts in local authority expenditures following cuts in public expenditure generally.

On the other hand, the departments have both faced increased demand for their services and had additional responsibilities placed upon them. For example, the National Health Reorganization Act of 1973 placed hospital social workers into the social services department and required local authorities to co-operate with the new health authorities in the provision of joint health and welfare services. Provisions for the physically handicapped have also been increased.

The professionalization of social work

Both the increased service reponsibilities and the financial pressures have brought problems. Not least have been those concerned with the professional status of social workers, an issue that has taken a number of forms.

In part, the problem is that social workers, unlike doctors or lawyers, lack a long history of professionalism. Expert knowledge, long training periods, tests of competence, regulation of behaviour ('a code of ethics'), and sanctions against rule-breakers are all involved in the idea of a profession. Thus doctors, dentists and lawyers all undergo long periods of training and testing, and can be struck off their professional register for incompetence or unethical behaviour.[26] It is difficult to see social workers in quite the same light, however well intentioned the British Association of Social Workers may be. Furthermore, given the large part played by voluntary groups in the provision of social services, claims to professional status by social workers are likely to be weakened. Social workers, like a number of others who claim professional status such as planners and housing managers, are on the bottom rungs of the professional ladder; in other words, like a number of others, social workers are experiencing the early stages of what might best be called the professionalization process, whereby they are moving away from the ranks of the largely unpaid, untrained enthusiastic part-time amateur towards those of the paid, trained full-time professional.

The professional status of social workers is of particular significance in the urban political system because of the extent of their control over access to the resources of the local welfare services. Social workers, by virtue of their casework approach, have considerable discretion in terms of deciding not only *who* gets access to the welfare resources but also what resources individual recipients shall get. Social workers not only have to establish the claimant's need for benefit, but they also have to determine the claimant's right to benefit through their interpretation of the maze of rules and regulations governing the provision of the benefits.[27] Clearly, in such a situation social workers will be expected to perform these tasks in as objective a fashion as possible, and such objectivity might be expected to result from the attainment of professional qualification following a period of training.

Not unnaturally, given the imprecise nature of social services, the question of objective interpretation of claimants' rights to and needs for welfare is highly debatable, causing divisions among social workers themselves. For some, a strict and objective interpretation of the rules, sympathetically done, is both possible and desirable. For others, often described as radical social workers, their task is to manipulate the welfare system to the advantage of their clients. In essence, this group is perhaps subscribing to the view that only those in conditions of poverty and deprivation know best what their needs are or how best they can escape their condition. This view is one often expressed by those groups concerned to protect and promote the rights of those seeking welfare benefits. Many organized groups, such as claimants' unions and other welfare rights organizations, have come into this arena in recent years, being especially concerned to see that claimants not only know their rights but also are able to obtain them. Many of these groups view social workers with suspicion, regarding them as professional 'do-gooders' more than as willing allies against a system that keeps the poor and deprived in their condition permanently.

Nevertheless, it would be true to say that groups and social workers adopting this kind of position constitute only a minority of the groups and social workers involved in providing the social services. Most are concerned with a far less conflictual interpretation of the welfare system. Furthermore, in terms of recipients of local social services, those who constitute what are sometimes called the hard-core welfare cases are also only a minority of the cases with which social workers deal or who are receiving some benefit from the local social services. In other words, many of those with whom the local welfare system deals receive only selected or temporary benefits. For example, old age pensioners may receive 'meals on wheels' but no other benefits, or the physically handicapped get benefits applying to them alone. Some of the homeless with whom social workers deal may be only temporarily unable to house themselves, and so on.

The multiply deprived and community development

Despite this situation, however, there still remain a number of people, frequently to be found in urban areas, whose circumstances are such that they require substantial support from all the welfare agencies of the state. Often they are stigmatized by social workers (to whom they are well known), who label them as 'deviant', or 'hard-core unemployables' or whatever. They are a minority whose 'problems' cross all the internal divisions of any social services department: the children are known to the worker concerned with children, the parent(s) to those concerned with housing matters, and the police and local probation service may also know the household, as will the local social security and supplementary benefits officers. In areas where there are concentrations of coloured residents, it is likely that at least some of this minority will be black.

For social workers, these 'problem families' (to use another social work label) represent a major difficulty, if only because of the scale and breadth of their multiple deprivation. This deprivation seems beyond the scope of the local social services provision, and those in this condition are often those, for whatever reason, least able to help themselves. Thus, not only are the benefits inadequate, but those receiving them may be least able to make use of whatever benefits are provided. Furthermore, given the variety of different 'explanations' for the condition of 'problem families', solutions seem ever distant.

Nevertheless, in order to tackle some of the worst aspects of multiple deprivation, particularly in the inner areas of Britain's cities, since 1968 the central government has initiated a series of programmes, from education priority areas through urban aid programmes to the current inner-city partnerships and programmes. One experiment of particular interest here has been the various community development projects set up in 1969 under the aegis of the Home Office. Designed as a 'neighbourhood-based experiment aimed at finding new ways of meeting the needs of people living in areas of high social deprivation',[28] twelve projects were established in places like Batley (West Yorks), Benwell (Newcastle), Hillfields (Coventry), Vauxhall (Liverpool) and Canning Town and Southwark in London. Each project had two teams: one for research, designed to illuminate the needs of the particular area with which they were concerned, and one an action team (employed by the co-operating local authority), concerned with developing the community's ability to cope with its problems and to seek better co-ordination of locally delivered services.

As Edwards and Batley note, since the community development projects were originally conceived by central government,[29] their organization and aims reflected current official thinking about the causes and nature of urban deprivation. But as they progressed through their (initially five-year) lives many of the projects came to realize that their assumption that deprivation was a result of the individual pathology of their community populations was false. They came to adopt a far more critical perspective, concluding in one report that the 'State's fight against deprivation has been exposed . . . as empty rhetoric'[30] calling one of their reports *Gilding the Ghetto*. As an example, that report quoted Liverpool, where by 1974 nearly £1¾ million had been spent on 146 different urban aid projects. Yet the problems of inner Liverpool still appear insoluble, partnerships notwithstanding. CDP, like other radical critics, saw the failure of the various urban experiments of the 1960s and 1970s as the failure of the state in the capitalist system. Perhaps not unexpectedly, given their critical position, one by one the community development projects have been wound down, until in the end even its sponsoring Urban Deprivation Unit, which published many of the CDP's critical reports, was closed down.

Yet the action side of community development, the idea of helping local neighbourhoods to develop their skills, to understand their problems better and to cope with them, continues to hold considerable sway among those who argue for wider public involvement in service provision by local authorities. From this perspective, the voluntary sector would have a major part to play in determining the nature of *all* local services, and in their delivery. As a result, even those groups that have been critical of present local social services, such as welfare rights groups, would be involved in the policy-making processes designed to secure the level of social services necessary in a particular community.

The voluntary sector

'Welfare rights' groups are, however, only a small number of the plethora of organized groups and workers who make up what is called the voluntary sector in social work. Voluntary social work takes many forms and is constantly changing. It has a long history, but is perhaps particularly associated with Victorian philanthropy and its charitable good works. Often, too, voluntary organizations have pioneered the provision of a service that subsequently acquired statutory recognition. Not infrequently, there has been conflict between the voluntary sector and the new professional social worker in the local authority. The latter sees the former as 'amateur and inefficient', though perhaps well intentioned, while volunteers are critical of the 'bureaucratic inflexibility' of the professionals.

As far as the voluntary sector is concerned, we need to follow the important distinction made by Jones *et al.*[31] between voluntary workers, who are *not* paid for the social work they do, and voluntary organizations, who operate outside of the state welfare system, free to pursue their own policy goals. Voluntary workers may work for a voluntary organization or the local welfare authority. Voluntary organizations, particularly if they are of any size, are likely to employ professionally trained social workers.

Voluntary workers undertake a variety of tasks, ranging from direct service giving, such as hospital visiting or taking handicapped children on an outing, through running a voluntary organization, fund-raising or working with self-help groups (Alcoholics Anonymous is a good example), to pressure group activity seeking to influence local and central government policies and their implementation. Many individuals clearly undertake these different kinds of work, and bring a variety of skills to bear upon the problems with which they seek to deal. Indeed, most professional social workers would recognize the important contribution that these volunteers have made and continue to make to the provision of social services.

Attempts to classify voluntary organizations in the welfare sector are difficult. The organizations run from the large international variety, such as the Red Cross or UNICEF, to national bodies operating largely in an international context, such as Oxfam, to national ones operating mainly within Britain, such as Age Concern or the RSPCC. Then there are many local organizations that are affiliated to larger national or even international bodies: service clubs such as Rotary or Lions, church groups and women's organizations such as the Women's Institute or Women's Royal Voluntary Service. Last but not least, there are many local groups existing for purely local purposes: local charities are perhaps the best example of this latter kind. The result of this variety is that local authority social services departments will have to deal with a vast number of organized groups, as any director of services knows. As a consequence, given the complexity and range of organizational structures, powers and responsibilities to be found in this voluntary sector, it is frequently difficult to establish practical working relationships between it and the bureaucracies of central and local government. Furthermore, given that one of the important features of the voluntary sector is its ability to call on extensive resources at short notice and its adapt-ability in the face of changing problems, these organizations are capable of both defying the state welfare system and mounting an alternative provision if necessary. The problem of co-ordinating these organizations with the local welfare system is therefore a considerable one.

What might be called 'national disasters', such as floods or earthquakes, provide a good example of the problem. In the event of such an occurrence, all the welfare groups in the voluntary sector within the area concerned are likely to seek to be involved in dealing with the problems: they will want both to help and to be seen to be helping, for such is one of the main reasons for their existence. Offers of help, in all its various forms, pour into the local social services department, itself trying to estimate the extent of damage and assistance needed. Voluntary organizations appear on the scene, giving assistance where they feel it is needed most, but often without having contacted the local social services department or whatever co-ordinating agency there may be. The result can often be chaos!

However, many local authorities have developed liaison and co-ordination arrangements with the voluntary sector, and many voluntary organizations have developed links and co-ordination strategies both among themselves and with the local social services departments. Social workers, if not employed by the voluntary organizations, are likely to be among their membership ranks, as are local councillors, whose own group membership is frequently more extensive than most individuals. Many local authorities have their own Council of Social Service, on which are represented most if not all the organizations within the local voluntary sector. In this way, the sector is brought into the policy-making arena, perhaps able to influence policy at an early stage and to take part in its implementation. In Newton's terms, such groups become 'established', recognized for the contribution that they are able to make to the delivery of the welfare service.[32] In achieving this state, however, such groups run the danger of what their critics call 'selling out', of being 'incorporated into' the welfare system, or being encapsulated within it. As such, these groups are seen no longer as independent of the state system, but rather as part and parcel of it. In consequence, they are unable to be critical of what the welfare system has to offer, but have to accept (and operate within) the system and its benefits. It is this fear of incorporation or encapsulation that leads many radical groups concerned with welfare to operate outside the local service network, frequently conflicting with the latter's professional, state-oriented workers and raising critical ideas about what the state welfare system does.

Nevertheless, wherever the voluntary sector stands in relation to the state-organized welfare system, it remains true that its existence has played and continues to play an important role. Many of the present services were initiated by the voluntary sector, which perhaps continues to perform some tasks that the state is unwilling or unable to perform. Looking after battered wives, helping drug addicts and dealing with what are virtually closed communities such as Pakistani women are all examples. In this way, they perhaps echo a long tradition about the nature and scope of government in Britain, namely that the state, particularly in its central form, cannot do everything. Certainly the voluntary sector can and does perform an important publicity function, informing the public about many of the issues involved in welfare provision and helping to develop attitudes towards the many stigmatized groups in society who are dependent upon the social services. Last, but by no means least, the voluntary sector may perform an important critical role *vis-à-vis* the state in particular and society in general, even allowing for the problems of incorporation to which we have referred.

The importance of the voluntary sector has been recognized both by the movement nationally, with its creation of the Volunteer Centre in 1973, and by central government earlier, with its creation of the Voluntary Services Unit within the Home Office in 1972. Both are concerned with promoting and developing voluntary groups operating in the welfare system, with the latter being also particularly concerned with promoting co-ordination of the voluntary group with the central government departments involved in the welfare system. In part developments such as these must be seen as related to the general governmental response to the mood of the late 1960s and early 1970s, assumed to be one demanding more widespread public participation in the process of government and in the provision of services. Whatever the motives involved, be they encouragement or control of the voluntary sector, the latter has maintained, if not increased, its importance.

The crisis of the welfare state

As we enter the 1980s, and given the current depressed state of the British economy and a central government concerned with reducing the role of the state in the welfare sector, it seems likely that the voluntary sector's importance in identifying, publicizing and tackling welfare problems will increase rapidly. Not the least reason for this lies in one remaining question to be considered here, namely the rapidly increasing financial strain placed upon both central and local governments by the increasing scope of the welfare state.

Given the increase in expenditure on welfare generally and local social services specifically over recent years, it is not surprising that considerable concern has been expressed about the burden this expenditure places upon central and local government. The concern has been expressed by both conservative and radical critics alike, the former because of their dislike of extensive welfare provision, their preference for selective rather than universal benefits, and because of their desire to reduce government expenditure and the scope of state activity generally. All these are themes familiar to those who paid any attention to the 1979 election campaign in Britain.

The radical critics' concern is more complex, but perhaps by now no less familiar, for expenditure on welfare and social services is very much part of the collective consumption of public goods and services. Whether or not such expenditure is regarded as part of 'the social wage' or as part of the means whereby the working class(es) are 'pacified' or misdirected away from their 'true interests', radical critics of the welfare system are most likely to be concerned either by the extent of people's dependence on welfare benefits or by the possibility of reductions in the level of welfare expenditure. Ian Gough[33] has provided one of the best analyses of the welfare system from this radical perspective. He points to the very rapid increases in expenditure on all aspects of the welfare state, of which the personal social services are but one part, and to the growing proportion of the labour force employed in delivering the services comprising the welfare system. Again, the personal social services loom large.

The growth in social expenditure lies in four immediate reasons. First, there are rising relative costs, since the cost of most welfare services, such as housing, education and personal social services, have all risen faster than the general level of prices. Second, demographic changes in post-war Britain, particularly the post-war population bulge and the continuing increase in the proportion of elderly people in the population, have made their contribution. Third, old services have been improved and new ones introduced. And lastly, but perhaps most importantly, changing definitions of need in relation to welfare services have added to levels of social expenditure. The essential point, however, is that all these changes have resulted in an increasing transfer of public goods and services from a declining working population (on whom the taxes to pay for public goods increasingly fall) to a rapidly increasing non-working population. And increasingly the state, at both central and local levels, has faced the problem of financing these increases in welfare expenditures; this gives rise to what has been called 'the fiscal crisis of the state'. The welfare system thus faces two problems: rising demands for services, and financial difficulties in paying for these services. The result, regardless of the complexion of government in Britain during the 1970s, has been 'cuts' in welfare services as well as generally increasing levels of taxation, a mixture enriched by the severity of inflation itself, fuelled partly by government borrowing to finance its own (largely welfare) expenditures. As a consequence, there has been too little capital left for investment in the productive sector (itself often regarded unfavourably as a means of increasing profits or accumulating capital), with the result that the British economy has lagged further and further behind its competitors. So the crisis in the welfare system is linked to the crisis in contemporary capitalism.

Regardless of one's political perspective (and the analysis above would also be accepted in part by Conservative critics), the impact of the cuts in state expenditure has been considerable, with 1975 being very much a key year. Using government expenditure figures, Gough shows how expenditure on welfare services switched from a growth of 14 per cent between 1973 and 1975 to a drop of 1 per cent in 1975–7. The personal social services were most severely affected: growing 17 per cent in 1973–5 and contracting 11 per cent in 1975–7. Furthermore, the cuts were most heavily felt by local government, which faced a 9 per cent cut in expenditure in 1975–7 compared with an 8 per cent increase in 1973–5. Central government comparable figures were 1973–5, + 13 per cent; 1975–7, − 3 per cent.

Cuts on this sort of scale mean inevitable hardship, which in all probability has fallen most on those least able to cope. The Labour Government of 1974–9, under pressure from the unions, did its best to mitigate the worst effects of the cuts as its part of the Social Contract. With various job creation schemes, its inner-city programme and its revamping of the rate support grant, Labour did attempt to direct welfare resources to the areas where they were most needed, yet probably at the continued expense of much needed investment in industry and technological development.

With the arrival of a Conservative Government committed to monetarist rather than Keynesian economics, cuts in welfare and government expenditure have taken a harsher nature. While we know little as yet about the impact of recent cuts and of their distribution among different sectors of the population, it seems likely that, as always, those best able to weather the storms of service cuts, inflation and continued economic decline will be the more prosperous middle classes and those of the working class employed in the more buoyant economic sectors. Notwithstanding the effects of the unions, particularly those in the public sector where unionization has proceeded apace, to maintain the level of welfare provision, inevitably the immediate future must see continuing falls in service levels. Not only the personal social services, but also other public goods such as housing, education and transport, will be provided at lower levels in real terms than has been the case in the past. Understanding who gets the cuts, as well as who receives service benefits, has thus become an important issue, and one to which we turn in our next chapter.

9 Policy consequences and policy solutions

In the previous three chapters, we have attempted to review the major issues and decisions involved in three service areas – planning, housing and the social services – that have been very much at the centre of urban politics in post-war Britain. The issues they pose have also been central to much of British politics generally, and in all three cases we have clearly seen the penetration of the locality by the centre. In other words, the politics of central government are closely related to the political processes of the city and vice versa.

Three other themes are also implicit in much of the discussion of our selected policy arenas. First, particularly in relation to both planning and the social services, the role of the professional officer at both central and city levels underlies much of the policy-making discussion. In other words, what constitutes good or appropriate planning or social work practice and policy depends very much on the professional's perspective. The same comment could apply to other local services, such as education, or highways/public transport.

Second, there is the all-pervading influence of finance, particularly from the centre. The level of central finance affects the design and quantity of public housing, or planners' (in)ability to operate in urban land markets, or the extent and means by which city governments all try and help the less fortunate residents.

Lastly, there is the role and place of the non-governmental sector, be it in the form of a multinational corporation or an ordinary citizen, in shaping and influencing the decisions and policies of those authorities' decision-makers. The role of the voluntary sector in social service provision, the influence of property developers on planning and housing policies, or of 'homeless' squatters and building societies on housing policy, are all examples.

These, together with other perhaps more minor themes, are ideas to which we shall return later in this chapter. Meanwhile, it is to a consideration of the consequences of policy, to what we have called the policy outcomes, to which we now turn. In essence, this discussion seeks to answer who gets what, where, when and how in the city as a result of the public policies adopted by its government. At a mundane, but not unimportant, level this means answering questions about which streets get cleaned, how frequently refuse is collected, how quickly police arrive at the scene of a crime or which areas are most heavily policed, as well as asking questions about teacher/pupil ratios in schools, housing programmes and so on. Furthermore, we should be concerned with attempting to answer questions as to whether or not policy intentions have been fulfilled, or whether particular policies have had unintended consequences. In housing, for example, we have seen how policies designed to control rents and give tenants security of tenure have been successful only with the unintended consequence of bringing about a rapid decline in the amount of accommodation available for private rent, leaving a gap which public sector housing has been unable to fill completely. In planning, we have seen how Green Belt policies contributed to the rise in land prices. In social services, we have seen how different definitions of the welfare problem lead to different policy solutions which in turn have different consequences.

Lastly, in evaluating policy outcomes we also need to consider their distributional consequences: do some groups do better than others out of certain policy preferences, intentionally or unintentionally, or do policies redirect resources away from one group to another, or from one class to another? In housing, for example, we have seen how the owner-occupier and the developer have been the greatest beneficiaries of various housing policies, whatever the intentions of the policy-makers.

It would be ideal if one could point to detailed accounts of policy outcomes arising from a number of studies in Britain. Unfortunately, however, few studies of the kind that would allow us to demonstrate vividly some of the issues involved have as yet been made. Indeed, most of the examples come from America, and even these still raise questions about both the conceptualization of and the methodological approaches to the problem involved. One good example of this kind of work is that of Levy *et al.*'s study, *Urban Outcomes*, which examines the distribution of educational, library and highway services in Oakland, California.[1] The book analyses in detail what the city authorities allocate in terms of money, people and facilities for these three services, generally showing that the better-off areas tend to get more resources than do the less well-off ones, though this is moderated by the different needs of the different groups. What clearly emerges from this work, as well as from others,[2] is the importance of the rules governing distributional decision-making and of the local bureaucracy in this process. Similarly Jones, in his article on Detroit, describes the hub of bureaucratic service decisions that determine ultimate levels of service.[3]

In Britain one or two geographers and other social scientists have started to map the distribution of urban outputs for particular services in particular cities.[4] However, to date much of the work here, as in America, has focused specifically on outputs rather than on their consequences or outcomes and has been concerned with variations in service provision between local authorities rather than with specific cities.[5] In this area, British studies have been particularly concerned with trying to measure the extent to which service levels vary because of differences in the *party* control of local councils, though some are also strongly suggestive of the importance of bureaucratic influences on outputs.[6] One problem with much of this work, as critics like Dearlove have noted,[7] is that it is of a highly statistical, quantitative nature, often located in rather poorly developed theoretical frameworks, and lacking in the kind of insights that might arise from work of a more qualitative nature. As Newton and Sharpe correctly note,[8] what is needed as far as output studies are concerned are studies that cover longer periods of time than do most of the existing ones, as well as a more careful unpacking or disaggregation of service links together with an extension of the measures currently employed for political variables: party control, voter turnout and so on are rather poor measures in this respect.

Doing this kind of work will enable us to see how service levels vary between cities and local authorities over time in a quantitative sense. It would allow us, for example, to see whether, for whatever reasons, inner-city authorities do spend less on or receive lower levels of services than do their suburban or rural counterparts consistently over time. In part this will allow us to begin an evaluation of the service performance of different kinds of authorities, but what it will not do is tell us very much about the performance of local governments in particular places. Thus, for example a careful cross-sectional time series-based study of outputs might allow us to rank Salford with Manchester or Walsall with Wolverhampton against Leicester or Exeter, but it will not tell us much about the distribution of those outputs within particular cities or parts of cities, or about the *outcomes* of these outputs.

Yet it is obvious to anyone who walks or drives around any city in

Britain today that different areas within them do get different levels of public goods and services and that these have different consequences. Within the Borough of Trafford, for example, one can compare the area of Stretford with that of Bowdon, or within Cheshire one can compare the district of Widnes with that of Chester, or the East End with the West End of London: areas within the same authority or local government, yet still poles apart in terms of environment, quality of life, level of public services received, and so on.

If the differences within cities and local authorities are at least visually obvious, then they should be measurably so, and thus one should be able to examine, demonstrate and explain variations in service levels between particular neighbourhoods within the same city. Much of the variation may well be hidden from view – for example, knowing pupil–teacher ratios for individual schools in a city or the numbers of doctors per thousand head of population – but we can *see* where old and new schools are located, where the parks are and so on.

Some of the variations between areas in the city are likely to be easily explained. For example, suburban areas, being largely residential, have fewer pollution problems, with the result that city government is likely to spend less on pollution control in those areas than in older, more congested and central areas. In other cases, there may be a kind of substitution effect. For example, there may be fewer parks in middle-class areas than in working-class ones, if only because the middle-class may have greater opportunities and resources to make use of other leisure/recreational facilities whether provided by public or private sectors.[9]

Much of this is, of course, speculation. But analysing and understanding the distribution within cities of public outputs and outcomes is important if we want to begin to evaluate the performance of city governments and if we wish to relate that performance to our normative ideas about the goals and purpose of government generally.

Two other aspects of this problem are also important. First, we need to know a lot more about what kinds of demands people make of their authorities in overall service terms and to what extent they are currently satisfied with their present conditions and service levels. Both aspects present considerable problems to the researcher and the decision-makers concerned,[10] particularly in terms of relating satisfaction with present levels of service to demands for improvement in service levels. Certainly, there is evidence to show that many people are actually quite satisfied with the level of service provisions in relation to many city services,[11] just as there is evidence (from the same source) to indicate dissatisfaction. Furthermore, there is the question as to whether or not people actually perceive an 'objective' improvement in their service as subjectively better or more satisfactory. Thus, for some people, the addition of hot and cold running water, a bath and inside lavatory may be 'very nice', but they may equally well describe the house and its condition before such improvements as 'very nice'. In other words, one issue with which analyses of the distribution of public goods and services in urban areas will have to deal is that of relating such a distribution to people's perceptions of and felt needs for such goods and services, and of course relating questions of costs to the benefits of changing existing distributions.

A second aspect of the analysis of urban outputs and outcomes relates to a question that has underlain both explicitly and implicitly much of what has been said beforehand, namely to what extent can governments, both national and local, control their environments; to what extent are they subordinate to or dependent upon them; and to what extent can they influence or shape the nature of the distribution of public goods and services? Much of the recent debate in the 1970s about governmental policy for the city, in Britain as elsewhere, has centred on this issue, both in academic and official circles. The assumption by government has been what we might expect, namely that it can manage its environment and shape the nature of urban outputs and outcomes. By contrast, critics, particularly those of a Marxist persuasion, have argued for a contrary view; non-Marxists point to the severe economic, financial and political constraints under which city governments operate, while Marxists consider that the general subversion of state institutions to the economic sector under capitalism means that the state can operate only in the interests of the capitalist class, and that much of the crisis of contemporary capitalism lies in the failure of the state to perform its functions. The point at issue, here, however, is that, regardless of the perspective, analyses of urban outputs and outcomes have to include assessments of the extent of state/governmental influence over those outputs and outcomes. Clearly, as we have seen in relation to some services, city governments can affect outcomes, by, for example, their control over the access to and allocation of council housing or certain personal social services. But do they have the same control over an area like planning, or industrial location? The experience of the 1970s of structure planning and some local planning would suggest not, perhaps leading one to make somewhat pessimistic assessments of current governmental attempts to cope with the problems of inner-city deprivation and decline. Indeed, one might go so far as to suggest that the realization that governments have limited ability to control or manage their turbulent environment is the major lesson to be learnt from the experience of the 1970s, whether one is considering city governments or national ones.

This leads inevitably to yet another methodological and conceptual problem, namely the need to distinguish not only outputs from outcomes, but public from private outputs and outcomes. Such a distinction encourages us to explore the relationship between the actions (and their consequences) of public sector agencies and those of the private sector. Ultimately, the sum total of what people get in terms of living in a Western city is a result of the interplay between public and private sectors, and the two may not necessarily be pulling in the same direction at any one time, despite the assertions of Marxist theorists about the need for the state to act in the interest of the dominant capitalist economic class. What is important, however, is unpacking the total set of outcomes, so that we can begin to evaluate the different impacts of governmental and private sector activities on people and problems. For example, do we know precisely the costs and benefits to different groups of the development of hypermarkets, often brought about through the partnership of a private retail sector seeking to maximize economics of scale and a public sector hoping to revitalize some of its shopping facilities? This is not to advocate the wider use of the economists' cost–benefit analysis approach,[12] but to point to the need for the kind of urban impact analyses that are currently being undertaken in the United States under the auspices of the Department of Housing and Urban Development. These studies attempt to evaluate systematically the effect of the whole range of state (governmental) policies on the economic health and welfare of urban areas. Such research is very much underdeveloped here.

In other words, to understand how the actions of the local and central state (in all its manifestations) affect the life of cities and their residents, we need far more thoroughgoing and total analyses than have been developed so far in *any* of the social sciences, let alone from political science alone. It is a path along which a number of social scientists from a number of disciplines have begun to tread, often joined by a number of practitioners who are also aware of the need to follow the consequences of policy actions and implementation. Perhaps it is this area of social/public policy analysis that is likely to be the most exciting and to see the fastest breakthroughs in conceptual and methodological terms in the 1980s, even though one remains somewhat sceptical and pessimistic about the possibilities. This is largely because of the complexity of the real world and its problems, with which such analyses have to cope, and for which only limited success can be foreseen.

If we can realistically be only somewhat speculative about the nature and causes of urban outputs and outcomes, are there other areas or urban politics about which we can be more certain? At the beginning of this chapter, attention was drawn to four themes that underlie much of the earlier discussion in this book.

First, there has been the penetration of the locality by the centre and vice versa. Britain is very much a centralized state, and for all its local and territorial variations it remains true that in political and policy terms the centre and the locality are closely linked. Looking after all aspects of their intergovernmental relations, and not just those with central government, is a primary task for all public urban decision-makers in Britain. In Young's terms, a primary task for local governors is 'managing their political environment'.[13] The complexity of central–local government relations is well demonstrated by some of the recent conceptual and empirical work in the field drawing upon inter-organizational analysis.[14] All point to the use of bargaining resources and power among the governmental institutions involved and the extent to which these institutions are dependent on each other. Looked at historically and speaking relatively, what has happened to British local government and politics in the twentieth century is that it has been 'delocalized', and nowhere is this more apparent than in the cities.[15] Indeed, the linkage reaches its most formal state with the inner-city partnerships created to tackle the major problems of the most heavily deprived areas of cities like Glasgow, Liverpool, Manchester, London and Birmingham. As we shall see shortly, there is a strong financial dimension to the relationship, both through the grants central government provides to finance current expenditure and through its sanctioning of capital spending programmes, as well as the centre's need to control public sector expenditure (and especially that of local government) as part of its strategy for economic management generally. Furthermore, the centre may be more directive, persuasive or whatever in relation to its most favoured policy areas, or in those areas where it particularly hopes governmental action will have favourable consequences.

Yet it would be wrong to see this central–local relationship in pure agency terms: local authorities are far from being the pure agents of the centre, doing as they are bid.[16] Neither are they completely autonomous of the centre, nor can they fairly be described as partners with central government. The truth of the matter is that local authorities are likely to act as agents or parties of central government, or to exercise discretion or act autonomously, according to their perspective on any particular issue, and on how central government (in its many forms) also decides to act in relation to that particular issue. Hence the idea that the two sides are mutually dependent upon each other, and with other bodies with which they also interact. Both sides will bring their respective resources to bear and exercise their influence on each other through a variety of channels and in a variety of ways, each according to its particular objective, yet neither will be able to operate quite independently of the other.

Our second theme, questions of finance, illustrates the interplay between the centre and the locality extremely well. Local authorities raise some of their finance from local taxes (rates) and by charging for services, but the bulk of current expenditure is supplied by central government in the form of grants, particularly the Rate Support Grant. Given the size of public sector expenditure and its rapid growth in recent years, the centre is particularly concerned to maintain control over local authority expenditure for purposes of economic management, whether of the Keynesian or monetarist variety. Yet in recent years it has only been the imposition of cash limits (which effectively set upper levels to the supplementary grants local authorities receive to cover additional costs brought about by inflation and wage settlements) that has given the centre the kind of control it has sought to maintain. By contrast, its control over capital expenditure has been far greater, through the exercise of loan sanction, but even here the centre would probably have preferred tighter control.

From the centre's perspective, it is largely the Treasury that is concerned with financial control for purposes of economic management. Though it is likely to be able to obtain support from service departments, the latter may prefer to encourage local authority spending, in order that departmental policies are successfully implemented. By contrast, local authorities either may resent central government attempts to control them, and be prepared to raise rates or charges in order to maintain services, or else may be prepared to accept the fact that they must 'play the tune' called by the piper if they are to receive the finance necessary to provide the services.

The nature of this central–local conflict is being clearly demonstrated at this time, with the Conservative-controlled Local Authority Associations strongly opposing the Conservative Government's attempt to change the grant provisions through their Bill. With the proposed block grant, central government theoretically would be prepared to control not only the overall size of local authority expenditure but also that of individual authorities. In effect, the new Bill would allow the centre to punish those authorities who chose to deviate from the centre's norm by financing increased expenditure by means of increased rates or higher service charges. It remains to be seen how this conflict will be resolved.

Given the current government's desire to reduce the level of public sector expenditure – that is, to reduce the scope of state action – financing local services is of crucial importance. We have seen some of this in our discussion of the personal social services and of the cuts in public expenditure more generally. Clearly, reductions in the level of central government grants, together with control over the level of an individual authority's expenditure, must mean reductions in service levels. Such a move is most likely to be strongly resisted by the more service and expenditure-orientated authorities, which will most likely be Labour-controlled. By contrast, Conservative-controlled authorities may be more willing to accept cuts in service levels, other things being equal. Nevertheless, given the widespread belief in local discretion and autonomy that exists among local councillors and officials generally, any attempt by the centre that threatens local discretion is likely to be strongly opposed by all authorities, regardless of party political line. Hence the opposition to the government's proposed Bill in early 1980.

What is perhaps more problematic in this context, however, is the fact that since reorganization local government in Britain has become a large-scale enterprise, with all the financial implications that follow from this increase in scale of operation. It may well be that both the scale and complexity of many local authority operations have not been fully grasped by many of those responsible for local authority decision-making, be they in central government or in the cities. Indeed, this argument may even hold at the shire district level, where the scale of operation is still larger than in most of the former urban and rural districts of pre-reform days. After all, most data show that the personnel of local government have not changed radically since reorganization: perhaps a case of old wine in new bottles.[17] The extent to which the moves towards efficiency in local government have made the question of local democracy/discretion/autonomy apparently irrelevant is a theme to which we should return in our concluding remarks, but we have already noted something of the changing balance of power between elected and appointed officials in our earlier discussion, particularly in terms of the planning and social work fields.

In both of these, our third theme, namely the growing importance of the paid official in local decision-making, is well illustrated. Of all the changes in twentieth-century urban politics, the rise of the paid official is perhaps the most important.[18] It seems that the officer is likely to dominate decision-making in many areas of local authority work: planning, education, transport and highways, social work and environmental health all provide examples where elected representatives are dependent to a greater or lesser extent on the advice, information and expertise provided by their officers. By contrast, policy arenas like housing or leisure are both more likely to see heavier councillor involvement and are both areas where the professionalization of the officer class is relatively underdeveloped. Yet both subjects are complex ones, and, in the case of the latter, there is the possibility that increasing and widening public leisure provision, particularly by local authorities, may result as a consequence of technological changes and their impact on employment levels.

In other words, it seems unlikely that the work of urban governors is going to become any easier. We have seen in our discussion of both planning and social work that the ability of the professional to manage his environment is limited. The assumptions of planners, for example, about future levels of population and economic activity have had to be drastically revised in the light of experience in the 1970s, while despite the many attempts to eradicate or alleviate the worst excesses of relative deprivation and poverty, both remain major urban problems for which the activities of most social workers seem mere palliatives. In the transport field, the private car, often with only the driver in it, still remains the main method of transporting people, despite escalating fuel costs and the best efforts of transport planners to encourage shifts towards the use of public transport. Only recently, for example, did the central government deem it necessary to overrule British Rail proposals to close some lines in order to make economies, closures that would probably have meant even greater hardship in rural areas which already face considerable deprivation in terms of transport and personal mobility.[19]

The point of issue, however, is less the professional's competence in dealing with complex matters than the extent to which the politicians, at both local and national level, have either given up or lost control over decisions and policies that are *essentially political* in nature. At both levels, decisions about cuts in expenditure on services involve decisions about priorities of expenditure: should more (or less) be spent on roads *vis-à-vis* housing or education? Which is more important – encouraging new industrial development or dealing with homelessness? Issues such as these involve judgements of a political nature in which the views of the professional officer are worth no more than those of the humblest councillor. In a system that claims to be representative and responsible, surely the expectation is that such judgements will be made by *elected* members, not on the basis of the professional's values but on that of the values held by elected decision-makers responsible to the people at large.

However, even if such an expectation were to be more clearly fulfilled than it is at present, there still remains one theme that has been implicit in much of what we have discussed so far. This refers to the relationship between the public and the private sector, between the state and the economy, between city governments and the major economic interests therein. It involves all the ideas of a mobilization of bias, of decisions and non-decisions, that we examined earlier. The discussion of all three service sectors has shown how difficult it is for the state, be it local or central, to control its environment, assuming this is what those elected to office seek to do. Such an assumption may well be false, since, for example, those elected members of a Conservative disposition may well have non-interventionist values concerning the proper scope and role of government: a stress on private provision, on market forces, on individualistic explanations of 'misfortune' – all are likely to lead councillors to pursue non-interventionist policies. Beliefs about the value of the pursuit of profit and the accumulation of capital may well lead city governors, as well as those at the centre, to develop policies that will favour such processes, making them easier to fulfil. Where the state in its manifestations adopts such a posture and policies, it can be considered a willing partner to the capitalist mode of production so prevalent in Western societies. It may be, however, that the state is subordinate to that mode of production, as Marxists would argue, in which case it is little more than a more or less willing/unwilling agent of capitalism. Miliband's instrumentalist analysis[20] would seem to fit this kind of model, and indeed allows for the state to act as an unwilling agent. Thus, for example, Labour governments in the 1970s may be considered to have acted so as to preserve the capitalist system more or less intact, willingly and consciously or otherwise, despite the continuing rise in unemployment levels, prices and inequalities in the distribution of wealth.

The problem with both the partner/agent analogies is that they are essentially too simplistic, and, like the normative theories from which they derive, ultimately unfalsifiable. In reality, the relationship between the state and the economy is a good deal more complex than either model would suggest. The whole experience of local government in Britain during the 1970s, and particularly of city government, has been to suggest that it is extremely difficult for government to control and manage their economic environments. Indeed, this argument applies as much at central government level as it does at the local. We have seen how the complexity and interdependence of housing has meant many housing policies rather than one, culminating in a Green Paper strong on analysis and weak on prescription. Planners have found that the assumptions on which the planning system has been based have subsequently proved misleading, while the different explanations of poverty and deprivation have resulted in many different solutions being adopted, but failing to solve the problem. In both housing and planning, we have seen how local authorities, and particularly city governments, have often willingly assisted the developer and builder in reconstructing city centres for commercial purposes and building tower blocks in the sky in which few want to live. Even if these developments have been of some benefit to city residents, undoubtedly the major rewards have gone to the property interests, as has been recognized by the interests of finance capital in their rush to join the property boom. National and local governments of both political hues have stressed owner-occupation, where the benefits have been greatest, as an ideal, with apparently little thought for the interests of those unable to get into the market. Similarly, in a variety of ways from their approval of individual planning applications to grand strategic plans, local planners have generally recommended policies that favour middle-class and capital interests, and may well find themselves overthrown if they do otherwise.[21] Radical social workers find themselves in a minority, conflicting with the professional outlook of most of their colleagues, when it comes to suggesting major changes in approaches to social work. In other words, professional officers and councillors alike have generally been unwilling to change the mobilization of bias in Britain which exists largely in favour of the basic values and tenets of the capitalist system. And if this is true of the local level, it has been at least equally so at the national level, even under governments of a Labour persuasion. In other words, city politics in Britain, like those at the national level, are about maintaining the capitalist system. As we said earlier, the urban economic environment in Britain is largely a capitalist one: we must expect city governments to respond to changes in that environment in a fashion that is mutually acceptable unless there is to be a severe dislocation between the economic and political sectors.

Such a conclusion should not be surprising. British politics has been characterized as gradualist, conservative, unwilling or reluctant to change for years. The dominant ideology remains that of capitalism, albeit with a large state component within it. Such a view is perfectly compatible with either liberal or social democratic ideas about the nature of society, ideas that are dominant elements in the prevailing ethics or ideology about the scope and nature of government, the relationship between the economic and political sectors and indeed that between the individual and the state.

In addition, of course, these ideas are also central to the normative debate about the nature and purpose of government, both local and central, and about what constitutes 'the good life', justice, equity in a society such as ours. They involve debates about the size and scale of local government, and about the extent to which it should be autonomous or have discretion. At this level arguments about local democracy also become relevant: what part should individuals and groups play in deciding the future of the community and the level of public services to be provided? Furthermore, questions about the distribution and redistribution of public goods and services, of life chances, or of rewards for effort or merit are very much at the core of the issues of the day, just as much as questions about the future directions of economic activity in Britain. And local government, and particularly that of the cities, has a part to play in the resolution of these normative questions. And so the circle is closed: we began by raising some normative issues, we end by returning to them.

In between times, the concepts, ideas and tools of social (and particularly political) science have been used to illuminate the kinds of changes that are taking place in city politics, in the kinds of policy arenas with which city governments are concerned, and with some of the normative issues involved. At the outset, we also stressed the complexity of the real world, and the difficulty that exists in attempting to understand it. Even at the risk of simplification, hopefully the analysis presented here has helped to make that complexity easier for the reader to grasp and at the same time illuminated some of the many issues and problems with which those in the city deal.

Notes and references

Chapter 1   Political theory, political practice and public policy

1   A useful introductory discussion of this question can be found in B. J. L. Berry, *The Human Consequences of Urbanisation*, London: Macmillan 1973.
2   See Berry, *Human Consequences*, chs. 2 and 3, pp. 27–115.
3   Aristotle, *The Politics*, Harmondsworth: Penguin 1962.
4   For a discussion of the relationship between size and democracy, see R. A. Dahl and E. Tufte, *Size and Democracy*, London: Oxford University Press 1974; R. A. Dahl, 'The city in the future of democracy', in L. Feldman and M. Goldrick, *Politics and Government of Urban Canada*, Toronto: Methuen 1972; and K. Newton, *Is Small Really So Beautiful? Is Big Really So Ugly?*, Studies in Public Policy CSPP no. 19, Glasgow: Strathclyde University 1978.
5   J. S. Mill, *Representation Government*, London: Dent 1968.
6   This point is well discussed in C. Pateman, *Participation and Democratic Theory*, London: Cambridge University Press 1970, pp. 32–5.
7   R. A. Dahl, *Who Governs?* New Haven, Conn.: Yale University Press 1961, especially ch. 19, pp. 223–8.
8   See K. P. Poole, *The Local Government Service*, London: Allen & Unwin 1978, and N. Hepworth, *The Finance of Local Government*, rev. ed., London: Allen & Unwin 1978, for a discussion.
9   Dahl, *Who Governs?*
10   W. Sayre and H. Kaufman, *Governing New York City*, New York: Norton 1960.
11   See, for example, Dahl, *Who Governs?*, and N. Polsby, *Community Power and Political Theory*, New Haven, Conn.: Yale University Press 1963.
12   F. Hunter, *Community Power Structure*, Chapel Hill, NC: University of North Carolina Press 1953; P. Bachrach and M. S. Baratz, *Power and Poverty*, London: Oxford University Press 1970.
13   D. Harvey, *Social Justice and the City*, London: Edward Arnold 1973.
14   M. Castells, *The Urban Question*, London: Edward Arnold 1977.
15   C. W. Mills, *The Power Elite*, London: Oxford University Press 1953; and Hunter, *Community Power Structure*.

16 For a discussion see P. Saunders, *Urban Politics: a Sociological Approach*, London: Hutchinson 1979, particularly ch. 1, pp. 21–65.

17 See, for example, C. Cockburn, *The Local State*, London: Pluto 1977.

18 Early contributions to the rapidly growing body of literature include A. Ranney, *Political Science and Public Policy*, Chicago: Markham 1968; I. Sharkansky, *Policy Analysis in Political Science*, Chicago: Markham 1970, and T. R. Dye, *Understanding Public Policy*, 2nd ed., Englewood Cliffs, NJ: Prentice-Hall 1975.

19 Dye, *Understanding Public Policy*, p. 1.

20 Ranney, *Political Science and Public Policy*, pp. 3–22.

21 See for example, J. Lewis and R. Flynn, 'The implementation of urban and regional planning policies', in *Policy and Politics*, vol. 7, no. 2, pp. 123–44.

22 N. Boaden, *Urban Policy Making*, London: Cambridge University Press 1971.

23 L. A. Froman Jr, 'The categorisation of policy contents', in Ranney, *Political Science and Public Policy*, pp. 41–54.

24 T. J. Lowi, 'American business, public policy, case studies and political theory', *World Politics*, vol. 16 (July 1964), pp. 677–715; and his 'Decision-making versus policy-making', *Public Administrative Review* (May–June 1970), pp. 314–25, together with 'From systems of policy, politics and choice,' *Public Administration Review* (July–August 1972), pp. 298–310.

25 H. Lasswell, *Politics, Who Gets What, When and How*, New York: Meridian 1958.

Chapter 2   Analysing city politics

1 An example of this traditional mode of writing is P. G. Richards, *The Reformed Local Government System*, London: Allen & Unwin 1968. More interestingly, see R. Rhodes, Appendix 1, *SSRC Report on Central-Local Government Relations*, London: SSRC 1979.

2 As exemplified by the work of R. A. Dahl, *Who Governs?* New Haven, Conn.: Yale University Press 1961, and F. Hunter, *Community Power Structure*, Chapel Hill, NC: University of North Carolina Press 1953.

3 Associated mainly with the work of David Easton: see his *A Framework for Political Analysis*, Englewood Cliffs, NJ: Prentice-Hall 1965 and *Systems Analysis of Political Life*, New York: John Wiley 1965.

4 In the urban politics field, American examples include R. Lineberry and I. Sharkansky, *Urban Politics and Public Policies*, 3rd ed., New York: Harper and Row 1977, and D. Morgan and S. Fitzpatrick, *Urban Political Analysis*, New York: Free Press 1972. A British example which implicitly adopts a systemic framework is N. Boaden, *Urban Policy Making*, London: Cambridge University Press 1971, as does J. Stanyer, *Understanding Local Government*, London: Fontana 1976.

5   See, for example, J. Dearlove, *The Politics of Policy in British Local Government*, London: Cambridge University Press 1973, and R. A. Pahl, *Whose City?* Harmondsworth: Penguin 1975, especially chs. 11–13.

6   M. Castells, *The Urban Question*, London: Edward Arnold 1977.

7   On this subject generally see *Report of the (Layfield) Committee on Local Government Finance*, Cmnd 6453, London: HMSO 1976. A standard text is N. Hepworth, *The Finance of Local Government*, rev. ed., London: Allen & Unwin 1978.

8   See, for example, D. Moynihan, *Maximum Feasible Misunderstanding*, New York: Free Press 1970; P. Barach and M. Baratz, *Power and Poverty*, London: Oxford University Press 1970.

9   See SSRC, *Report of the Panel on Central-Local Government Relations*, London: SSRC 1979.

10   See M. Danielson, *Metropolitan Politics: A Reader*, 2nd ed., Boston: Little, Brown 1971.

11   Not for nothing did Robert Wood call his book on New York *1400 Governments* (Cambridge, Mass.: Harvard University Press 1961).

12   See, for example, classically, *Report of the* (Redcliffe-Maud) *Royal Commission of Local Government in England*, Cmnd 4040, London: HMSO 1969. An academic example is W. Robson, *Local Government in Crisis*, London: Allen & Unwin 1966. For an interesting contrary view see J. Dearlove, *The Reorganisation of British Local Government*, Cambridge: University Press 1979.

13   For details see P. Richards, *The Reformed Local Government System*, 3rd ed., London: Allen & Unwin 1978.

14   ibid.

15   K. Young and J. Kramer, *Strategy and Conflict in Metropolitan Housing*, London: Heinemann 1978; M. Harloe *et al.*, *The Organisation of Housing*, London: Heinemann 1974.

16   See, for example, Boaden, *Urban Policy Making*; B. Davies, *Social Needs and Resources in Local Services*, London: Michael Joseph 1968: J. Alt, 'Some social and political correlates of county borough expenditures', *British Journal of Political Science*, vol. 1, no. 1 (1971) pp. 49–62; F. R. Oliver and J. Stanyer, 'Some aspects of the financial behaviour of county boroughs', *Public Administration*, vol. 47 (1969), pp. 169–84. This literature and its limitations are well reviewed in K. Newton and L. J. Sharpe, 'Local outputs research: some reflections and proposals', *Policy and Politics*, vol. 5, no. 3 (1977), pp. 61–82.

17   Report of the Bains Committee: *The New Local Authorities: Management and Structure*, London: HMSO 1972; and similarly the Report of the Paterson Committee on *Management Structure in the New Scottish Local Authorities*, Edinburgh: Scottish Office 1973.

18   Dahl, *Who Governs?* and Hunter, *Community Power Structure*. See also K. Newton, 'City Politics in Britain and the United States', *Political Studies*, vol. 17, no. 2 (1969), pp. 208–18; P. Saunders, 'They make the

rules', *Policy and Politics*, vol. 4 (1975), pp. 31–58; B. Green, 'Community decision making in Georgian city', unpublished PhD thesis, Bath University 1967, for a British discussion and examples.

19   Bachrach and Baratz, *Power and Poverty*.

20   ibid., p. 39.

21   ibid., p. 44; R. Wotifinger, 'Non-decisions and the study of local politics', *American Political Science Review*, vol. 65 (1971), pp. 1063–80; K. Newton, 'Democracy, community power and non-decision making', *Political Studies*, vol. 20., no. 4 (1972), pp. 484–7.

22   See M. Crenson, *The Unpolitics of Air Pollution*, Baltimore: John Hopkins Press 1971; Saunders, 'They make the rules', is a particularly good British example, as is his fuller work: P. Saunders, *Urban Politics: A Sociological Analysis*, London: Hutchinson 1979.

23   The phrase is from E. E. Schattschneider, *The Semi-Sovereign People*, New York: Holt, Rinehart and Winston 1960.

24   As an example, J. Q. Wilson, *City Politics and Public Policy*, New York: John Wiley 1968.

25   ibid., p. 2.

26   Easton, *Framework for Political Analysis*.

27   An interesting third example is K. Deutsch, *The Nerves of Government*, London: Collier Macmillan 1966.

28   See, for example, G. Almond and S. Verba, *The Civic Culture*, Boston: Little, Brown 1963.

29   One notable exception is H. Kaplan, *Urban Political Systems*, New York: Columbia University Press 1968, a study of Toronto.

30   Examples include Lineberry and Sharkansky, *Urban Politics and Public Policies*; Morgan and Fitzpatrick, *Urban Political Analysis*. J. Stanyer, *Understanding Local Government*, London: Fontana 1976, is a British example of the use of systemic thinking in this field.

31   Dahl, *Who Governs?*, strangely ignores the federal government's part in New Haven's politics, an odd omission given its importance in terms of providing finance for urban redevelopment programmes. R. Rhodes, Appendix 1, *Report of the Panel on Central-Local Government Relations*, London: SSRC 1979, is an interesting attempt to conceptualize this problem, as is K. Young, 'Environmental management in local politics', in D. Kavanagh and R. Rose, *New Directions in British Politics*, London: Sage 1977, pp. 141–66.

32   From Boaden, *Urban Policy Making*, p. 22.

33   Crenson, *Unpolitics of Air Pollution*.

34   Dearlove, *Reorganisation of British Local Government*, p. 75.

35   Boaden, *Urban Policy Making*, p. 2.

36   Dearlove, *Reorganisation of British Local Government*.

37   K. Young, 'Values in the policy processes', *Policy and Politics*, vol. 5, no. 3 (1977), p. 2.

38   Young and Kramer, *Strategy and Conflict*.

39   J. G. Davies, *The Evangelistic Bureaucrat*, London: Tavistock 1972.
40   N. Dennis, *Public Participation and Planners' Blight*, London: Faber 1972.
41   See J. Rex and R. Moore, *Race, Community and Conflict*, London: Oxford University Press 1967. R. Pahl, *Whose City?*, Harmondsworth: Penguin 1975.
42   R. Pahl, 'Managers, technical experts and the state', in M. Harloe (ed.), *Captive Cities*, London: John Wiley 1977, pp. 49–60.
43   See Harloe's introduction in ibid., pp. 1–48.
44   Castells, *The Urban Question*, and, more recently, *Cities, Classes and Power*, London: Macmillan 1978.
45   I draw here particularly on the discussion in Saunders, *Urban Politics*, and his paper, 'Community power, urban managerialism and the "local state" ', given at the CES 'Urban Change and Conflict' conference, Nottingham 1979 (to be published in M. Harlow, ed., *Urban Change and Conflict*; London: Heinemann 1980).
46   See J. Lojkin, 'Contribution to a Marxist theory of capitalist urbanisation', in C. Pickvance, *Urban Sociology: Critical Essays*, London: Tavistock 1976.
47   See Saunders, *Urban Politics*, p. 117.
48   R. Pahl, 'Collective consumption and the state in capitalist and state socialist societies', in R. Scase, *Industrial Society: Class, Cleavage and Control*, London: Tavistock 1977.
49   Saunders, *Urban Politics*, p. 123.
50   P. Collinson, *The Cutteslowe Walls*, London: Faber 1963.
51   Saunders, *Urban Politics*, p. 124.
52   R. Miliband, *The State in Capitalist Society*, London: Weidenfeld & Nicolson 1969.
53   Saunders's 'Community power, urban managerialism and the local state' is a good attempt at tackling the question of relative autonomy within this perspective.
54   See R. Flynn, 'Managing consensus: the infrastructure of policy making in planning', CES *Urban Change and Conflict*; and N. Boaden, M. Goldsmith, W. Hampton and P. Stringer, *Participation and Planning in Practice*, Oxford: Pergamon (forthcoming) outlines some of the problems involved.
55   In general the work of C. Offe, particularly his 'The theory of the capitalist state and the problem of policy formulation', in L. Lindbergh, R. Alford, C. Crouch and C. Offe, *Stress and Contradiction in Modern Capitalism*, New York: Lexington 1975.
56   C. Pickvance, 'On the study of urban social movements', in his *Urban Sociology: Critical Essays*.
57   See Harloe's introduction in his *Captive Cities*.
58   One exception is the work of Pat Dunleavy – see, for example, his 'Protest and quiescence in urban politics: a critique of some pluralist and

structuralist myths', *International Journal of Urban and Regional Research*, vol. 1 (1977), pp. 193–218.

Chapter 3 Environmental change and the city

1 See K. Young, 'Environmental management in local politics', in D. Kavanagh and R. Rose, *New Trends in British Politics*, London: Sage 1977, pp. 141–66. For another example, see J. D. Stewart, *The Responsive Local Authority*, London: Charles Knight 1974.

2 The use here of the political environment is in the analytic, systemic sense, in that there have understandably been changes in national British politics that have had an impact on urban political processes.

3 A. G. Champion, 'Evolving patterns of population distribution in England and Wales, 1951–1971', *Institute of British Geographers*, Transactions, New Series vol. 1, no. 4 (1976), pp. 401–20.

4 The term is from P. Hall, R. Thomas, H. Gracey and R. Drewett, *The Containment of Urban England*, vol. 1, London: Allen & Unwin 1973.

5 On this latter, see C. M. Law and A. M. Warnes, 'The changing geography of the elderly in England and Wales', *Institute of British Geographers*, Transactions, New Series, vol. 1, no. 4 (1976), pp. 453–71. This work shows movement of the elderly particularly to the South coast (now known among planners as the Costa Geriatrica); the South-West and parts of the North-West and East Anglia.

6 M. Clawson and P. Hall, *Planning and Urban Growth*, London: RFF/Johns Hopkins University Press 1973, p. 99.

7 This exodus tended to accelerate towards the end of this period, and the decline has continued since.

8 Champion, 'Evolving patterns of population distribution'. See also Hall *et al.*, *Containment of Urban England*, for an earlier analysis.

9 Law and Warnes, 'Changing geography of the elderly'.

10 As many officials in these areas know, subsequently these idyllic retirement dreams can lead to problems of isolation, loneliness and poverty, as inflation eats into the carefully husbanded savings or spouses die.

11 See the figures in *The Inner Area Studies: Final Reports by the Consultants*, London: HMSO 1977.

12 See *Social Trends, 1979* London: HMSO 1979, p. 34.

13 One of the problems in this field has been some planners' reluctance to accept that population and economic growth are no longer the norm. When decline became more readily apparent in the early 1970s, some planners could be heard to use the phrase 'negative growth' rather than face the reality of decline and its implications.

14 All figures taken from *Economic Trends*, 1979 edition, London: HMSO 1979.

15 H. Newby, C. Bell, D. Rose and P. Saunders, *Property, Paternalism and*

Power, London: Hutchinson 1978, especially chs. 2 and 3, pp. 42–145.

16 *Public Employment in the U.K.*, Glasgow: CSPP Strathclyde University 1980, for a detailed discussion.

17 For a discussion of some of these, see T. A. Broadbent, *Planning and Profit in the Urban Economy*, London: Methuen 1977, especially ch. 2, pp. 29–90.

18 A. R. Prest and D. J. Coppock, *The U.K. Economy: A Manual of Applied Economics*, 6th ed., London: Weidenfeld & Nicolson 1976, p. 221.

19 P. Hall, *Urban and Regional Planning*, Harmondsworth: Penguin 1974, pp. 128–9.

20 ibid., p. 133.

21 ibid., p. 133.

22 For a discussion, see J. E. S. Hayward and M. Watson, *Planning Politics and Public Policy*, Cambridge: University Press 1975, especially pp. 217–36 and 295–315.

23 Hall, *Urban and Regional Planning*, p. 146.

24 ibid., p. 150.

25 B. Moore and J. Rhodes, 'Evaluating the effects of British regional economic policy', *Economic Journal*, vol. 83 (1973), pp. 87–110; quoted in T. A. Broadbent, *Planning and Profit in the Urban Economy*, London: Methuen 1977, p. 77.

26 See Broadbent, *Planning and Profit*, p. 39.

27 *Social Trends, 1979*, London: HMSO 1979, p. 88.

28 An excellent discussion of some of these policies can be found in D. A. McKay and A. W. Cox, *The Politics of Urban Change*, London: Croom Helm 1979, especially ch. 7, pp. 233–71; and in their 'Confusion and reality in public policy making', *Political Studies*, vol. 26 (December 1978), pp. 491–506. Another account can be found in J. Edwards and J. R. Batley, *The Politics of Positive Discrimination*, London: Tavistock 1978. Much of this section draws on A. W. Cox, 'Administrative inertia and inner city policy', *Public Administration Bulletin*, no. 29 (1979), pp. 2–17.

29 See, for example, CPRS, *A Joint Framework for Social Policies*, London: HMSO 1975; *The Inner Area Studies: Final Reports by the Consultants*, London: HMSO 1972; and *Policy for the Inner Cities*, Cmnd 6845, London: HMSO 1977.

30 CDP, *The Costs of Industrial Change* and *Gilding the Ghetto*, London: Home Office 1977.

31 See, for example, P. Gripaios, 'Industrial decline in London: an examination of its causes', *Urban Studies*, vol. 13 (1976), pp. 261–71; also *Change and Decay: Final Report of the Liverpool Inner Area Study*, London: HMSO 1977.

32 See *Social Trends*, no. 9 (1979), London: HMSO, p. 187. Most of the data quoted below are drawn from this source, unless otherwise stated.

33 Figures from *Social Trends*, no. 10 (1980), London: HMSO, pp. 257, 259.

Chapter 4   Changes in city politics 1: the reactions of the political community

1   See, for example, J. Garrard, *The English and Immigration*, London: Institute of Race Relations/Oxford University Press 1972 on English reactions to late nineteenth-century Jewish immigration.

2   P. Stringer, *The Press and Publicity for Public Participation*, interim Research Report no. 12, Linked Research Project into Public Participation and Structure Planning, London: DOE 1978.

3   R. A. Dahl, *Who Governs?* New Haven, Conn.: Yale University Press 1961, p. 223.

4   W. A. Hampton, *Democracy and Community*, London: Oxford University Press 1970; and M. Goldsmith and P. Saunders, *The Tale of Lewis the Cat*, interim Research Report no. 9, Linked Research Project into Public Participation and Structure Planning, London: DOE 1975, both discuss this point.

5   See W. A. Hampton and R. Walker, *The Individual Citizen and Public Participation*, interim Research Report no. 13, Linked Research Project into Public Participation Structure Planning, London: DOE 1978. See also R. Drake and R. Walker, *Local Government and Public Participation*, London: Leonard Hill 1977.

6   An interesting comparison between the two countries is made by L. J. Sharpe, 'American democracy reconsidered, parts 1 and 2', *British Journal of Political Science*, vol. 3, nos. 1 and 2 (1973), pp. 1–28 and 129–68.

7   L. J. Sharpe (ed.), *Voting in Cities*, London: Macmillan 1967.

8   S. L. Bristow, 'Local politics after re-organisation: the homogenisation of local government in England and Wales', *Public Administration Bulletin*, no. 28 (December 1978), pp. 17–33.

9   ibid., p. 21.

10   Thus in 1968–9 hundreds of long-serving Labour councillors fell under the electoral axe as the Wilson Government of 1964–70 reached its most unpopular levels. Their Conservative successors, however, disappeared in 1971–3, the peak of the Heath Government's unpopularity.

11   K. Newton, 'Turnout and marginality in local elections', *British Journal of Political Science*, vol. 2, no. 2 (1972), pp. 251–5.

12   B. Pimlott, 'Local party organisation turnout and marginality', *British Journal of Political Science*, vol. 3, no. 2 (1973), pp. 252–5; and W. B. Grant, 'Size of place and local Labour strength', *British Journal of Political Science*, vol. 2, no. 2 (1972), pp. 259–69.

13   See, for example, D. Fraser, *Urban Politics in Victorian England*, London: Macmillan 1979, especially Part 4, pp. 237–78.

14   L. J. Sharpe, 'Leadership and representation in local government', *Political Quarterly*, vol. 37 (1966), pp. 149–58.

15   See M. Goldsmith and P. Saunders, 'Participation through public

meetings: the case of Cheshire', interim Research Paper no. 9 and P. Stringer and S. Ewens, 'Participation through public meetings: the case of Lancashire', Interim Research Paper no. 2, Linked Research Project into Public Participation and Structure Planning, London: DOE 1975–6.

16   K. Newton, *Second City Politics*, Oxford: Clarendon 1976, especially chs. 3 and 4.

17   J. Case, 'Interest group activity at the local level: five case studies', unpublished MSc. thesis, University of Salford 1971; and A. K. Moss, 'Local pressure groups: a comparative study', unpublished MSc. thesis, University of Salford 1977.

18   J. D. Dearlove, *The Politics of Policy in English Local Government*, London: Cambridge University Press, especially ch. 8.

19   Newton, *Second City Politics*, pp. 85–8.

20   Dearlove, *Politics of Policy*, p. 171.

21   D. Easton, *A Framework for Political Analysis*, Englewood Cliffs, NJ: Prentice-Hall 1965, pp. 116-17.

22   See N. Boaden and C. Collins, *Consultations with Organisations in the Merseyside Structure Plan*, Interim Research Paper no. 6, Linked Research Project into Public Participation and Structure Planning, Department of the Environment 1975, for a discussion of group involvement in the Merseyside structure plan.

23   A point discussed in N. Boaden, M. Goldsmith, W. Hampton and P. Stringer, *Public Participation and Planning in Practice*, Oxford: Pergamon (forthcoming).

24   J. Bulpitt, *Party Politics in English Local Government*, London: Longmans 1967, especially ch. 1.

25   D. Fraser, *Urban Politics in Victorian England*, Leicester: University Press 1976; and E. P. Hennock, *Fit and Proper Persons: Ideal and Reality in Nineteenth Century Urban Government*, London: Edward Arnold 1973.

26   G. W. Jones, *Borough Politics*, London: Macmillan 1969; and T. J. Nossiter, *Influence Opinion and Political Idioms in Reformed England*, Brighton: Harvester 1975.

27   This section draws on work done under the direction of the author under an SSRC Grant into politics in Salford between 1830 and 1970. See M. Goldsmith, *Politics in Salford, 1830–1970: A Report to SSRC* (1971).

28   R. Rose, *The Problem of Party Government*, Harmondsworth: Penguin 1976, provides a good discussion of membership and other party matters.

29   Dearlove, *Politics of Policy*. See also P. Saunders's study of Croydon, *Urban Politics*, Hutchinson 1979. See Bulpitt, *Party Politics in English Local Government*, pp. 40–58 for brief discussion of Salford.

30   A point made by Dylis Hill, 'Communication in the local political community: regional and neighbourhood pressures', paper presented to

the Political Studies Association Annual Meeting, Reading, 1973.
31 See for example, D. Murphy, *The Silent Watchdog*, London: Constable 1976; W. H. Cox and D. Morgan, *City Politics and the Press*, London: Cambridge University Press 1974, and I. Jackson, *The Provincial Press and the Community*, Manchester: University Press 1972.
32 Stringer, *Press and Publicity*.
33 ibid., p. 5.
34 Murphy, *Silent Watchdog*; Cox and Morgan, *City Politics and the Press*.
35 Cox and Morgan, *City Politics and the Press*, pp. 145–7.

Chapter 5   Changes in city politics 2: the regime and the authorities

1   Following D. Easton, *A Framework for Political Analysis*, Englewood Cliffs: Prentice-Hall 1965, pp. 116–17.
2   ibid., pp. 53–4.
3   The government of London was reformed in 1963. In some ways, it is perhaps easiest to treat London as *sui generis*, it perhaps having more in common with other capital cities than with the rest of urban Britain.
4   See for example, M. N. Danielson (ed.), *Metropolitan Politics: A Reader*, 2nd ed., Boston: Little, Brown 1971. By comparison there has been considerable local government reform in the USA's immediate northern neighbour, Canada, particularly in the Province of Ontario. See D. J. Higgins, *Urban Canada: its Government and Politics*, Toronto: Macmillan 1977 for a discussion.
5   Royal Commission on Local Government in Greater London, 1957–60, *Report*, Cmnd 1164, London: HMSO 1960.
6   On Metropolitan Toronto, see H. Kaplan, *Urban Political Systems*, New York: Columbia University Press 1965; and A. Rose, *Governing Metropolitan Toronto*, Berkeley, University of California Press 1972.
7   See, for example, F. Smallwood, *Greater London: The Politics of Metropolitan Reform*, New York: Bobbs Merrill 1965 and G. Rhodes (ed.), *The New Government of London*, London: Weidenfeld & Nicolson 1972.
8   Royal Commission on Local Government in England, 1966–1969, *Report*, Cmnd 4040, London: HMSO 1969.
9   See particularly B. Wood, *The Process of Local Government Reform 1966–74*, London: Allen & Unwin 1976; J. Brand, *Local Government Reform in England*, London: Croom Helm 1974, and P. G. Richards, *The Reformed Local Government System*, 3rd ed. London: Allen & Unwin 1978.
10 See Wood, *Process of Local Government*, pp. 17–18.
11 See, for example, Royal Commission on Local Government in England, Research Studies, vol. ix, *Community Attitudes Survey: England*, London: HMSO 1969; and W. A. Hampton, *Democracy and Community*, London: Oxford University Press 1970.

12   Wood, *Process of Local Government*, p. 30.
13   See, for example, some of the evidence of the central government departments to the English Royal Commission.
14   The generally accepted fourth criterion is that of financial viability, but discussion of finance was specifically excluded from the terms of reference of both the English and Scottish Royal Commissions.
15   Wood, *Process of Local Government*, p. 57.
16   See Royal Commission on Local Government in England, 1966–1969, *Report*, vol. 2.
17   An idea he had advocated earlier. See D. Senior, 'The city region as an administrative unit', *Political Quarterly*, vol. 36, no. 1 (1965), pp. 82–91.
18   Ministry of Local Government and Regional Planning, *Reform of Local Government in England,* Cmnd 4276, London: HMSO 1970.
19   Rural District Councils Association, *The Democratic Alternative to Maud*, London: RDCA 1969.
20   This is discussed in J. M. Lee, *et al.*, *The Scope of Local Initiative*. London: Martin Robertson 1974.
21   For a detailed analysis of the reactions to the Redcliffe-Maud report see Wood, *Process of Local Government*, ch. 3, pp. 63–89.
22   Department of the Environment: *Local Government in England: Government Proposals for Reorganisation*, Cmnd 4584, London: HMSO 1971.
23   Wood, *Process of Local Government*, p. 96.
24   For details see ibid., pp. 191–4.
25   See S. L. Bristow, 'The criteria for local government reorganisation and local authority autonomy', *Policy and Politics*, vol. 1, no. 2 (December 1972).
26   See Wood, *Process of Local Government*, ch. 6, pp. 128–61 for details.
27   See Rhodes, *New Government of London* and K. Young and J. Kramer, *Strategy and Conflict in Metropolitan Housing*, London: Heinemann 1978.
28   See S. Leach and N. Moore, 'County/district relations in shire and metropolitan counties', *Policy and Politics*, vol. 7, no. 2 (1979), pp. 165–80.
29   On this subject, see Social Sciences Research Council, *Report of the Panel on Central–Local Government Relations*, London: SSRC 1979, and its subsequently sponsored research. Also see Central Policy Review Staff, *Relations Between Central Government and Local Authorities*, London: HMSO 1977; the (Layfield) *Report of the Committee of Enquiry into Local Government Finance*, Cmnd 6453, London: HMSO 1976; and J. A. G. Griffiths, *Central Departments and Local Authorities*, London: Allen & Unwin 1966.
30   See Layfield Report, particularly ch. 2.
31   See G. W. Jones, 'Local government finance in Great Britain', in J. Lagroye and V. Wright (eds.), *Local Government in England and France,*

London: Allen & Unwin 1979, pp. 165–82. Currently the Conservative Government's Local Government Bill seeks to increase central control over the expenditure of individual authorities while at the same time reducing its control over some aspects of capital expenditure.

32 This has particular implications for central government's control over public expenditure generally, which is why in recent years the Treasury has sought to increase its control over local government expenditure.

33 See R. Rhodes, Appendix 1, SSRC *Panel Report on Central–Local Government Relationships*, London: SSRC 1979, for a well developed model along these lines.

34 See P. Saunders, *Urban Politics*, London: Hutchinson 1979, pp. 273–97; and J. Dearlove, *The Politics of Policy in English Local Government*, London: Cambridge University Press 1973.

35 B. Hindess, *The Decline of Working Class Politics*, London: Paladin 1971.

36 W. I. Grant, *Independent Local Politics in England and Wales*, London: Saxon House 1976, and S. L. Bristow, 'Local politics after reorganisation: the homogenisation of local government in England and Wales', *Public Administration Bulletin*, no. 28 (December 1978), pp. 17–33.

37 J. M. Lee, *Social Leaders and Public Persons*, Oxford: Clarendon Press 1963.

38 See Hindess, *Decline of Working Class Politics* and Saunders, *Urban Politics*, ch. 7. pp. 273–96.

39 See J. Gyford, *Local Politics in England*, London: Croom Hall 1976, ch. 2, pp. 25–58 for a discussion.

40 K. Newton, *Second City Politics*, Oxford: Clarendon Press 1976, particularly ch. 6, pp. 114–44.

41 ibid., p. 140.

42 ibid., p. 141.

43 See, for example, I. Gordon, 'The recruitment of local politicians', *Policy and Politics*, vol. 7, no. 1 (January 1979), pp. 1–38; and C. A. Collins, 'Considerations on the social background and motivation of councillors', *Policy and Politics*, vol. 6, no. 4 (1978), pp. 425–47.

44 See R. A. Pahl, *Whose City?*, Harmondsworth: Penguin 1975; J. G. Davies, *The Evangelistic Bureaucrat*, London: Tavistock 1972; N. Dennis, *Public Participation and Planning Blight*, London: Faber 1972.

45 Town planning perhaps provides a good example of a profession where this has happened.

46 Dennis, *Public Participation and Planning Blight*.

47 Dearlove, *The Politics of Policy in English Local Government*.

48 Report of the Bains Committee, *The New Local Authorities: Management and Structure*, London: HMSO 1972.

49 R. Hambleton, *Policy Planning and Local Government*, London: Hutchinson 1978.

50 ibid., p. 69.

51 ibid., p. 239.
52 See P. Davidoff, 'Advocacy and pluralism in planning', in A. Faludi, *A Reader in Planning Theory*, Oxford: Pergamon 1973.

Chapter 6   Policy arena 1: housing

1 A. Murie, P. Niner and C. Watson, *Housing Policy and the Housing System*, London: Allen & Unwin 1976 on this point particularly.
2 J. Rex and R. Moore, *Race, Community and Conflict*, London: Oxford University Press, 1967; J. Rex, *Race, Colonialism and the City*, London: Routledge & Kegan Paul 1973, and, most recently, J. Rex and S. Tomlinson, *Colonial Immigrants in a British City*, London: Routledge & Kegan Paul 1979.
3 See, for example, J. Lambert, C. Parris and B. Blackaby, *Housing Policy and the State*, London: 1979.
4 ibid.
5 One of the myths/realities for would-be council tenants may be the belief that it is necessary for them to pay 'a little extra' to obtain a tenancy.
6 See Lambert *et al.*, *Housing Policy and the State*, ch. 3, pp. 36–62.
7 W. Harvey Cox, *Cities: The Public Dimension*, Harmondsworth: Penguin 1976.
8 See M. Goldsmith and P. Saunders, *Public Participation and Local Planning* (forthcoming).
9 See *Guardian* (12 July 1979).
10 For example, P. R. Williams, 'The role of institutions in the inner London housing market: the case of Islington', *IBT Transactions*, New Series, vol. 1 (1972), pp. 72–82; and C. Hamnett, 'Improvement grants as an indicator of gentrification in inner London', *Area*, vol. 5, no. 3 (1973), pp. 252–61. Interestingly, the process of rural gentrification appears to have received little attention, but see C. Bell, H. Newby, D. Rose and P. Saunders, *Property, Paternalism and Power*, London: Hutchinson 1978.
11 See W. Grant, *Independent Local Politics in England and Wales*, London: Saxon House 1977, ch. 4, pp. 86–104, for a discussion.
12 For an interesting discussion of this point see P. Saunders, *Urban Politics: A Sociological Analysis*, London: Hutchinson 1979, especially chs. 4 and 6.
13 N. Wates, *The Battle for Tolmers Square*, London: Routledge & Kegan Paul 1977, p. 162.
14 ibid., p. 159.
15 ibid., p. 161.
16 R. Bailey, *The Squatters*, Harmondsworth: Penguin 1973, pp. 183–90.
17 Whether Bailey's third claim – namely that some working people have taken control of their own lives – is fully justified seems more doubtful:

see Bailey, *The Squatters*, p. 189.

18　See, for example, demands made by some housing authorities that homeless families should have lived within a local authority for a minimum period of time before qualifying as homeless. Failure to meet this qualification results in the homeless family being returned to their previous area of residence.

19　Murie, Niner, and Watson, *Housing Policy and the Housing System*, particularly chs. 4 and 7.

20　See S. Lansley, *Housing and Public Policy*, London: Croom Helm, 1979 ch. 2, pp. 46–70.

21　ibid., p. 93.

22　See for example, A. Altshuler, *The City Planning Process*, Ithaca, NY: Cornell University Press 1965; A. J. Catanese, *Planners and Local Politics*, London: Sage 1974, and O. P. Williams *et al.*, *Suburban Differences and Metropolitan Policies*, Philadelphia: University of Pennsylvania Press 1965.

23　Saunders, *Urban Politics*, esp. ch. 6.

24　K. Young and J. Kramer, *Strategy and Conflict in Metropolitan Housing*, London: Heinemann 1978.

25　*DOE Housing Policy: A Consultative Document*, Cmnd. 6853, London: HMSO 1977.

26　ibid., p. 50.

27　Lansley, *Housing and Public Policy*, p. 218.

28　See, for example, S. L. Elkin, *Politics and Land Use Planning*, London: Cambridge University Press 1974, ch. 3.

29　Wates, *Battle for Tolmers Square*.

30　O. Marriott, *The Property Boom*, London: Hamish Hamilton 1967, especially chs. 9 and 14.

31　See particularly P. Ambrose and R. Colenutt, *The Property Machine*, Harmondsworth: Penguin 1975.

32　See Lansley, *Housing and Public Policy*, particularly pp. 104–219.

Chapter 7　Policy arena 2: planning

1　O. P. Williams, *Metropolitan Political Analysis*, New York: Free Press 1971.

2　This initial criticism culminated in the influential report of the Planning Advisory Group: *The Future of Development Plans*, London: HMSO 1965.

3　For example see N. Dennis, *Public Participation and Planning Blight*, London: Faber 1972 and J. G. Davies, *The Evangelistic Bureaucrat*, London: Tavistock 1972.

4　See, for example, H. Gans, *People and Plans*, Harmondsworth: Penguin 1972; and P. Davidoff, 'Advocacy and pluralism in planning', in A. Faludi, *A Reader in Planning Theory*, Oxford: Pergamon 1973.

5   P. Hall, R. Thomas, H. Grey and R. Drewett, *The Containment of Urban England*, London: PEP/Allen & Unwin 1973.

6   Ministry of Works and Planning, *Report of the Committee on Land Utilisation in Rural Areas*, Cmnd 6378, London: HMSO 1943.

7   Royal Commission on the Distribution of the Industrial Population, *Report*, Cmnd 6153, London: HMSO 1940.

8   *Final Report on the New Towns Committee*, Cmnd 6876, London: HMSO 1946.

9   Hall *et al.*, *Containment of Urban England*, vol. 2, p. 35.

10 As is noted by Donald Foley: see his *Controlling London's Growth: Planning the Great Wen, 1940–60*, Berkeley: California University Press 1963.

11 Hall *et al.*, *Containment of Urban England*, pp. 85–9.

12 See for example, O. Marriott, *The Property Boom*, London: Hamish Hamilton 1968; P. Ambrose and R. Colenutt, *The Property Machine*, Harmondsworth: Penguin 1976; and S. Elkin, *Politics and Land Use Planning*, London: Cambridge University Press 1973.

13 N. Wates, *The Battle for Tolmers Square*, London: Routledge & Kegan Paul 1976; and P. Cook, 'Capital relation and state dependency', in G. Rees, *Poverty at the Periphery* (forthcoming).

14 See G. Cherry, *The Evolution of British Town Planning*, London: Leonard Hill 1974, p. 153 for details.

15 ibid., p. 153.

16 Hall *et al.*, *Containment of Urban England*, vol. 2, p. 226.

17 The following section draws heavily on Wates, *Battle for Tolmers Square*, pp. 24–6, and on Ambrose and Colenutt, *Property Machine*, p. 27.

18 Ambrose and Colenutt, *Property Machine*, p. 27.

19 Quoted in ibid., p. 28.

20 For a fuller discussion of the Land Commission see Hall *et al.*, *Containment of Urban England*, vol. 2, pp. 222–44.

21 ibid., pp. 76–84.

22 For many years development control was seen as the least glamorous job, thus it was unattractive to the most able planners, who preferred to be involved in broad strategic planning. More recently, however, its importance has been recognized – see for example, J. B. McLoughlin, *Planning and Development Control*, London: Faber 1973. Currently it is perhaps the major planning function in these rather negative times.

23 See Davies, *Evangelistic Bureaucrat*, and Dennis, *Public Participation and Planning Blight*.

24 The largest of the new towns, the unnamed Central Lancashire New Town (CLNT), based on Leyland-Chorley and designated in 1970, has subsequently been considerably scaled down so that growth there will be far below that originally envisaged. See P. Levin, *Government and the Planning Process*, London: Allen & Unwin 1976, for an interesting

discuss⸱on of CLNT's origins and of the decision to expand Swindon.

25 See Hall *et al., Containment of Urban England*, vol. 2, pp. 329–59 and R. Thomas, *London's New Towns*, London: PEP Broadsheet 510, 1969 and his *Aycliffe to Cumbernauld*, London: PEP Broadsheet 516, 1959.
26 Hall *et al., Containment of Urban England*, vol. 2, p. 358.
27 ibid., p. 391.
28 ibid., p. 393.
29 ibid., p. 395.
30 See, for example, J. M. Lee, *Social Leaders and Public Persons*, Oxford: Clarendon Press, 1967 and J. M. Lee, *et al., The Scope for Local Initiative*, London: Martin Robertson, 1974, especially ch. 2, pp. 23–52.
31 Hall *et al., Containment of Urban England*, vol. 2, pp. 405–9.
32 ibid., p. 408.
33 Planning Advisory Group, *Future of Development Plans.*
34 Some of these criticisms are to be found in Davies, *Evangelistic Bureaucrat*; Dennis, *Public Participation and Planning Blight* and in the 'urban managerial' writings of Ray Pahl. See for example, R. A. Pahl, *Whose City*, Harmondsworth: Penguin, 1975. See also L. Alison, *Environmental Planning*, London: Allen & Unwin, 1974, which is also relevant as is Gans, *People and Plans* – a critique from within the American profession.
35 *Report of the Committee on Public Participation in Planning, People and Planning*, London: HMSO 1969.
36 P. Levin and D. Donnison, 'People and Planning', *Public Administration*, vol. 49, Winter 1969, pp 473–9.
37 See, for example, N. Boaden, *et al.*, 'Public Participation in Planning Within A Representative Local Democracy', *Policy and Politics*, vol. 7, no. 1, 1979, pp. 55–68.
38 The legislation also allows for Subject and Action Area plans, though these too have been less commonly employed by planning authorities.
39 M. Drake, *et al., Aspects of Structure Planning*, London: CES 1975.
40 ibid.
41 Cherry, *Evolution of British Town Planning*, p 192.
42 M. Hill, Appendix 2 on Implementation, *SSRC Panel Report on Central Local Government Relations*, London: SSRC 1979.
43 Much of what follows draws heavily on the author's work for the Department of the Environment on Public Participation in Planning. See, for example, N. Boaden, *et al.*, 'Public Participation and Planning Stringer, *Planning and Participation in Practice*, Oxford: Pergamon, forthcoming.
44 See Boaden *et al.*, 'Public Participation in Planning'.
45 For a discussion of this point see N. Boaden and N. Collins, *Consultation with Organisations in the Merseyside Structure Plan*, Interim Research Paper 6, Linked Research Project into Public Participation and Structure Planning, London: DOE 1975.

Chapter 8 Policy arena 3: social services

1 See, for example, M. Castells, *The Urban Question*, London: Edward Arnold 1977; and C. Cockburn, *The Local State*, London: Pluto 1977.

2 For a discussion of another service, see D. Regan, *Local Government and Education*, London: Allen & Unwin 1978.

3 D. Fraser, *The New Poor Law in the Nineteenth Century*, London: Macmillan 1977; and *The Evolution of the British Welfare State*, London: Macmillan 1978 provides an introduction to the subject.

4 See, for example, their *The Poor and the Poorest*, London: Bell 1965. Most recently, of course, Peter Townsend has published the results of his major study on poverty: P. Townsend, *Poverty in the United Kingdom*, Harmondsworth: Penguin 1979.

5 For a discussion see, for example, I. Gough, *The Political Economy of the Welfare State*, London: Macmillan 1979.

6 See, for example, the influential work by the geographer David Harvey and his *Social Justice and the City*, London: Edward Arnold 1973.

7 J. Locke, *Of Civil Government*; J. J. Rousseau, *The Social Contract and Discourses.*

8 J. Rawls, *A Theory of Justice*, Oxford: Clarendon Press, 1972.

9 ibid., pp. 302–3.

10 W. G. Runciman, *Relative Deprivation and Social Justice*, Harmondsworth: Penguin 1972.

11 ibid., p. 291.

12 ibid., p. 316.

13 Harvey, *Social Justice and the City.*

14 A. Weale, *Equality and Social Policy*, London: Routledge & Kegan Paul 1978.

15 K. Jones, J. Brown and J. Bradshaw, *Issues in Social Policy*, London: Routledge & Kegan Paul 1978, p. 8.

16 ibid., p. 10.

17 Interestingly, given the fact that education is the service that is the largest element in local authority budgets, there have been some suggestions that it be transferred to the centre.

18 I. Gough, *The Political Economy of the Welfare State*, London: Macmillan 1979, p. 2.

19 *Report of the* (Seebohm) *Committee on Local Authority and Allied Personal Social Services*, Cmnd 3703, London: HMSO 1968.

20 P. Hall, *Reforming the Welfare*, London: Heinemann 1976, shows that the number of elderly rose by 30 per cent overall between 1951 and 1971, rising from 13.6 to 16 per cent of the total population. This section draws heavily on her excellent study of the reforms associated with Seebohm.

21 ibid., pp. 8–9.

22 Space prohibits a fuller discussion of these issues: see R. Holman, *Poverty: Explanations of Deprivation*, London: Martin Robertson 1978.

23 See the *Report of the Committee on Social Workers in the Local Authority Health and Welfare Services* (Younghusband Committee Report), London: HMSO 1959, p. 123 for an example of such a claim.
24 Hall, *Reforming the Welfare*, p. 19.
25 Particularly in 1965; see ibid., pp. 22–3.
26 Critics, however, point to the difficulties ordinary members of the public have in proving incompetence or unethical behaviour on the part of some of these professions and their tendency to close ranks in the face of criticism of their professionalism.
27 Quite clearly, this discretion also has financial implications. Taking a child into care on the recommendation of a social worker may add £60 a week to a local authority budget. For a discussion see T. A. Booth, *Planning for Welfare*, Oxford: Martin Robertson 1979, especially Howard Glennerster's contribution, pp. 3–22.
28 See CDP, *Gilding the Ghetto*, London: Home Office 1977.
29 R. Batley and J. Edwards, *The Politics of Positive Discrimination*, London: Routledge & Kegan Paul 1978.
30 See *Gilding the Ghetto*, p. 63.
31 Jones *et al., Issues in Social Policy*, p. 70.
32 K. Newton, *Second City Politics*, Oxford: Clarendon Press 1978, p. 66.
33 Gough, *Political Economy of the Welfare State.*

Chapter 9   Policy consequences and policy solutions

1 F. S. Levy, A. J. Meltsner and A. Wildavsky, *Urban Outcomes: Schools, Streets and Libraries*, Berkeley: University of California Press 1974.
2 For a review see R. Rich, 'Neglected issues in the study of urban service distributions: a research agenda', *Urban Studies*, vol. 16, no. 2 (1979), pp. 143–56.
3 B. D. Jones, 'Distributional considerations in models of government service provision', *Urban Affairs Quarterly*, vol. 12, no. 3 (March 1977), pp. 219–312. See also G. Antunes and K. Mladenka, 'The politics of local services and service distribution', in L. Masotti and R. Lineberry (eds.), *The New Urban Politics*, Cambridge, Mass: Ballinger 1976.'
4 See, for example the work of Alan Burnett (Portsmouth Polytechnic) on Portsmouth and his paper to the SSRC seminar on Urban Political Geography, Warwick University, September 1979.
5 See, for example N. Boaden, *Urban Policy Making*, London: Cambridge University Press 1971; B. Davies, *Social Needs and Resources in Local Services*, London: Michael Joseph 1968; J. Danziger, *Making Budgets*, London: Sage 1979; J. A. Alt, *Politics and Expenditure Models* and the review by K. Newton and L. J. Sharpe, 'Local outputs research: some reflections and proposals', *Policy and Politics*, vol. 5, no. 3 (March 1977), pp. 61–92. For an American summary and review, see B. Hawkins, *Urban Politics and Policies*, New York: Bobbs Merrill 1972.

6   See, for example R. J. Nicholson and N. Topham, 'The determinants of investment in housing by local authorities', *Journal of the Royal Statistical Society*, Series A, vol. 134, no. 3 (1971), pp. 273–303; and 'Urban road provision in England and Wales', *Policy and Politics*, vol. 4 (1976), pp. 3–29.

7   J. Dearlove, *The Politics of Policy in Local Government*, London: Cambridge University Press 1973, pp. 61–9.

8   Newton and Sharpe, 'Local outputs research', p. 79.

9   An interesting example of this point has been made in conversation by a number of planners over the location of sports or leisure centres. The argument is that such facilities should be located in deprived areas since this will first encourage the participation of the local residents in new leisure activities (e.g. squash) and second will attract (middle-class) residents from other areas who want to make use of the new facilities and will spend money to do so *and in* the deprived area. This kind of positive discrimination is thus theoretically seen as having both direct and indirect benefits. This author awaits the empirical proof!

10   See, for example, I. Gordon, 'Subjective social indications and urban political analysis', *Policy and Politics*, vol. 5, no. 3 (March 1977), pp. 93–112; and the special issue of the journal edited by T. N. Clark, *Citizen Preferences and Urban Public Policy*, Sage Contemporary Social Science Issues, vol. 34, London: Sage 1978.

11   See, for example, the results of a survey undertaken in north-east Lancashire authorities reported in P. Stringer, 'Tuning into the public', *D.O.E. Linked Research Project into Public Participation in Structure Planning*, interim Research Paper no. 14 Sheffield, 1978, especially pp. 17–25.

12   For a critical discussion, see P. J. O. Self, *Econocrats and the Policy Process*, London: Macmillan 1975.

13   K. Young, 'Environmental management and local politics', in D. Kavanagh and R. Rose, *New Trends in British Politics*, London: Sage 1977.

14   See, for example, R. A. W. Rhodes, 'Research into central-local relations in Britain: a framework for analysis', SSRC *Central–Local Government Relationships: a Report*, London: SSRC 1979, Appendix 2; K. Hanf and F. W. Scharpf, *Inter-organisational Policy Making: Limits to Coordination and Central Control*, Sage Modern Politics Series, vol. 1, London: Sage 1978; and M. Crozier and J. C. Thoenig, 'The regulation of complex organised systems', *Administrative Science Quarterly*, vol. 2 (1976), pp. 547–70.

15   For a discussion of this point see M. Goldsmith, 'England: the changing system', in J. Lagroye and V. Wright (eds.), *Local Government in Britain and France*, London: Allen & Unwin 1979, pp. 10–27.

16   For some of this literature, see O. A. Hartley, 'The relationship between central and local authorities', *Public Administration*, vol. 49

(1971), pp. 439–56; N. Boaden, *Urban Policy Making*, London: Cambridge University Press 1971, especially chs. 1 and 2; N. Boaden, 'Central departments and local authorities: the relationship examined', *Political Studies*, vol. 28 (1970), pp. 175–86. The classic study remains J. A. G. Griffith, *Central Departments and Local Authorities*, London: Allen & Unwin 1966.

17 There are dangers here of falling into what might be called the efficiency trap. Having changed the system, ostensibly to make it more efficient, the proponents of efficiency might argue for a change in the *type* of person making the decisions. For an excellent discussion of this view see J. Dearlove, *The Reorganisation of British Local Government*, Cambridge: University Press 1979.

18 See Goldsmith, 'England: the Changing System', pp. 18–19, for a discussion of this point.

19 The energy and transport fields perhaps provide some of the best examples of the current complexity of decision-making that faces central and local government, as well as demonstrating some of the inadequacies of such decisions. See, for example, J. Tyme, *Motorways against Democracy*, London: Macmillan 1978; and R. Gregory, *The Price of Amenity*, London: Macmillan 1971.

20 R. Miliband, *The State in Capitalist Society*, London: Weidenfeld & Nicolson 1969.

21 For an example of this point, see R. Darke, 'Public participation and state power: the case of South Yorkshire', *Policy and Politics*, vol. 7, no. 4 (October 1979).

Further reading

These notes on further reading are designed to introduce students to the labyrinth of the literature on urban studies, much of which is rapidly assuming an inter- or multi-disciplinary nature. It is designed to highlight major references related to the themes discussed in the book, particularly the literature drawn from political science. As introductions to that literature, students would do well to read John Gyford's useful text, *Local Politics in Britain* (Croom Helm 1976); Jeff Stanyer, *Understanding Local Government* (Fontana 1976); and Ken Newton, *Second City Politics* (Oxford University Press 1976), while R. L. Lineberry and I. Sharkansky (eds.), *Urban Politics and Public Policy*, 3rd ed. (Harper & Row 1978), provides an introduction to the American literature and the subject. At a somewhat higher level, students will find interesting Peter Saunders, *Urban Politics: a Sociological Interpretation* (Hutchinson 1979), and John Dearlove, *The Politics of Policy in Local Government* (Cambridge University Press 1973), and *The Reorganisation of British Local Government* (Cambridge University Press 1979). Hawley *et al.*, *Theoretical Perspectives on Urban Policy* (Prentice-Hall 1976), brings some new ideas to the American scene.

Few references are made to journal articles in these notes, though their importance cannot be overestimated. Such journals as *Policy and Politics, Public Administration, Public Administration Bulletin, Political Studies, International Journal of Urban and Regional Research, Local Government Studies* and *British Journal of Political Science* and *Urban Studies* frequently contain articles of relevance, as do the main sociology, geography, economics and planning journals. The *American Political Science Review* and the regional American political science journals, *Public Administration Review, The Public Interest*, the various policy journals and *Urban Affairs Quarterly* are all useful journals, as are the twice-yearly *Urban Affairs Annual Reviews* published by Sage.

Chapter 1:   Political theory, political practice and public policy in the city

Useful books which touch on similar issues to those raised in this chapter include Harvey Cox's *Cities: The Public Dimension* (Penguin 1976), and Murray Stewart's edited collection: *The City* (Penguin 1973). From an

American perspective, Edward Banfield, *The Unheavenly City Revisited* (Little, Brown 1974) asks some awkward questions, while Anthony Downs, *Opening up the Suburbs* (Yale 1973) has an alternative view; Peter Hall, *The World's Cities* (Weidenfeld & Nicolson 1978), Brian Berry, *The Human Consequences of Urbanisation* (Macmillan 1973), and T. H. Elkins, *The Urban Explosion* (Macmillan 1973), all provide background material.

The most useful literature on democracy and local government includes D. Hill, *Democratic Theory and Local Government* (Allen & Unwin 1973), together with the section of articles in L. Feldman and M. Goldrick (eds.), *Politics and Government of Urban Canada,* 3rd ed. (Methuen 1979). Mill's original statements are to be found in his essay, *Representative Government* (Oxford University Press 1975), and much of the debate is usefully examined in C. Pateman, *Participation and Democratic Theory* (Cambridge University Press 1970). An empirically based study covering this topic is Bill Hampton's *Democracy and Community* (Oxford University Press 1970).

Models designed to explain city politics are discussed more fully under Chapter 2. A good introduction to the elitest–pluralist debate is to be found in G. Parry, *Political Elites* (Allen & Unwin 1969), while the Marxist perspective is usefully summarized by Peter Saunders in *Urban Politics: A Sociological Interpretation* (Hutchinson 1979).

The literature on public policy is developing fast. Useful introductions include T. Dye, *Understanding Public Policy,* 2nd ed. (Prentice-Hall 1975); R. Hofferbert, *The Study of Public Policy* (Bobbs Merrill 1975); A. Ranney (ed.), *Political Science and Public Policy* (Markham 1968); and J. Anderson, *Public Policymaking* (Nelson 1975). Important contributions from Britain include W. Jenkins, *Policy Analysis* (Martin Robertson 1978); R. Rose (ed.), *The Dynamics of Public Policy* (Sage 1976); P. Hall, H. Land, R. Parker, A. Webb, *Change, Choice and Conflict in Social Policy* (Heinemann 1975); and B. Smith, *Policy Making in British Government* (Martin Robertson 1976). Some of the normative issues involved in policy studies are examined in M. Rein, *Social Science and Public Policy* (Penguin 1976), and M. Bulmer (ed.), *Social Policy Research* (Macmillan 1978). J. V. May and A. Wildavsky (eds.), *The Policy Cycle* (Sage 1978) provides a useful collection taking an overview of the policy process. The question of policy implementation is examined in J. L. Pressman and A. Wildavsky: *Implementation* (University of California Press 1973), and E. Bardach, *The Implementation Game* (MIT Press 1977), while an interesting British contribution is Michael Hill, *Implementation,* Appendix 2 (SSRC Report of the Panel on Central–Local Government Relations, SSRC 1979). J. Levy, A. Meltsner and A. Wildavsky, *Urban Outcomes* (University of California Press 1974) is an enthralling empirical attempt at policy analysis and evaluation.

Chapter 2: Analysing city politics

On the general state of the study of urban politics in Britain, see K. Young,

Essays in the Study of Urban Politics (Macmillan 1975), which is an accurate reflection at that time, as is the special issue of *Policy and Politics*, March 1977. A useful collection of articles covering the general state of the art is W. D. Hawley, *et al., Theoretical Perspectives on Urban Politics* (Prentice-Hall 1976).

Though there is no clear statement of the institutional model *per se*, many of its central concerns remain the focus of much of political science and of traditional writers on the subject of local government. P. G. Richards, *The Reformed Local Government System* (Allen & Unwin 1975), is a good example of this tradition, while J. Stanyer, *Understanding Local Government* (Fontana 1976), has a useful second chapter. More recently, R. A. W. Rhodes has been developing the use of organization theory in the study of local government and politics, particularly on the subject of central–local government relations: his Appendix to the SSRC *Panel Report on Central–Local Government Relations* (SSRC 1979), is particularly relevant.

The community power model literature is vast. Students will still find it useful to consult some of the original materials: F. Hunter, *Community Power Structure* (University of North Carolina Press 1953); R. A. Dahl, *Who Governs?* (Yale 1961), and N. Polsby, *Community Power and Political Theory* (Yale 1963). Useful readers on the subject include C. M. Bonjean *et al., Community Politics* (Free Press 1971), and W. D. Hawley and F. M. Wirt (eds.), *The Search for Community Power* (Prentice-Hall 1968). On decisions and non-decisions particularly, see P. Bachrach and M. S. Baratz: *Power and Poverty* (Oxford University Press 1970), as well as M. Crenson, *The Unpolitics of Air Pollution* (Johns Hopkins University Press 1971). For a British perspective, P. Saunders, *Urban Politics: a Sociological Interpretation* (Hutchinson 1979) is most important, as is S. Lukes, *Power: a Radical View* (Macmillan 1974), together with K. Newton, 'Democracy, community power and non-decision making', *Political Studies*, vol. 20, no. 4 (1972).

Systems analysis and its application to politics is best examined at its source: D. Easton, *A Framework for Political Analysis* (Prentice-Hall 1965), and *A Systems Analysis of Political Life* (Wiley 1965). For its application to American urban politics, see R. L. Lineberry and I. Sharkansky, *Urban Politics and Public Policy*, 3rd ed. (Harper & Row 1977) and D. R. Morgan and S. Fitzpatrick, *Urban Political Analysis* (Free Press 1972). For British applications, with variations, see J. Stanyer, *Understanding Local Government* (Fontana 1976), and N. Boaden, *Urban Policy Making* (Cambridge University Press 1971).

The managerial thesis is most succinctly stated in Pahl's paper in D. T. Herbert and D. M. Smith, *Social Problems and the City* (Oxford University Press 1979) and in his *Whose City?* (Penguin 1975). M. Harloe (ed.), *Captive Cities* (Wiley 1977), has useful contributions. In political science, see J. Dearlove, *The Politics of Policy in English Local Government* (Cambridge University Press 1973), as well as K. Young, and J. Kramer, *Strategy and Conflict in Metropolitan Housing* (Heinemann 1978). Boaden, *Urban Policy*

Making, is also relevant. Empirical studies involving the thesis also include
P. Norman, 'Managerialism: a review of recent work', in M. Harloe (ed.),
Proceedings of Conference of Urban Change and Conflict (CES 1975); P.
Williams, 'The role of institutions in the inner London housing market',
Transactions of the Institute of British Geographers (n.s.) vol. 1 (1976), as well
as J. G. Davies, *The Evangelistic Bureaucrat* (Tavistock 1972); N. Dennis,
Public Participation and Planning Blight (Faber 1972), and J. Lambert *et al.,*
Housing Policy and the State (Macmillan 1978).

Marxist writings abound. They are most usefully reviewed by P. Saunders,
Urban Politics. Important landmarks include M. Castells, *The Urban*
Question (Edward Arnold 1975), and his *City, Class and Power* (Macmillan
1979); C. Cockburn, *The Local State* (Pluto 1976), and C. Pickvance, *Urban*
Sociology: Critical Essays (Tavistock 1976). Harloe's introduction to the
Captive Cities volume is an important review, and a journal which frequently
examines issues from a Marxist perspective is the *International Journal of*
Urban and Regional Research: see especially the first issue in 1977. Useful
contributions are to be found in L. N. Lindberg *et al., Stress and*
Contradiction in Modern Capitalism (Lexington Books 1975) as well as C.
Crouch, *State and Economy in Contemporary Capitalism* (St Martin's 1979)
and J. Holloway and S. Picciotto: *State and Capital* (Edward Arnold 1978).

Chapter 3: Environmental change and the city

Much of the discussion in this chapter draws on an examination of official
government data in the form of population and production censuses as well
as such publications as *Social Trends* and *Economic Trends*, published
annually by HMSO.

P. Hall *et al., The Containment of Urban England* (Allen & Unwin 1973),
together with his *Urban and Regional Planning* (Penguin 1974), and his work
with Marion Clawson, *Planning and Urban Growth* (RFF/Johns Hopkins
1973), are good secondary sources of areal change and some aspects of
regional policy. They are well supplemented by Champion's article,
'Evolving patterns of population distribution in England and Wales,
1951-71', in *Transactions of the Institute of British Geographers* (n.s.), vol. 1,
no. 4 (1976).

The section on industrial and economic changes can be expanded by a
reading of A. R. Prest and D. J. Coppock (eds.), *The U.K. Economy: A*
Manual of Applied Economics (Wiedenfeld & Nicholson 1976). T. A.
Broadbent, *Planning and Profit in the Urban Economy* (Methuen 1977), is also
generally useful and, with reference to regional policy, Hall, *Urban and*
Regional Planning, is also a good introduction. Gavin McCrone, *Regional*
Policy in Britain (Allen & Unwin 1971), is a useful historical review to that
point. G. C. Cameron and L. Wingo (eds.), *Cities, Regions and Public Policy*

(RFF/Oliver and Boyd 1973), is also helpful. More critically, see S. A. Holland, *The Regional Problem* (Macmillan 1976).

For the Urban Programme and Inner Cities work see J. Edwards and J. R. Batley, *The Politics of Positive Discrimination* (Tavistock 1978); D. A. McKay and A. W. Cox, *The Politics of Urban Change* (Croom Helm 1979), as well as A. M. Cox, 'Administrative inertia and inner city policy', *Public Administration Bulletin*, no. 29 (1979). Important also are CPRS, *A joint framework for social policies* (HMSO 1975); *The Inner Area Studies: Consultants' Final Reports* (HMSO 1976), and Cmnd 6845, *Policy for the Inner Cities* (HMSO 1977). For a radical critique of much of this urban aid programme, see particularly: CDP, *The Costs of Industrial Change*, *Profits Against Housing*, and *Gilding the Ghetto* (Home Office 1977).

Social change and social structure are well dealt with by the annual report on *Social Trends* (HMSO). See also A. H. Halsey, *Change in British Society* (Oxford University Press 1978); J. Westergaard and H. Resler: *Class in a capitalist society* (Penguin 1976); A. John, *The Social Structure of Modern Britain*, rev. ed. (Pergamon 1979). E. Butterworth and D. Weir (eds.), *Social Problems of Modern Britain* (Fontana 1972), is a useful introduction to some of the issues discussed. On changing leisure patterns, see K. Roberts, *Contemporary Society and the Growth of Leisure* (Longman 1979); on poverty, see P. Townsend, *Poverty in the UK* (Penguin 1979); and on race, see R. Miles and A. Phizacklea, *Racism and Political Action in Britain* (Routledge & Kegan Paul 1979).

The ungovernability thesis is discussed essentially in T. Nairn, *The Break Up of Britain* (New Left Books 1975); A. King, 'Overload: problems of governing in the seventies', *Political Studies*, vol. 23 (1975), and his edited book, *Why is Britain becoming harder to govern?* (BBC 1976), and R. Rose, 'Ungovernability: is there a fire behind the smoke?', *Political Studies*, vol. 27 (1979). A. H. Birch, *Political Integration and Disintegration in the British Isles* (Allen & Unwin 1977), is also relevant.

Chapter 4   The reactions of the political community

The literature on participation is vast and something of a dangerous morass. L. Milbrath, *Political Participation* (Rand McNally 1965), remains a basic text, while some of the ideas outlined here are developed in N. Boaden, M. Goldsmith, W. Hampton and P. Stringer, *Public Participation and Planning in Practice* (Pergamon 1980). R. Darke and R. Walker, *Local Government and Public Participation* (Leonard Hill 1977), is also useful. One of the best texts on political socialization is R. E. Dawson and K. Prewitt, *Political Socialisation*, 2nd ed. (Little, Brown 1977), but D. Marsh's article, 'Political socialisation: the implicit assumptions questioned', *British Journal of Political Science,* vol. 1, no. 4 (1971), remains an excellent reminder of the difficulties with the concept.

On local elections, see L. J. Sharpe (ed.), *Voting in Cities* (Macmillan

1967); K. Newton, *Second City Politics* (Oxford University Press 1976), ch. 2; W. A. Hampton, *Democracy and Community* (Oxford University Press 1970), chs. 7, 8; and S. Bristow, 'Local politics after reorganisation', *Public Administration Bulletin*, no. 28 (December 1978). On turnout and marginality, see K. Newton, 'Turnout and marginality in local elections', *British Journal of Political Science*, vol. 2, no. 2 (1972); B. Pimlott, 'Local party organisation, turnout and marginality', *British Journal of Political Science*, vol. 3, no. 2 (1973); W. B. Grant, 'Size of place and labour strength', *British Journal of Political Science*, vol. 2, no. 2 (1972).

Organized groups are most extensively examined by K. Newton, *Second City Politics*, chs. 3 and 4; and J. Dearlove, *The Politics of Policy in English Local Government* (Cambridge University Press 1973), while W. A. Hampton, *Democracy and Community* ch. 9, and M. Stacey, *et al., Power, Persistence and Change* (Routledge & Kegan Paul 1975), ch. 4, contain local case discussions. Betty Zisk, *Local Interest Politics: One Way Street* (Bobbs Merrill 1973), provides a useful American contrast.

The literature on local political parties and urban politics remains scant. J. Bulpitt, *Party Politics in English Local Government* (Longman 1967), remains the pioneering work. K. Newton, *Second City Politics*, ch. 5; W. A. Hampton, *Democracy and Community*, ch. 9; and M. Stacey *et al., Power, Persistence and Change*, ch. 4, have useful case study material. J. Gyford, *Local Politics in Britain* (Croom Helm 1976), ch. 3, covers most of the available literature up to that point.

On the role of the media, D. Murphy, *The Silent Watchdog* (Constable 1976), remains one of the best studies, with H. Cox and D. Morgan, *City Politics and the Press* (Cambridge University Press 1974) not far behind. Ian Jackson, *The Provincial Press and the Community* (Manchester University Press 1972), is an earlier useful contribution.

Chapter 5:   The regime and the authorities

There is not a great deal of literature on the relationship between decisions made in the private sector with those in the public sector as far as urban politics is concerned, though D. Fraser, *Urban Politics in Victorian England* (Leicester University Press 1976); and H. J. Dyos and M. Wolff, *Victorian City* (Edward Arnold 1971), have useful chapters on the nineteenth century. One recent publication which does get near to the issues involved is CDP, *The Costs of Industrial Change* (1977).

On local government reform, B. Wood, *The Process of Local Government Reform, 1966–74* (Allen & Unwin 1976); J. Brand, *Local Government Reform in England* (Croom Helm 1974), and J. Dearlove, *The Reorganisation of British Local Government* (Cambridge University Press 1979), are all essential, while the London case is examined by F. Smallwood, *Greater London: the politics of metropolitan reform* (Bobbs Merrill 1965), and G.

Rhodes, *The Government of London: the Struggle for Reform* (Weidenfeld & Nicolson 1970).

On local government finance and central–local relations, see SSRC Panel Report, *Central–Local Government Relations* (SSRC 1979); *Report of the (Layfield) Committee of Enquiry into Local Government Finance* (HMSO 1976), especially Appendix 6; while J. A. G. Griffiths, *Central Departments and Local Authorities* (Allen & Unwin 1966), remains the major empirical study. CPRS, *Relations between Central Government and Local Authorities* (HMSO 1977), is also useful. N. Boaden, *Urban Policy Making* (Cambridge University Press 1971), attempts to measure statistically the effect of central control over local authorities. N. Hepworth, *The Finance of Local Government* (Allen & Unwin 1971), is the basic text on local government finance, while G. W. Jones, 'Local government finance in Great Britain', in J. Lagroye and V. Wright, *Local Government in England and France* (Allen & Unwin 1979), provides a useful summary of the major elements.

The distinction between decisions and non-decisions was first made by P. Bachrach and M. S. Baratz. Their *Power and Poverty* (Oxford University Press 1970) is most useful, as is M. Crenson, *The Unpolitics of Air Pollution* (Johns Hopkins University Press 1971), though for a counter-view, see Charles O. Jones, *Clean Air* (Pittsburgh 1975). Important articles include R. Wolfinger, 'On issues and non-issues in the Study of Power', and the comment by Fred Frey, in *American Political Science Review*, vol. 65 (1971); G. Parry and P. Morriss, 'When is a decision not a decision?', in I. Crewe, (ed.), *British Political Sociology Yearbook*, vol. 1 (1974), and N. Polsby, 'Empirical investigations of the mobilisation of bias in community power research', together with Newton's comment and Polsby's reply, in *Political Studies*, vol. 27, no. 4 (1979). P. Saunders, *Urban Politics* (Hutchinson 1979) is also relevant.

The literature on councillors is growing rapidly, a reflection of interest in the subject of local political leadership and its selection. J. Gyford, *Local Politics in Britain*, (Croom Helm 1976) ch. 2, and K. Newton, *Second City Politics* (Oxford University Press 1976), ch. 6, are useful. G. W. Jones, *Borough Politics* (Macmillan 1969), and J. M. Lee, *Social Leaders and Public Persons* (Oxford University Press 1963), demonstrate the changing nature of political leaders, while G. W. Jones and A. Norton, *Political Leaders in Local Authorities* (INLOGOV 1979), has some interesting portraits of some local leaders. J. Dearlove, *The Politics of Policy in English Local Government* (Cambridge University Press 1973), is important on councillor role perceptions and their job socialization, while W. Grant, *Independent Local Politics in England and Wales* (Saxon House 1977), documents the decline of independent councils and councillors. Two recent articles of relevance are I. Gordon, 'The recruitment of local politicians', *Policy and Politics*, vol. 7, no. 1 (1979), and C. A. Collins, 'Considerations on the social background and motivation of councillors', *Policy and Politics*, vol. 6, no. 4 (1978).

On paid officials, K. Newton, *Second City Politics*, ch. 7, is a good counter to the claims made here on officer power. For that view see R. Pahl, *Whose City?* (Penguin 1975), and M. Harloe, *Captive City* (John Wiley 1977), as well as J. G. Davies, *The Evangelistic Bureaucrat* (Tavistock 1972), and N. Dennis, *Public Participation and Planning Blight* (Faber 1972). C. A. Collins, R. R. Hinings and K. Walsh, 'The officer and the councillor in local government', *Public Administration Bulletin*, no. 28 (1978), is a useful article. On the post reorganization internal reforms, see R. Hambleton, *Policy Planning and Local Government* (Hutchinson 1978); the Bains Committee Report, *The New Local Authorities: Management and Structure* (HMSO 1972); J. Dearlove, *The Reorganisation of English Local Government*, especially part 2.

Chapter 6: Housing

Useful introductions to the study of housing in Britain are to be found in D. Donnison, *The Government of Housing* (Penguin 1967), and moıe recently J. B. Cullingworth, *Essays on Housing Policy* (Allen & Unwin 1979). A basic text, utilizing the idea of housing markets, is A. Murie *et al., Housing Policy and the Housing System* (Allen & Unwin 1977), while J. Lambert *et al., Housing Policy and the State* (Macmillan 1978) explicitly explores the ideas of access and allocation. These are implicitly examined in J. Rex and R. Moore, *Race, Community and Conflict* (Oxford University Press 1967), and in M. Harloe, *et al., The Organisation of Housing* (Heinemann 1974).

The development of council housing is well discussed in S. Merrett, *The State and Housing* (Routledge & Kegan Paul 1979), whereas the National CDP, *Whatever Happened to Council Housing?*, and the Conference of Socialist Economists, *Political Economy and the Housing Question* (CSE 1975), look at the subject from a critical perspective. S. Lansley, *Housing and the Public Policy* (Croom Helm 1979), provides another useful recent overview. Housing improvement is discussed by J. T. Roberts, *General Improvement Areas* (Saxon House 1976), and by P. Williams, 'The role of institutions in the inner London housing market', *Transactions of the Institute of British Geographers* (n.s.), vol. 1 (1976), and C. Hamnett, 'Improvement grants as an indicator of gentrification in inner London, *AREA*, vol. 5, no. 3 (1973). Useful sections are to be found in Lansley, *Housing and the Public Policy* and Merrett, *The State and Housing*.

The role of particular housing institutions, such as building societies and estate agents, is discussed in Harloe, *The Organisation of Housing*, and J. Ford, 'The role of the building society manager in the urban system', *Urban Studies*, vol. 12 (1975), and by P. Williams, 'Building Societies and the Inner City', *Transactions of the Institute of British Geographers* (n.s.), vol. 3 (1978).

On homelessness, see R. Bailey, *The Squatters* (Penguin 1973) and *The Homeless and the Empty Houses* (Penguin 1977); while N. Wates, *The Battle for Tolmers Square* (Routledge & Kegan Paul 1977), provides some graphic illustrations of their problems. The problem of the ratepayers revolt is discussed in W. I. Grant, *Independent Local Politics in England and Wales* (Saxon House 1977), and their strength well demonstrated by P. Saunders, *Urban Politics* (Hutchinson 1979).

Questions about housing finance are covered in A. Nevitt, *Housing, Taxation and Subsidies* (Nelson 1966); Murie *et al., Housing Policy and the Housing System*, as well as in Lansley, and Merrett, *The State and Housing*. They are also examined in National CDP, *Profits Against Housing* (CDP 1976), and in S. Duncan, 'The housing question and the structure of the housing market', *Journal of Social Policy*, vol. 6 (1977). The way in which some of the conflicts over housing were resolved in one London borough is well researched by K. Young and J. Kramer, *Strategy and Conflict in Metropolitan Housing* (Heinemann 1977).

Chapter 7: Planning

The major source of planning in post-war Britain remains P. Hall *et al., The Containment of Urban England*, 2 vols. (PEP/Allen & Unwin 1973). Abbreviated versions of the material can be found in his *Urban and Regional Planning* (Penguin 1975), and M. Clawson and P. Hall, *Regional Planning in Britain and America* (RFF 1973). Also useful is D. McKay, and A. Cox, *The Politics of Urban Change* (Croom Helm 1979). On planning history, theory and planning ideology, see W. Ashworth, *The Genesis of Modern British Town Planning* (Routledge & Kegan Paul 1954); G. Cherry, *The Evolution of British Town Planning* (Leonard Hill 1974); D. Eversley, *The Planner in Society* (Faber 1973); P. Cowan (ed.), *The Future of Planning* (Heinemann 1973); A. Faludi, *Planning Theory*, and *Reader in Planning Theory* (Pergamon 1973); J. G. Davies, *The Evangelistic Bureaucrat* (Tavistock 1972); N. Dennis, *Public Participation and Planning Blight* (Faber 1972); M. Bruton, *The Spirit and Purpose of Planning* (Hutchinson, 1973); and Royal Town Planning Institute, *The Future of Planning* (1977). On city redevelopment and the property boom, much can be learnt from such case studies as O. Marriott, *The Property Boom* (Hamish Hamilton 1968); S. Elkin, *Politics and Land Use Planning* (Cambridge University Press 1973); P. Ambrose and B. Colenutt: *The Property Machine* (Penguin 1976), and N. Wates, *The Battle for Tolmers Square* (Routledge & Kegan Paul 1976). John Ratcliffe's *Land Policy* (Hutchinson 1976) provides a planners' perspective, while T. A. Broadbent's *Planning and Profit in the Urban Economy* (Methuen 1977) provides an economist's view on the overall planning system. New Towns policy is well discussed in Hall, *Containment*, and interesting case studies are provided by M. Harloe, *Swindon, a Town in Transition* (Heinemann 1975), and P. Levin, *Government and the Planning Process* (Allen & Unwin 1976). Public participation and planning is well covered by Skeffington, Report of the Committee on Public Participation, in *Planning, People and Planning*

(HMSO 1969); J. M. Simmie, *Citizens in Conflict* (Hutchinson 1974); A. Thornley, *Theoretical Perspectives on Planning, Participation* Progress in Planning series (Pergamon 1976); R. Darke and R. Walker, *Local Government and the Public* (Leonard Hill 1977), as well as N. Boaden *et al., Public Participation and Planning in Practice* (Pergamon 1980). On current problems in planning, see, among others, M. Drake *et al., Aspects of Structure Planning* (CES 1976), *Planning Newspaper*, and such journals as the *Town Planning Review, Progress in Planning* and *Regional Studies.*

Chapter 8: Social services

On the development of the welfare state see D. Fraser, *The New Poor Law in the Nineteenth Century* (Macmillan 1972), and his *The Evolution of the British Welfare State* (Macmillan 1973). Penelope Hall's *The Social Services of Modern England* (Routledge & Kegan Paul 1975) provides an excellent introduction to present day social services, while the York *Yearbook of Social Policy* (Routledge & Kegan Paul) is a useful annual review.

The question of poverty is well covered by R. Holman, *Poverty* (Martin Robertson 1978), but see also Peter Townsend and Brian Abel-Smith, *The Poor and the Poorest* (Bell 1965), and Townsend's major study, *Poverty in the United Kingdom* (Penguin 1979). Other works of interest include CDP, *Gilding the Ghetto* (CDP 1977); and P. Marris and M. Rein, *Dilemmas of Social Reform*, 2nd ed. (Pelican 1974), which has useful US comparisons.

Interesting work on social justice, equality, universality and selectivity includes J. Rawles, *A Theory of Justice* (Clarendon Press 1972); W. G. Runciman, *Relative Deprivation and Social Justice* (Penguin 1972); A. Weale, *Equality and Social Policy* (Routledge & Kegan Paul 1978); D. Harvey, *Social Justice and the City* (Edward Arnold 1973). The work of Richard Titmuss is also crucial; see, for example, *Essays on the Welfare State* (Allen & Unwin 1958). These issues are usefully summarized in K. Jones, J. Brown and J. Bradshaw, *Issues in Social Policy* (Routledge & Kegan Paul 1978).

The Seebohm Report and the subsequent reform of the personal social services are well covered by Phoebe Hall's *Reforming the Welfare* (Heinemann 1968), on which this section draws heavily, though Seebohm *(Report of the Committee on Local Authority and Allied Social Services)* is obviously important reading itself. Problems of planning in/for social services are tackled by K. Judge, *Rationing Social Services* (Heinemann 1978); H. Glennester, *Social Service Budgets and Social Policy* (Allen & Unwin 1975); and T. A. Booth (ed.), *Planning for Welfare* (Blackwell 1979).

Professionalism in social work and professionalism generally is discussed in P. Elliott, *The Sociology of the Professions* (Macmillan 1972), and P. Halmos, *The Faith of the Counsellors* (Constable 1965). Michael Hill, *The State, Administration and the Individual* (Fontana 1976), is useful introductory material. P. Halmos, 'Professionalisation and Social Change', *Sociological Review Monograph*, no. 20 (1973), is also helpful.

Multiple deprivation and community development has generated a vast literature. Runciman, *Relative Deprivation and Social Justice*; CDP, *Gilding the Ghetto*; Holman, *Poverty*, are all relevant, as is Marris and Rein, *Dilemmas of Social Reform*. The British community development programme is well analysed by J. Edwards and R. Batley, *The Politics of Positive Discrimination* (Routledge & Kegan Paul 1978), and in the various CDP publications themselves.

The voluntary sector is discussed in Jones *et al., Issues in Social Policy*, ch. 5, and by the Aves Report, *The Voluntary Worker in the Social Services* (Allen & Unwin 1969), and the Report of the Wolfenden Committee, *The Future of Voluntary Organisations* (Croom Helm 1977).

The 'crisis of the welfare state' has produced a number of authors, one of the most provocative being I. Gough, *The Political Economy of the Welfare State* (Macmillan 1979).

Chapter 9:   Policy consequences and policy solutions

Some of the suggested reading for Chapter 1 is also relevant here, such as T. Dye, *Understanding Public Policy* (Prentice Hall 1975); R. Hofferbert, *The Study of Public Policy* (Merrill 1975); J. Anderson, *Public Policy Making* (Nelson 1975); W. Jenkins, *Policy Analysis* (Robertson 1978); J. May and A. Wildavsky, *The Policy Cycle* (Sage 1978); J. Pressman and A. Wildavsky, *Implementation* (California 1973); E. Bardach, *The Implementation Game* (MIT Press 1977); M. Hill, *Implementation* (SSRC 1979); and J. Levy, A. Meltsner and A. Wildavsky, *Urban Outcomes* (California 1974).

On the distribution consequences of urban policy, see R. L. Lineberry, *Equality and Public Policy* (Sage 1977); R. L. Lineberry (ed.), *The Politics and Economics of Public Services* (Sage 1978). R. L. Lineberry and L. H. Masotti (eds.), *The New Urban Politics* (Ballinger 1976), has some useful contributions.

Geographers have made a number of interesting contributions; see, for example, D. Harvey, *Social Justice and the City* (Edward Arnold 1973), and K. R. Cox, *Urbanisation and Conflict in Market Societies* (Methuen 1978), while in Britain, S. Pinch, 'Local authority provision for the elderly', in D. T. Herbert, and D. M. Smith (eds.), *Social Problems and the City: geographical perspectives* (Oxford University Press 1979), and his 'Patterns of local authority housing allocation in greater London', *Transactions of the Institute of British Geographers* (n.s.), vol. 3 (1978), and A. Burnett, *Political Demands and Public Services* (IBG Urban Geography Study Group 1978), are examples. The work of R. C. Rich, *Urban Studies*, vol. 16 (1979), and in Lineberry, *Politics and Economics*, repays attention.

But the main studies of outputs in Britain still remain N. Boaden, *Urban Policymaking* (Cambridge University Press 1971); B. Davies, *Social Needs and Resources in Local Services* (Michael Joseph 1968); J. Danziger, *Making Budgets* (Sage 1979); and the articles by J. L. Alt, 'Politics and expenditure models', *Policy and Politics*, vol. 5 (1977). The same issue has another critical review by K. Newton and L. J. Sharp, 'Local output research: some reflections and proposals', and K. Newton, 'Community Performance in Britain', in *Current Sociology*, vol. 22 (1976), is also worthwhile. For interesting work from an economic perspective, see R. J. Nicholson and N. Topham, 'The determinants of investment in housing by local authorities', *Journal of the Royal Statistical Society*, series A, vol. 134 (1971) and 'Urban road provision in England and Wales', *Policy and Politics*, vol. 4 (1976); and J. LeGrand and D. Winter, 'Towards an economic model of local government behaviour', *Policy and Politics*, vol. 5 (1977). The American literature is usefully summarized in B. Hawkins, *Urban Politics and Policies* (Bobbs Merrill 1972), while Fried's contribution, 'Comparative urban policy and performance', in F. I. Greenstein and N. W. Polsby (eds.), *The Handbook of Political Science*, vol. 6 (Addison-Wesley 1976), remains seminal.

On measuring citizen preferences, T. N. Clark (ed.), *Citizen Preferences and Urban Public Policy* (Sage 1978); and R. W. Gettser and P. D. Schumaker, 'Contextual bases of responsiveness to citizen preferences and group demands', *Policy and Politics*, vol. 6 (1978), are useful American contributions, and I. Gordon, 'Subjective social indicators and urban political analysis', *Policy and Politics*, vol. 5 (1977), is a British contribution.

For an optimistic view of cities' ability to control or manage their environments see K. Young, 'Environmental management in local politics', in D. Kavanagh and R. Rose (eds.), *New Trends in British Politics* (Sage 1977), and his work with J. Kramer, *Strategy and Conflict in Metropolitan Housing* (Heinemann 1978), and J. D. Stewart, *The Responsive Local Authority* (Charles Knight 1974).

The rest of the argument is carried on at a normative level. Other books which similarly engage this level include H. Cox, *Cities: the Public Dimension* (Penguin 1976); E. Banfield, *The Unheavenly City Revisited* (Little, Brown 1974); P. Hall, *Issues in Urban Society* (Penguin 1978), as well as some of the essays in C. Lambert and D. Weir, *Cities in Modern Britain* (Fontana 1976).

Index